W9-CNN-517

BRITAIN AND THE NETHERLANDS
IN EUROPE AND ASIA

Britain and the Netherlands in Europe and Asia

Papers delivered to the
Third Anglo-Dutch Historical Conference

Edited by

J. S. Bromley and
E. H. Kossmann

Macmillan
London · Melbourne · Toronto
St Martin's Press
New York
1 9 6 8

Editorial matter © J. S. Bromley and E. H. Kossmann
Text © Macmillan and Co Ltd

Published by
MACMILLAN AND CO LTD
Little Essex Street London W C 2
and also at Bombay Calcutta and Madras
Macmillan South Africa (Publishers) Pty Ltd Johannesburg
The Macmillan Company of Australia Pty Ltd Melbourne
The Macmillan Company of Canada Ltd Toronto
St Martin's Press Inc New York

Library of Congress catalog card no. 68–27096

Printed in Great Britain by
ROBERT MACLEHOSE AND CO LTD
The University Press, Glasgow

PIAE MEMORIAE

PETRI GEYL

PRAECEPTORIS PRUDENTIS

SCRIPTORIS PRAECLARI

AMICI EGREGII

GRATO ANIMO

DEDICATUM

Contents

MAPS

Preface

With the exception of Chapters 2 and 5, which were specially written for it, this book consists of papers presented to the Third Anglo-Dutch Conference of Historians, which took place in London between 19 and 24 September 1966. The editors wish to record their keen sense of obligation to the organisers of that meeting – especially to Professors C. R. Boxer and S. T. Bindoff and to Mrs Alice Carter – as well as to the Marquess of Salisbury, the Trustees of the National Maritime Museum, the University of London and several of its constituent Colleges, whose hospitality they were fortunate to enjoy.

There is another debt of gratitude which it is fitting to record. While the Netherlands Ministry of Education has generously continued to meet some of the expenses of the Dutch membership, it is not the practice of the British government to subsidise conferences of this kind. This one accordingly owed much to the kindly interest of the Shell Transport and Trading Company, Unilever, and Philips Industries, all of whom affirmed their belief in the value of academic traffic across the North Sea and in the relevance of historical study.

In spite of unavoidable changes of publisher and format, the present volume may be regarded as the third in the series 'Britain and the Netherlands' which was launched in 1960 by Chatto & Windus, with the backing of St Antony's College, Oxford, and continued in 1964 by J. B. Wolters of Groningen, acting for the Historical Institute of the University of Utrecht. A small addition to the title on this occasion is intended as a rough indication of the two major enquiries which formed the programme of the 1966 Conference.

The first of these might be described as the study, still in its infancy, of changing attitudes in Britain and the Netherlands to

9

the respective situations, at times even to the *raison d'être*, of the two countries in the highly unstable power-complex which remains so prominent a feature of modern European history, however much we should wish to stress (and still need to explore) the cultural and institutional sympathies implied in the concept of a Western civilisation. It is to be hoped that English and Dutch historians will one day be able to confer on the subject of their cultural and institutional environments, so much akin as the world goes and yet so strangely and subtly diverse; and there is need to explain further the contrasts of national mentality which may strike the attentive reader in the pages here presented. He will readily understand why their bias is towards Anglo-Dutch relations in particular, and perhaps concede that these were of outstanding importance, at least from the sixteenth to the nineteenth century, to western Europe as a whole.

The history of Anglo-Dutch relations is of course filled with tensions and misunderstandings. For the origin of these, as everyone knows, the rivalry between two trading powers in Asia had much to do, although there is still a great deal that we do not know about the 'fort and factory' stage of European intervention in the Far East. Less familiar to most people is the mutual distrust bequeathed by the East India Companies to the territorial empires which they founded. It seems hardly too much to say that the later history of Netherlands India is only now being written, while recent work has thrown a fresh light on British activity in South-East Asia during the nineteenth century. The character of both empires, and not least the motivation which gave rise to them and influenced the imperial policy-making itself, is still open to judgement. Meanwhile, historians face problems which to the unwary may appear no more interesting than yet another foregone conclusion in the chain of inevitability: the recent and in many respects obscure history of the 'retreat from empire'. This group of questions constitutes the second main theme of our volume.

Since all the questions here discussed are large in proportion to the scope of a single chapter, and in many cases are questions under active revision by scholars, it has been decided to add short reading lists as an initial guide for the benefit of students or amateurs who may be stimulated to further enquiry. An attempt has been made to include representative collections of printed source materials as well as monographs and general histories in these 'bibliographies', but of necessity they are as a rule highly selective. The place of publication is London unless otherwise stated.

J. S. B.

October 1967

E. H. K.

Abbreviations

ARA   Algemeen Rijksarchief
BKI   *Bijdragen tot de Taal-, Land- en Volkenkunde van Neder-landsch-Indië. Uitgegeven door het Koninklijk Instituut voor de Taal-, Land- en Volkenkunde van Nederlandsch-Indië*
BM   British Museum
CCM   *A Calendar of Court Minutes etc. of the East India Company 1635–1679*, ed. E. B. Sainsbury (Oxford, 1907–38)
EFI   *The English Factories in India, 1618–1621 [1622–1623, etc.]* ed. W. Foster [Sir C. Fawcett, etc.] (Oxford, 1906 [1908, etc.])
EIC   East India Company
IOL   India Office Library, London
PEC   *Parlementaire Enquêtecommissie Regeringsbeleid, 1940–1945* (The Hague, 1956)
RGP   Rijks Geschiedkundige Publicatiën
VKI   *Verhandelingen van het Koninklijk Instituut voor Taal-, Land- en Volkenkunde van Nederlandsch-Indië*
VOC   Vereenigde Oostindische Compagnie

1 The Netherlands and Europe in the Seventeenth and Eighteenth Centuries

J. W. SMIT

IT is well known how the old idea of the order of the Christian commonwealth was gradually replaced during the seventeenth and eighteenth centuries by a concept of Europe as a cultural and political entity. The awareness of a common religious and cultural heritage was closely related to the conception of a European power-system, though not altogether congruent with it. But in spite of its inherent vagueness, the 'interest and balance of Europe' had become by the end of the seventeenth century a term rich in diplomatic propaganda value and an idea to which politicians could commit themselves or at least pay lip-service.[1] Before the end of the next century men had learned to speak of Europe as – in the words of Edmund Burke – 'a diplomatic Republic of Europe' in which 'no citizen could be an exile in any part', a 'society of nations' in which no single state could act without considering the peace and interest of the entire community.[2]

It is my purpose to examine the influence of the concept of Europe upon the foreign policy of the Dutch Republic. Rather surprisingly, we find that in the judgement of most historians that influence never really existed. No one, of course, doubts that the Republic under William III of Orange played a major part in the establishment of the European balance of power against the expansion of Louis XIV. But at the same time this European commitment is seen as a personal policy of the King-Stadholder, imposed upon a mercantile patriciate itself devoted to

[1] F. Chabod, *Storia dell'idea d'Europa* (Bari, 1961) ch. ii; J. Ter Meulen, *Der Gedanke der internationalen Organisation in seiner Entwicklung*, 3 vols (The Hague, 1917–40) I 38–42.

[2] E. V. Gulick, *Europe's Classical Balance of Power* (Cornell University Press, 1955) II, 21–2.

13

profit and incapable of lofty political ideas.[1] Not long ago, in a penetrating study of the influence of the over-mighty province of Holland in the shaping of general Dutch foreign policy, Professor Boogman came to the conclusion that the trading interests of Holland thrust upon the Republic a policy of neutrality and avoidance of alliances which was in striking contrast with the general expansionist maxims of seventeenth-century politics. In his view, the Republic turned its back on the Continent in order to tend the interests of its world-wide seaborne trade.[2] Developing this theme, Professor Kossmann has sought to explain the European commitment in the Dutch propaganda of William III's time as an importation from England alien to the Dutch tradition.[3]

The general trend of Boogman's argument cannot be challenged, and I shall more than once have occasion to produce evidence in support of it. His structural approach, which investigates the interest-groups behind foreign policy, is fruitful and should be pursued. On the other hand, Dutch foreign policy is as intricate a phenomenon as Dutch political institutions. Even the policy advocated by the province of Holland itself was the result of a number of interests, often conflicting, among towns of varying importance, balanced and arbitrated by politicians whose personal ideas played an important role. Holland, moreover, was not the only force in the shaping of Dutch policy: the princes of Orange and the other provinces had their own interests and ideas to defend, and they often defended them successfully.

The time for a full structural analysis of the historic trends in Dutch foreign policy has certainly not yet come. So I must use, although with a bad conscience, the traditional terminology for the agents by which it was shaped: Holland, Amsterdam, Orangists, Calvinists and so on. I will first analyse Dutch attitudes to Europe from the standpoint of ideas, of what may be called the image of the nature and interest of the Dutch community in international affairs – in modern phraseology, the image of

[1] R. Fruin, *Verspreide Geschriften*, 10 vols (The Hague, 1900–5) IV 48; J. A. van Hamel, *Nederland tusschen de Mogendheden* (Amsterdam, 1918) 147 ff.

[2] J. C. Boogman, 'Die holländische Tradition in der niederländischen Geschichte,' *Westfälische Forschungen*, XV (1962) 96 ff.

[3] E. H. Kossmann, *In Praise of the Dutch Republic* (Inaugural Lecture, University College London, 1963) 16.

national identity. Secondly, we shall explore the terminology and
the rhetoric in which the aims of foreign policy were stated by
contemporaries, ranging from non-commitment to sophisticated
concepts of a European balance of power and of a common
European interest. Finally, I propose to examine the variety of
diplomatic forms with which experiments were made: the choice
for or against neutrality, the simple commercial treaty, arbitration, defensive or offensive alliance, coalition – all indicating
degrees of involvement in the evasive and changing concept of
Europe.

Although I shall have little to say about the eighteenth century,
we may well introduce our problem with two quotations from
that period. In 1794, when time was already running out for the
Republic, the Council of State, in its customary explanatory
memorandum on the military budget, declared it to be its
important duty 'to consider the state of affairs of the whole of
Europe together with that of the Republic itself, being an important link in the chain of European powers'.[1] This statement, and
others of the same sort, betray an acute awareness of the existence
of a system as wide as Europe in which the Republic had its own
place and its own function to fulfil. Such a declaration is certainly
to be expected in an age which had learned to recognise the
European power-system as a reality, and from an Orangist
government traditionally committed to an active Dutch role in
Europe. A few years earlier, however, we find a quite different
pattern of thought in the memoirs of the Amsterdam burgomaster Rendorp, who was no anti-Orangist and who had even
collaborated with the Orangists to crush a democratic revolt.
Rendorp, meditating on the basic conditions of Dutch foreign
policy, says bluntly that, since war indisputably spells nothing but
disaster for nations dependent on trade, it is of vital interest to the
Republic, more than to any other state, to avoid any involvement
in defensive alliances; he does not even mention offensive ones.
Fortunately, he continues, no country is in a better position than
the Republic to abstain from all foreign relations except those
which are purely commercial. Then, reviewing the seventeenth-
century history of the Netherlands, he reproaches both the Grand
Pensionary John de Witt and the Stadholder William III for their

[1] G. W. Vreede, *Inleiding tot eene Geschiedenis der Nederlandsche Diplomatie*
(Utrecht, 1856) I 118.

15

entanglement in what he calls the political actions of princes: an entanglement which, after the bloody and costly War of the Spanish Succession, had produced nothing but an expensive and useless Barrier in the Southern Netherlands and some even more useless territorial accretions. There exists, he emphasises, an essential difference between the interest of the Dutch Republic, which consists in peace and neutrality, and the interest of monarchs, who always wish to increase their influence on the state of all Europe and who are easily governed by the incalculable demands of princely honour.[1]

I have cited these two conflicting views at some length because they are the expression, from authoritative sources, of two archetypal patterns of thought about the role of the Republic in European affairs. They represent the polarised solutions to a deeply felt and constantly disquieting problem: the ambiguity of the Dutch position as a first-rate commercial power without a corresponding territorial and demographical basis. It was the problem of a nation seeking its security in peace, in a world which granted no profit without power, no safety without war.

When we turn now to the very beginning of the seventeenth century, we find an attitude towards international affairs which is still relatively uncomplicated. The Netherlands in rebellion against the Spanish world-power did not enjoy the advantage of a long tradition in international affairs. Before the Revolt, foreign policy had been the exclusive prerogative of the Habsburg princes, and the only consistent policy of the provinces had been to pay up as little as possible for Habsburg adventures. The province of Holland, which now dominated the policy of the rebels, had previously cultivated only one main foreign interest: the free fishing and trade rights in the North Sea and the Baltic – in short, the safety of the seas.

The rebellion had led to a war of sheer survival or extinction, and it was clear that France and England, with their clashing but mainly anti-Spanish interests in the Netherlands, were its natural allies. The war aims were simple: the security and monopoly of the Protestant religion, independence and sovereign status for all the Netherlands. This meant that an offensive war had to be carried on until the seventeen Netherlands provinces had been

[1] J. Rendorp, *Memoriën*, 2 vols (Amsterdam, 1792) I 33–8.

liberated. At the beginning of the seventeenth century this was not yet a programme of warmongers and expansionists, as would be the case later on. All the political pressure-groups were united in these war aims, which were the natural result of the revolutionary situation, and the policy enshrined in them was firmly carried out by the leader of the States of Holland, Oldenbarnevelt, and by Prince Maurice of Orange, the leader of the army, although we shall encounter them shortly in opposite camps.

Except for the reconquest of the Southern Netherlands, there were no territorial demands. On the eastern frontier the political leaders were set against any expansion; the requests of lesser German princes and territories to be admitted to the Union of Utrecht had been refused.[1] The Dutch were content to garrison crucial German fortresses and to keep the activities of the German border-territories under control. In this respect we may already speak of a policy of contraction (as opposed to expansion) which was to become a characteristic element of the later neutralist tradition. At the beginning of the century, however, the role the Netherlanders inevitably played in the struggle against the Habsburgs entailed a certain European vision. Rebels and foreigners alike felt, and stated, that in the Netherlands the fate of Europe was at stake. Yet the concept of Europe as a diplomatic system was still far from being realised. Europe then consisted of a number of small power-systems, sometimes loosely connected by a common opposition to the Habsburg menace. The term 'Europe' occurs in Dutch diplomatic correspondence, but more often we find its unsecularised forerunner 'Christendom', which in Dutch usage meant principally the Protestant powers. This, however, was not a workable guide for practical policy-making. Although the Netherlands tried to get assistance from the German princes and sent them dispatches often resembling sophisticated theological tracts,[2] they certainly wished to avoid entanglement in the problems of the Empire. Moreover, they did not neglect Catholic anti-Habsburg powers such as France and Venice, and they also established diplomatic relations with Turkey.[3] But

[1] P. J. van Winter, *De Zeven Provinciën* (Haarlem, 1954) 18 ff.
[2] A typical example is the letter of the Dutch envoy P. Brederode to Count Johann von Nassau in 1603, in G. Groen van Prinsterer (ed.), *Archives ou correspondance de la Maison d'Orange-Nassau*, 1ᵉ série, II (2) 262.
[3] K. Heeringa, *De eerste Nederlandsche gezant bij de Verheven Porte* (Utrecht, 1917).

although we see the gradual establishment of a net of diplomatic relations from the Baltic to the Levant, pertaining to the main interests of the state, we must come to the conclusion that all these connections were still rather casual and the result of passing expediency.

Dutch diplomacy was to lose its naïveté and its pragmatic character fairly soon. Even in the first decade of the seventeenth century an end to the war with Spain seemed to become a possibility. Staunch war-leaders like Oldenbarnevelt were willing to consider a peace on the basis of the *status quo*, that is, on the basis of the abandonment of the Southern Netherlands. In the political crisis that followed, the politicians and all politically interested people, among whom the ministers of the Church and the trading interests were prominent, had to review the fundamental conception of the new state with a fresh eye in order to reformulate their attitude to the acute problem of the conditions of war and peace. In the records of heated debates and in the paper war of the many pamphleteers, we can watch how the Dutch struggled to construct a concept of the interest of their state and thus bring order to the confusing reality of international relations. It became clear that in the Dutch situation the concept of state interest was a very ambiguous concept indeed.

An eighteenth-century Dutch politician once summed up the basic guarantees of Dutch independence in the following series: God, the water, Batavian heroism, the balance of Europe and jealousy between the great powers.[1] Except for the anachronistic idea of the balance of power – for which we may substitute the interest of anti-Habsburg Christendom – these were the elements which had occurred already in the discussions about war and peace from the beginning of the seventeenth century onwards. Let us examine them in the same order so as to illustrate how puzzling the problems were.

God, to begin with, was certainly no figurehead in Dutch history. He was very much present, devising crafty means to destroy the enemies of the state and chastising the sinners within the community who preferred worldly goods to His honour. For

---

For the objections against dealing with Turkey, see F. L. Baumler, 'England, the Turk and the Common Corps of Christendom', *American Historical Review*, L (1944–5) passim; for the same problem in the nineteenth century cf. Gulick, 15.

[1] J. Meerman, quoted in Vreede, 1.

the faithful, He led the state with a firm hand towards victory, almost as a second Israel. The radical Calvinists who felt themselves to be His mouthpiece were the most consistent supporters of the war. In 1608 a pamphlet was published entitled *The Triumph of War*, with the morbidly inappropriate sub-title, 'very pleasant and amusing to read'.[1] The booklet presents a rabid defence of the general principle of war and is aimed against Erasmus and his disciples, who are said to have been entirely misguided in their praise of peace. With grim pleasure the writer extols the Christian virtues of warfare, and he as well as many other writers emphasise the treacherous character of a peace that would leave the Southern Netherlands in the claws of the Papist beast. The very mention of Erasmus, however, hints at the fact that the peace party too could rely on a Christian tradition, and its propagandists made use of it. In the end, in 1618, an Orange-Calvinist *coup d'état* was necessary to make God speak in favour of war.

The next interest in our series, the water, was no less ambiguous as a guiding principle for Dutch foreign policy. In one sense it referred to the natural defence-line of the sea and the great rivers. In this meaning it could be used equally by the war party, to stress strategic strength, and by those who argued that it was only natural to withdraw behind such invincible barriers and to abandon European commitments. The water meant also seaborne trade. Yet at this time the interests of trade did not provide a self-evident guideline. The essential features of the economic system of Holland, its intermediary position between the Baltic and southern Europe, had already taken shape, and it was clear that this intricate system depended on peace. At the beginning of the century, however, the spectacular and promising warlike trade with the Indies was much more attractive for many investors than were the peaceful ways of traditional commerce; Amsterdam,

[1] *De Triumph van den Oorloch ende Mis-prijsinghe vanden Peys: seer ghenoechlyck ende cortswijlich om te lesen* (W. P. C. Knuttel, *Catalogus van de pamflettenverzameling*, no. 1478). This pamphlet is one of the few that seem to adhere to the idea of the *bellum perpetuum*. The idea of war as a natural condition of human society is more frequently to be found with colonial leaders such as Jan Pieterszoon Coen, governor-general in the East Indies, who stated quite bluntly (in 1614): 'We cannot carry on trade without war nor war without trade' (C. R. Boxer, *The Dutch Seaborne Empire* (1965) 96). This is the concept of the inexorable link between 'Profit and Power' which constitutes the theme of Charles Wilson's book of that title. Coen, however, limits the validity of his observation to the situation in the Indies.

later almost always the champion of peace, was at this stage more interested in colonial adventures and joined the war party.

If we pass over the item of Batavian heroism in our series, we come to the jealousy between the greater neighbours. The importance of that jealousy, mainly between England and France, was easy enough to understand, but in the framework of Dutch politics it provided no guidance. Involvement in the anti-Habsburg struggle – the programme of the Calvinists – meant taking the side of France, never an attractive prospect for Calvinist sympathisers; but England, though she might pose as the defender of Protestant Christendom, was remarkably inactive in continental affairs.

We can observe how in these early decades of the existence of the Republic two concepts of a 'natural' Dutch foreign policy, neutrality and European commitment, are struggling to find expression in workable formulations. In 1609 it was not a peace but a truce that was concluded, which presupposed the eventual continuation of the war. In 1618 the war party took over after the *coup d'état* of Prince Maurice, and Calvinism got its first chance to become the centre of a concept of national identity and national mission which was to inspire foreign policy. But even now it became clear that national interest was a many-sided thing. Among the victors of 1618, besides the true Calvinists and the colonial trading interests – who knew how to reap inordinate profits from the pursuit of the honour of God – we find also the princes of Orange, whose ideology was limited to the sincere belief that whatever was good for the House of Orange was in the interest of the state as well. Although after the war had reopened in 1621 the new official policy was one of Protestant solidarity throughout Europe, the Stadholder's faction used all its influence to prevent the Thirty Years War from developing into a general war of religion.[1] After 1625 the new Stadholder, Frederick Henry, became more and more involved in ties with the France of Richelieu. He concentrated on the liberation of the Southern Netherlands, not in order to establish the Reformation there, but to cash a premium promised by France: the free and sovereign possession of Antwerp for the House of Orange.

It is small wonder that this policy, threatening the vital interest of Amsterdam and the whole of Holland, met with increasing

[1] Vreede, I 87–8.

opposition. The Orangists and Calvinists, joining forces again, might argue in the States-General that it was in the interest of the state and of true religion to reconquer the South and so establish a Netherlands state powerful enough to guarantee the peace in Europe; but the time for a fully-fledged missionary Protestant European policy was past.[1] In comparison with the attitude now prevailing in the province of Holland, such a repetition of the traditional war aims sounded like inordinate expansionism. Holland did not want a restitution of the southern provinces, with the accompanying risk that trade would flow back to a liberated Antwerp. Its policy was to destroy whatever was left of an active interventionist policy in Europe. The hectic days of colonial pioneering were over. The established East Indian interests had found their place among many other interests in the framework of the general trade system of Holland.[2] The Baltic–Iberian network had regained its prominence in the minds of the responsible merchant-patriciate, and Amsterdam had returned to respectable and regular commerce. They wished to use the money spent by the Stadholder, in his campaigns in the Southern Netherlands, for the security of their trade in the Baltic, now threatened by Danish–Swedish enmity.

Besides his orientation towards the South and his relations with France – which for quite different reasons had also troubled his relations with the Calvinists – it was the prince's increasingly crypto-monarchical methods and manners, and later his family ties with the Stuarts, that gave birth to the opposition which finally developed a new conception of national identity and interest, and consequently to a fresh assessment of the proper place of the Republic in Europe. Holland and Amsterdam had already been critical of the alliance with France and Sweden in 1635. In 1648 they finally succeeded in imposing peace with Spain on Frederick Henry's successor, William II. A *coup d'état*

[1] This is the programme set forth in a memorandum of the provinces of Friesland and Groningen in 1633: see L. van Aitzema, *Saeken van Staet en Oorlogh* (The Hague, 1669–72) II bk. xiii, 20 ff.

[2] I. J. Brugmans, 'De Oost-Indische Compagnie en de welvaart in de Republiek', *Welvaart en Historie* (The Hague, 1950) 28 ff., proves that the East Indies trade was much less important than was generally believed. For Amsterdam's gradual disengagement from colonial adventures see W. J. van Hoboken, 'The Dutch West India Company', in J. S. Bromley and E. H. Kossmann (ed.), *Britain and the Netherlands* (1960) 41–61, and Boogman, 'Die holländische Tradition', 100.

by that prince in 1650 confirmed the worst expectations. It enhanced extremist formulations of the anti-monarchical and neutralist ideology which had been gaining ground and which had now developed into a consistent pattern of thought: the system of the so-called True Liberty. And then the sudden death of the Stadholder in 1650 left the government in the hands of the opposition.

We must look a little closer at the features of this ideology of True Liberty, not only because of its importance in the shaping of a new foreign policy, but also because it expressed the notions of Dutch interest so convincingly, and in a terminology so widely accepted that, even after the downfall of the Grand Pensionary De Witt's government in 1672, many adherents of the new leader William III still formulated their so-called new policy in the phraseology of True Liberty.[1] On the other hand, we shall come to the paradoxical conclusion that, even under De Witt, the dogma of True Liberty guided foreign policy only for a few years.

There are a few systematic expositions of the ideology of True Liberty, covering all aspects of interior and international policy, by theorists such as the brothers De la Court.[2] These do not date back further than the late 'fifties and early 'sixties. We can, however, find the same ideas much earlier, although less well defined and less well expressed, in pamphlets and in occasional utterances of politicians; and in these examples we may see to what extent their ideas had grown into the habits and thoughts of the leading group in Dutch politics after 1650 – and how these concepts determined, while also limiting, the politicians' capability of assessing political reality.

In its more sophisticated form, the system of True Liberty was an elaborate example of seventeenth-century interest-of-state theory. The core of the system is the inseparable connection between the economic nature of the Dutch state, its political constitution and its place in international affairs. Trade being put forward as the eminent interest of the state, it follows as self-evident that the form of that state must be republican and its

[1] See below, p. 25, n. 3.

[2] E. H. Kossmann, *Politieke Theorie in het zeventiende-eeuwse Nederland* (Amsterdam, 1960) ch. ii; P. Geyl, *Het stadhouderschap in de partijliteratuur onder De Witt* (Amsterdam, 1947).

character bourgeois. Trade, it is argued, cannot survive in a monarchy or under the government of a military nobility, because there the rule of law and justice is lacking.[1] In a pamphlet of 1646, the formative period of the ideology of True Liberty, it is said that

as long as the Nobility in France is in power, nothing is to be hoped for the common man; the commons there would be happy indeed if they could live under a Republic in which the common man does not suffer too much from wars and may live quietly in peace with his family in his own house.[2]

In 1644 the Directors of the Delft Chamber of the East India Company had already drawn the distinction between princely wars and the merchants' peace policy, an antithesis dear to the theorists of the next decades. The Directors write that

a merchant would do better honourably to increase his talent and send rich cargoes from Asia to the Netherlands, instead of carrying out costly territorial conquests, which are more suitable for crowned heads and mighty monarchs than for merchants greedy of gain.[3]

In 1673 Pieter de Groot, son of the great Hugo Grotius, asks:

What constitutes the wealth of the Republic? The opulence of its trade. And what is the source of that trade? Good government. For nothing is more attractive for the whole world than freedom of conscience and security of possessions. It is impossible that this freedom and this security of possessions would survive the government of a monarch.[4]

The brothers De la Court defend the eminently bourgeois idea of True Liberty even with rather democratic notions. These cynical followers of Descartes and Hobbes regarded self-interest and passion as the basis of human conduct, but at the same time they

[1] *Het interest van Holland ofte Gronden van Hollands Welvaren aangewezen door V.D.H.* [Pieter de la Court] (Amsterdam, 1662) ch. xxvi–xxxi; *Consideratiën van Staet ofte Politike Weeg-schaal* (Amsterdam, 1662) 112.

[2] H. J. van der Heim, *Het archief van den Raadpensionaris Antonie Heinsius* (The Hague, 1867) p. vii.

[3] Boxer, 95.

[4] F. J. L. Krämer (ed.), *Lettres de Pierre de Groot à Abraham de Wicquefort, 1668–74* (Werken Historisch Genootschap Utrecht, 3e serie, no. 5, 1894) 95.

developed the concept of the harmony of self-interests, possible only in a democratic community: 'When everyone looks after himself nobody gets lost', they say, and then they argue that the public interest as the sum of individual interests can be the supreme law only in a democracy, which in turn can exist only in small municipal communities. This was a well-known idea drawn from classical tradition, but it possessed a strikingly contemporary significance. The whole tendency of the system of True Liberty led to the conclusion that the smaller the state the better. City-republics, De la Court says, do not make offensive wars, there are no war-taxes, all the available wealth and energy may be spent on the advancement of culture: it is wealth combined with freedom that creates the arts, sciences and virtue.[1] In line with the classical tradition, renewed by Machiavelli, republican government is glorified by De la Court and his partisans – but later also by an Orangist author like Pieter Valkenier – as the true heritage of Europe, a heritage seriously threatened by un-European monarchism.[2] In a book of 1685, Pieter de la Court gloomily observes that more and more republics in his own lifetime have fallen victim to the monarchs – to such an extent that, were the process to continue for another century, all beneficial knowledge, the sciences, the arts, the virtues and wealth of man, even the number of people throughout the whole of Europe, would gradually decline.[3]

What we find here, and in many other examples, is thus the glorification of the small, peaceful and republican welfare state, and this is the true identity of the Dutch Republic.[4] As is well known, the small state, the embodiment of the Rule of Virtue, enjoyed a wide popularity in the political theory of the Enlightenment too. But there is a difference. The charming race of the

---

[1] *Consideratiën van Staet* ch. iv 549, 552, 567, 575–6.

[2] For the idea of Europe in Machiavelli see Chabod, 32 ff.; cf. De la Court, *Consideratiën*, 231–2. For the city-state as centre of culture see Chabod, 54; cf. De la Court, *Consideratiën*, 552. For Valkenier see his *'t Verwerd Europa*, 2 vols (Amsterdam, 1675) I 15–17, 134–6, 138, 313.

[3] Pieter de la Court, *Sinrijcke Fabulen* (Amsterdam, 1685), in the conclusion of the introduction.

[4] German pamphlets also contained the opinion that Holland's strength lay in her being a republic and 'schier nur eine Stadt': see R. E. von Gronow, *Die öffentliche Meinung in Deutschland gegenüber Holland nach 1648* (Marburg, 1914) 38–9.

Troglodytes in Montesquieu's *Lettres Persanes* lived happily in freedom until they became too numerous; when they decided to choose a king, the candidate for that high office accepted it with tears in his eyes, because his people had now lost their freedom and abandoned the government of virtue.[1] For Montesquieu the small welfare state was a lost paradise. The believers in True Liberty, on the contrary, felt quite confident that they could realise, or already had realised, that happy prospect: they had reached the Golden Age in their own lifetime.[2]

When we leave the realm of political speculation, sometimes quite unrealistic, and turn to the hard facts of political life, we notice how the foreign policy built on this pattern of thought failed completely within a few years of its creation. The Republic was no seafaring city-state, but a small and vulnerable territorial state with the wealth of a great power. It was its fate to be torn between its Atlantic – or global – and its European, continental commitments. This fate could be solved neither by the theorists nor by the practitioners of True Liberty. Yet, before turning to the story of practical policy, it is to be noticed that all the concepts so far illustrated from the works of the supporters of True Liberty could have been quoted from the book of one of the fiercest enemies of De Witt: Pieter Valkenier's *Europe Confused*. Although he disagreed with what he understood as the foreign policy of the Grand Pensionary, and with De Witt's anti-Orangist line of conduct, Valkenier formulated the basic interests and the identity of the Republic in the same phraseology as has just been described.[3] Here we have confirmation of the extent to which that ideology had become truly engrained in Dutch thought generally. True Liberty was no mere ideological mask for bourgeois interests: it was also a governmental ethos, a set of values which corresponded to the nature of Dutch society as a whole and inspired the policy of its leaders.

When we look at international policy as dictated by the idea of True Liberty, it is easy to see that this could hardly enhance any

---

[1] E. Sieber, *Die Idee des Kleinstaats bei den Denkern des 18. Jahrhunderts in Frankreich und Deutschland* (Basel, 1920) 11 ff.; Montesquieu, *Lettres Persanes*, XI–XIV.

[2] On the *topos* of the Golden Age applied to seventeenth-century Holland, see J. Heemskerck, *Batavische Arcadia* (Amsterdam, 1665) 310, 329.

[3] *'t Verwerd Europa*, I 16–17, 108–110.

policy of European involvement, in the first place. When De la Court extols Europe as the birth-place of the republican idea he has no missionary intentions, and instances of such are few indeed among his fellow-republicans: their ideal was not for export. Venice asked during the 'fifties for an exchange of ambassadors, arguing that

the two republics must be on guard against whatever Spain and France will attempt to the disadvantage of the Republics or to disturb the general peace in Christendom; this being the interest of the two Republics who have nothing else in view but to preserve their states in peace and tranquillity for the benefit of trade and navigation.[1]

'Benefit of trade' was the kind of language the Dutch understood, but exactly because of that interest the system of True Liberty prescribed complete neutrality, and the States-General remained deaf to the requests of the sister-republic. The official dogma after the peace of 1648 was thus non-commitment, disengagement, peace and contraction, in accordance with the motto 'qui a terre a guerre'.[2] It is a recurring theme in the early correspondence of De Witt and his fellow republicans that 'there must be peace and friendship with all kings, republics, princes, and also there must be peace among all those together, for all trouble and war is against the welfare of our Republic'.[3] And so were alliances. The sole aim of Dutch diplomacy in those first years after 1650 is the conclusion of mere treaties of navigation and commerce, in order to ensure an uninterrupted seaborne trade. As late as 1662, at a time when this policy had been radically changed, De Witt himself still wrote that the most advantageous thing for the state would be 'a simple treaty of commerce and navigation, without any obligation of mutual defence'.[4] It is also in line with the principles of True Liberty, and with the new conception of the identity of the state, that its leaders, though not insensible to the honour of their state, had a rather matter-of-fact attitude towards that kind of honour which in seventeenth-century opinion, and later still for Montesquieu, remains the distinctive quality of the

[1] *Brieven geschreven . . . tusschen den Heer Johan de Witt . . . ende Gevolmaghtigden van den Staedt der Vereenigde Nederlanden* (The Hague, 1723–25) I 10–11, 217.
[2] Ibid. 58.   [3] De Witt in 1653: ibid. 50.
[4] R. Fruin and N. Japikse, *Brieven van Johan de Witt,* II (Werken Historisch Genootschap Utrecht, 3ᵉ serie, no. 25, 1909) I 360.

monarchical form of government.[1] There are numerous instances of a feeling of impatience and contempt for the intricacies of diplomatic etiquette.[2] Thus Pieter de Groot writes:

The glory of treaties does not exist in grimaces but in conditions, and in that respect republics must always have more regard for the possessions of their subjects than for the splendour of their government, because they know that honour and money never flow into the same purse.[3]

And Witsen, Amsterdam burgomaster during the War of the Spanish Succession, expressed the same awareness of a unique Dutch mentality when he said that 'our Commonwealth has no use for ambition otherwise called the glory of arms, and because of its particular interests overseas, it does not need to make points of honour if this does not bring lasting profit'.[4]

This commercial mentality, however, is only one side of Dutch foreign policy in the age of De Witt. I have hinted several times at the inescapable discrepancy which lies at the bottom of the dogma of non-commitment and peace. Princes, in accordance with the bad name they had in Dutch political thought, were unwilling to collaborate for the benefit of the system of international peace with which the interests of the Republic were so closely bound. They did not understand their own interest, complained the Dutch, or rather, they neglected the true interest of their nations.[5] However that might be, the vulnerability of the Dutch economy became obvious whenever wars cut off one or more of the branches which were so intricately interwoven in its worldwide trade system.[6] Given the impossible reality of international relations, the principles of True Liberty often sound more like a

[1] Sieber, 11.

[2] J. Heringa, *De Eer en Hoogheid van de Staat* (Groningen, 1961) is an interesting book on the sensitivity of the Dutch to the honour of their state in the diplomatic world, but the basic Dutch lack of interest in ceremonial niceties would be an even more fascinating subject: e.g., the attitude of the Dutch ambassador Beverningh in F. W. C. P. van Bylandt, *Het diplomatiek beleid van Hieronymus van Beverningh* (The Hague, 1863) 39 ff. and 53.

[3] Krämer, *Lettres de Pierre de Groot*, 112 (6 March 1673).

[4] J. F. Gebhard, *Het Leven van Mr. Nicolaas Cornelisz. Witsen, 1641–1717*, 2 vols (Utrecht, 1881–2) I 461 (3 September 1703).

[5] Fruin and Japikse, *Brieven van De Witt*, II 46, 170.

[6] The vulnerability is fully explained in C. Wilson, *Profit and Power: a Study of England and the Dutch Wars* (1957) and in Boxer, *Dutch Seaborne Empire*.

desperate incantation than the realistic assessment of Dutch interest they were meant to be. The Dutch had to bargain and to beg for the international peace upon which their highly advanced trade system, but not that of other nations, depended.

One could, and did, seek safety in the typical device of the weak: the appeal to international law. It was indeed a traditional trait of Dutch policy to claim by legalistic remonstrances what could not be got by the use of power; the *œuvre* of Hugo Grotius is in a way merely the expression of the ambiguous position of his country.[1] In his own time, however, matter-of-fact politicians like Oldenbarnevelt had made only incidental use of Grotius's services. To Oldenbarnevelt, for instance, it made no difference whether England recognised the rights of the Dutch fishery on the basis of legal principle or else on the basis of historical precedent.[2] Grotius himself had performed a consummate act of legalistic contortionism by demanding rights for the Dutch on the basis of *mare liberum*, which he then denied to the English when it did not work in the Dutch interest.[3] John de Witt certainly did not handle the problems of international law in so casual a manner. The increasing involvement of England in European affairs turned the dangerous principle of *mare clausum* and its corollaries into a major concern of his diplomacy. De Witt instructed his ambassadors never to discuss, for example, the right of fishery or the regulation of neutral commerce in time of war on any footing other than that of natural and international law. Where limitations on neutral trade were under negotiation, he was careful to make sure that the Dutch did not offend against the very principles which must remain essential guarantees of their own welfare.[4]

The legalistic approach could not prevent the whole system of simple trade and navigation treaties from becoming increasingly ineffective when the international situation became less favourable.

[1] F. R. de Pauw, *Het Mare Liberum van Grotius en Patijn* (Brugge, 1960) 52-3, 73 ff.

[2] Ibid. 48, 72-80.

[3] Ibid. ch. ii. For another instance of Dutch efforts to limit international law cf. L. Ledeboer, *Het beroep op volkenrecht vóór 1667* (Leiden, 1932) 45. The juridical controversy between *mare liberum* and *mare clausum* – the sea open to all or under the dominion of a particular power – is clearly explained in T. W. Fulton, *The Sovereignty of the Sea* (Edinburgh, 1911) esp. 338 ff.

[4] *Brieven geschreven* 69–70 (De Witt to Boreel, 2 January 1654).

The First Anglo-Dutch War, Sweden's imperialism in the Baltic, and the continuing Franco-Spanish War all made it clear to De Witt that the dogma of neutrality did not work. Fully aware of the dangers in the European situation, De Witt gradually became the architect of a Dutch alliance system and the inventor of new diplomatic forms which make him, allowing for differences in their circumstances, a direct forerunner of William III. De Witt still strove for peace as the sole interest of his country, but he recognised that this interest was linked with those of many nations in Europe.

In 1658 he laid down his ideas in a long memorandum to the Amsterdam burgomaster, De Graeff: 'I must confess,' he writes, 'that I cannot see without fear how this state for some time has directed its affairs without any firm friendship or safe alliance with any of the greater powers. To continue in this manner will be dangerous.'[1] De Witt had no illusions about the great powers. England, in his opinion, never acted according to her real interest: she was a completely unreliable ally, and he put no more faith in France. But he was convinced that an alliance with the Habsburgs presented no better solution for Dutch problems. De Witt had a contempt for German affairs which was traditionally Dutch, on the one hand, but which on the other hand betrayed his fear of an entanglement in all continental affairs.[2] The principles of True Liberty prove their strength in the way they seem almost subliminally to have influenced De Witt and his collaborators, even when they felt that times were changing.

John de Witt's new alliance policy was not yet – this we must emphasise – a concept of a European balance of power; it was merely aimed at galvanising the unstable international situation by drawing England and France into joint arbitration enterprises. A specimen of this unorthodox diplomacy was his handling of the

[1] Fruin and Japikse, *Brieven van De Witt*, II 59 ff.

[2] On the traditional Dutch contempt for Germany see L. van Tongerloo, 'Een Hessisch diplomaat over de Staatse politiek ten opzichte van Duitsland (1630)', *Bijdragen en Mededelingen Historisch Genootschap*, LXXV (1961); Von Gronow, 39 and passim. Cf. Krämer, *Lettres de Pierre de Groot*, letter of 6 March 1673 for the judgement of Pieter de Groot; for a Swedish comment on the Dutch attitude towards Germany see the memorandum of the Swedish ambassador Appelboom in *Bijdragen en Mededelingen Historisch Genootschap*, XXVI 333 ff. For De Witt's low estimate of the power of the German princes and the Emperor see Fruin and Japikse, *Brieven van De Witt*, II 101.

Swedish–Danish conflict in the 'fifties, in which major Dutch interests were at stake. In opposition to Amsterdam, which wanted the immediate security of its vital interests by means of rapid naval action and annihilation of the Swedish fleet, De Witt quietly manœuvred England and France into mediation, although not in the traditional sense. He aimed at arbitration, with the provision of armed action in order to impose the settlement worked out by the mediators. The French and English ambassadors did not at first feel comfortable with what they called a dangerous precedent for the future.[1] This method, however, became more popular, and in 1667 the Dutch ambassador Meerman could write: 'It is nowadays no longer as unusual as it used to be to combine the offer of mediation with means of coercion.'[2] De Witt thus tried to avoid at all costs the establishment of a balance of power system in which France and England would eventually be found at the opposite ends of the scale. After the settlement in the Baltic he wished to conclude a double alliance with both England and France.

Again De Witt's conception broke down against a refractory reality. The power relations did not allow themselves to be arranged according to his scheme. During the 'sixties France and England became the decisive powers in western Europe, and for the Dutch the only possible way out of the dilemma was to enter into the balance system that was taking shape. In the event of having to choose between England and France, De Witt certainly preferred France, but at the same time a problem was developing that was to cause an even more direct involvement in European affairs: the fate of the Spanish Netherlands. From the early 'thirties onwards French expansionism to the north had troubled Dutch politicians. As De Witt points out, this had been the cause of the Dutch rupture with the French in 1648. At that point Mazarin, fighting alone against Spain, had not been in a position to do much about it. Now, visibly, the French set out to harvest the fruit of the Peace of the Pyrenees. De Witt tried to get French co-operation for the establishment of an independent South Netherlands Republic as a buffer-state; and this typical conservative politician even considered inciting a revolt against Spanish domination there, in order to create a justification for the im-

[1] N. Japikse, *Johan de Witt* (Amsterdam, 1915) 152–3.
[2] Vreede, *Inleiding*, I 30.

position of a new settlement, again by means of arbitration. Even
a partition of the Spanish Netherlands between France and the
Republic – a rather radical deviation from the idea of territorial
saturation and contraction – was taken into consideration.[1]
Nothing came of it, however, and after the Second Anglo-
Dutch War was over (1667), a French attack on the Spanish
Netherlands drew Dutch attention almost exclusively towards
the southern frontier. De Witt became completely involved in
the continental affairs he had tried to avoid. The Triple Alliance
with England and Sweden was not his desire, but on its conclusion
(1668) he insisted again on the importance of the appropriate use
of means of coercion. Dutch observers later in the century looked
on the Triple Alliance as the harbinger of the policy of coalition
against France.[2] Again, this was certainly not De Witt's intention,
but almost imperceptibly a situation had been created in which
the diplomacy of coalition was to become inevitable. The alliance
of 1668, effectively, was an arrangement lying between De
Witt's favourite idea of arbitration organised by all the great
powers, and the later conception of coalition as the machinery
for a balance of power. The balance of power system compre-
hending all Europe was still to be born, and that happened only
when the menace of Louis XIV's expansionism created the idea of
a common European interest.

Nevertheless, there was certainly no sudden revolution in
Dutch diplomacy when William III appeared on the scene in 1672.
Both De Witt and his greatest enemy were aware of the inescapable Dutch involvement in European politics. Yet they were
working in completely different circumstances. During the first
decade after the outbreak of the war of 1672 the former collaborators of De Witt, who had learned with him that the neutrality
of True Liberty was only wishful thinking, pursued the same goals
as the fallen Grand Pensionary. They learned to use concepts like
the 'peace and interest of Europe' and 'the security of Christendom' as natural elements in the security of the Republic itself, and
there is no need to explain that sense of European responsibility
by making it an ideological importation from England.[3] Even a

---

[1] Fruin and Japikse, *Brieven van de Witt*, II 46 ff. (letter to Cornelis de Graeff,
14 August 1658).

[2] J. Wagenaar, *Vaderlandse Historie*, xv 60.

[3] E.g., the Amsterdam regent Hasselaar in 1672: 'Not only towns and provinces

staunch neutralist like Pieter de Groot, reviewing the past in 1673, wrote that the other powers ought not to allow the weakening of the Republic – a state 'which had never had the intention of expanding its territory, but which had worked only to hold the affairs of Europe in such a condition that it would be impossible for the greater powers to decide unilaterally the fate of the small ones'.[1]

On the other hand, during that first decade of William III's government, there was still no complete acceptance of the idea of a balance of power to be found, nor of coalition as a necessary corollary of that European concept. Of this lack we find a striking example in the Treaty of Association between the Republic and Sweden in 1681. The idea underlying that treaty was again to combine in order to preserve the European *status quo* by means of a guarantee, signed by as many of the greater powers as possible; explicitly it was stated that France herself could join. The treaty was not the first attempt to create a general coalition against France, but the last effort to create an atmosphere in which such a coalition would be unnecessary. In that respect it was endorsed and defended by the Amsterdam politicians; Van Beuningen, their influential leader, was instrumental in this diplomatic effort, which failed because of the unwillingness of Charles II to join it.[2]

The history of William's relationship with the Holland politicians, and especially with Amsterdam, had already been full of conflicts; the most serious had yet to come, and it occurred precisely during these two years after the failure of the Treaty of Association. We have seen that Amsterdam had backed that policy, and we must explain why that town, again led by Van Beuningen, now opposed William's new coalition policy to the

---

but the whole of Europe is at stake', quoted in Valkenier, *'t Verwerd Europa*, I 648; and Witsen, quoted in Gebhard, *Leven van Witsen*, I 94–5. In Pieter Valkenier we find the inseparable link between the Republic and the whole of Europe throughout his book, along with the idea that the Republic holds the balance of Europe (*'t Verwerd Europa*, 192, 134–6, 144). The same holds true for Van Beuningen and Fagel. Certainly the perilous situation *c.* 1672 brought about the urge to identify the Dutch cause with the wider interest of Europe.

[1] Krämer, *Lettres de Pierre de Groot*, 246 (1673).

[2] For the interpretation of the Treaty of Association see W. J. M. van Eysinga, *Het Associatieverdrag van 10 oktober 1681* (Amsterdam, 1947) and the critical comments in M. A. M. Franken, *Coenraad van Beuningen's politieke en diplomatieke aktiviteiten in de jaren 1667–1684* (Groningen, 1966) 183 ff.

point of opening independent negotiations with France. The explanation usually given by Orangist historians is based on an assumed lack of understanding of the European situation among an Amsterdam patriciate which was only interested in the security of seaborne commerce.[1] It is certainly true that the Amsterdam politicians, unconsciously clinging to the simplicity of the idea of non-commitment, sometimes thought it advisable to acquiesce in French expansionism. During the 'eighties, for example, it was thought in some Amsterdam circles that a peace with Louis XIV would be possible on condition that he would leave the Southern Netherlands in peace and content himself with expansion in the Empire and Italy. The fact, however, that during the grave crisis in the relations of Amsterdam with William III in 1683 it was Van Beuningen who led the opposition – the very man who had worked so hard to get Charles II into the Treaty of Association – points towards another conclusion. The Amsterdammers were convinced that French expansionism must be checked, and they were even beginning to accept the necessity of a coalition. But they did not want to fight France before the essential condition for the formation of such a coalition, the collaboration of England, had been realised. It was no longer their anti-continental, or anti-European, tradition which kept them from following William III, but the 'anomalous' conduct of England. When, finally, the events of 1688 had assured them that England would collaborate, they backed the European policy of William, and they were even willing to sacrifice their cherished interest in an independent Dutch maritime power and to concentrate on war on the Continent, so alien to their diplomatic tradition. After William's death it was they, in fact, who carried out his policy. Their continental orientation and concern for territorial security grew into a truly obsessive preoccupation with the establishment of a Barrier in the Southern Netherlands, and even into demands for territorial expansion.[2]

We have reached the eighteenth century, and I intend to

[1] For a critical survey of the Orangist point of view see P. Geyl, 'Willem III en zijn tegenstanders', in *Kernproblemen van onze geschiedenis* (Utrecht, 1937).

[2] J. G. Stork-Penning, *Het Grote Werk* (Groningen, 1958) 451–65, defends the Dutch politicians against the English charges that they had demanded too much during the peace negotiations. On the concept of the Barrier see Werner Hahlweg, 'Barrière-Gleichgewicht-Sicherheit', *Historische Zeitschrift* CLXXXVII (1959) 75 ff.

be brief about it. Yet certain interesting developments must at least be mentioned, if only because they show that the neutralist tradition was far from dead – indeed, that it remained powerful enough to inspire Dutch foreign policy within the framework of a new European power-system. After the Peace of Utrecht, people like Heinsius and Slingelandt felt able to continue co-operation with England for the maintenance of the balance of power. Disappointment with the results of the peace, on the other hand, brought many people to seek refuge in a renewed glorification of non-commitment, and to formulate serious objections to the Barrier policy. The disasters incurred towards the end of the War of the Austrian Succession certainly demonstrate the inefficiency of the Barrier and the risks of European involvement.[1] For the time being, however, the result of that dangerous crisis was – as it had been in 1672 – the restoration of the House of Orange, and thus a continuation, even an intensification, of the alliance with England. But the politicians from the province of Holland and the business-men were interested in other affairs. It had become clear to them that neither the military nor the economic power of the state permitted an active foreign policy. It is significant that in the frequent discussions of this time about ways and means of restoring the Dutch economy, we once again hear voices likening the Dutch situation to that of the free commercial cities such as Hamburg, Danzig and so on.[2] And so, during the Seven Years War, the Republic withdrew completely from European affairs. Owing to the decline of Dutch importance and to the existence of a European balance of power, a situation had finally been created in which the diplomatic dogma of True Liberty seemed to function.

During the Anglo-French struggle in America, however, it was shown once more that neutrality could be maintained only by a display of power, and the obvious lack of Dutch maritime power made the commercial pressure-groups take refuge in an alliance with France; but this renewed participation in the balance of power led, no less than the English alliance, to disaster.

Once more let me recall the eighteenth-century voices quoted

[1] Alice C. Carter, 'The Dutch as Neutrals in the Seven Years' War', *The International and Comparative Law Quarterly* (July 1963) 818–34. Cf. below, Ch. 5.

[2] J. Hovy, *Het voorstel van 1751 tot instelling van een beperkt vrijhavenstelsel in de Republiek* (Groningen, 1966) 352.

at the beginning of this chapter. The principles laid down in the formula of the Council of State and in the memoirs of Burgomaster Rendorp must be interpreted in the light of the international power-relations of that period. But at the same time I hope to have demonstrated that they represent also, in opposing solutions, the outcome of two centuries of meditation upon the impossible conditions in which the Dutch community had to struggle – and to bargain – for life.

FURTHER READING

There is no specific literature on the problem of the idea of Europe in Dutch foreign policy, and only very little on the 'history of ideas' in Dutch diplomacy. Note should be taken of J. C. BOOGMAN, 'Die holländische Tradition in der niederländischen Geschichte', *Westfälische Forschungen*, XV (1962) and the useful elaboration of Boogman's ideas in the first chapter of M. A. M. FRANKEN, *Coenraad van Beuningen's politieke en diplomatieke aktiviteiten in de jaren 1667–1684* (Groningen, 1966). Of some value also is the rather partisan, Orangist approach of J. A. VAN HAMEL, *Nederland tusschen de Mogendheden* (Amsterdam, 1918). G. W. VREEDE, *Inleiding tot eene Geschiedenis der Nederlandsche Diplomatie* (2 vols, Utrecht, 1856–61) is antiquated but contains much valuable material.

The ideology of 'True Liberty' is analysed in P. GEYL, *Het stadhouderschap in de partij-literatuur onder De Witt* (Amsterdam, 1947) and in E. H. KOSSMANN, *Politieke Theorie in het zeventiende-eeuwse Nederland* (Amsterdam, 1960).

For the economic aspects of Dutch foreign policy see G. N. CLARK and W. J. M. VAN EYSINGA, *The Colonial Conferences between England and the Netherlands in 1613 and 1615* (2 vols, Leiden, 1940–51); C. WILSON, *Profit and Power: a Study of England and the Dutch Wars* (1957); C. R. BOXER, *The Dutch Seaborne Empire* (1965); J. E. ELIAS, *Het voorspel van den eersten Engelschen oorlog* (2 vols, The Hague, 1920); W. J. KOLKERT, *Nederland en het Zweedsche imperialisme* (Deventer, 1908); S. ELZINGA, *Het voorspel van den oorlog van 1672* (Haarlem, 1926); S. MULLER Fzn., *Mare Clausum* (Amsterdam, 1872).

A great number of biographical and monographical studies deal with aspects of foreign policy relevant to our essay. For the beginning of the seventeenth century see the chapters concerning foreign policy in J. DEN TEX, *Oldenbarnevelt* (3 vols, Haarlem, 1960–6, in progress). For the ages of Frederick Henry, De Witt and William III see P. GEYL,

Oranje en Stuart (Utrecht, 1939); N. JAPIKSE, *Johan de Witt* (Amsterdam, 1915); J. POELHEKKE, *De vrede van Munster* (The Hague, 1948); N. JAPIKSE, *De verwikkelingen tusschen de Republiek en Engeland van 1660–1665* (Leiden, 1900); N. J. JAPIKSE, *Willem III* (Amsterdam, 1930–3). For the eighteenth century see J. STORK-PENNING, *Het Grote Werk* (Groningen, 1958); A. GOSLINGA, *Slingelandt's efforts towards European Peace* (The Hague, 1915); P. GEYL, *Willem IV en Engeland tot 1748* (The Hague, 1924); and A. J. VAN DER MEULEN, *Studies over het ministerie Van de Spiegel* (Leiden, 1905).

2 English Attitudes to Europe in the Seventeenth Century

J. R. JONES

FOR most of the period from the death of Elizabeth until the Revolution of 1688 England's role in Europe was that of a peripheral power. She exerted comparatively little direct influence, less for example than Sweden and Turkey, and her policies were inconsistent, changing almost as often and as violently as the internal politics of the country. Obviously internal instability was largely responsible for external powerlessness, but there were other important factors which I wish to examine here. Because of the lack of informed opinion old attitudes persisted long after changing circumstances had made them obsolete; the 'Protestant' attitude to foreign affairs, which was dominant during most of the century, is the clearest example. The limited resources at the disposal of the Crown, combined with its insistence that, as foreign affairs were exclusively a matter for the prerogative, Parliament had no right to participate in the formulation of policies, or to receive confidential information, usually meant that an effective or credible foreign policy was impossible because of poverty. In particular, parliamentary and popular opposition to the raising of an army frequently hamstrung offensive action, and fostered suspicion at home to the point of precipitating major crises – as in 1625–8, 1666–7, 1673–4, 1678 and 1697–1700. Only in the case of economic policies was the Crown prepared, at times eager, to accept advice from its subjects, but it cannot be said that the courses of action which it followed were always consistent with either the interests of the nation or of the groups which had been consulted. No clear-cut picture emerges when one looks at the attempts which were made to follow what we would call mercantilist policies.

Almost from his accession James was unfavourably compared with Elizabeth by the majority of his subjects, who wanted him to take his place as the head of the Protestant interest in Europe.

James's rejection of this role was based on an older principle, a conception of Christendom which made peace with his fellow-rulers a Christian duty. To James, the King of Spain and the archdukes were his 'good brethren', to whose overtures for peace and amity he was bound to respond.[1] At the same time James sent emissaries to Huguenot assemblies and actively intervened with authority in Dutch religious politics. He instructed Dudley Carleton not to forget that 'you are the minister of that master whom God hath made the sole protector of his religion'.[2] This is the explanation. James was the protector and not the champion; his was a defensive, not an aggressive role. He consistently deplored aggression. In 1617 James supported Venice in her defiance of Spain, the Pope and the Jesuits, but in 1619 he cautioned his son-in-law Frederick against accepting the illegal offer of the Bohemian throne. Knowing how precarious was the state of peace, James frequently acted with success as a mediator; for instance, he was instrumental in ending the War of Kalmar between Sweden and Denmark, when Dutch mediation had failed. After helping to negotiate the Treaty of Xanten he denounced the Dutch seizure of Juliers and the expedition to Ravensberg, even though they could be justified as essential to the security of the United Provinces. His persistence with the Spanish marriage negotiations must also be seen in this context, as a despairing attempt to retain his position as the only mediator who could bring about a general European peace. Charles II made a less well known but equally ineffective attempt to act as a general mediator when, after 1674, England was the only power not involved in war. He suggested that this role would enable him to safeguard English interests and win both profit and honour, but the parliamentary opposition were as suspicious as their predecessors, seeing in it an excuse for not taking any decision or action that could be construed as anti-French.

Lack of power rendered James I's well-meant attempts at mediation ineffective. Charles I alternated between policies which were not only wildly inconsistent but which his poverty of resources exposed to humiliating failure. Under Buckingham an over-ambitious diplomatic campaign to put Charles at the head of a general Protestant alliance crumbled into failure with the

---

[1] Sir Ralph Winwood, *Memorials of Affairs of State* (1725) II 62–3.
[2] Dudley Carleton, *Letters* (1775) 6.

defeat before Cadiz. The desperate Huguenots of La Rochelle were pressed into accepting English assistance for which they had not asked, and then abandoned to die from hunger after the English had been driven from the Ile de Ré. In the 1630s neither Spain nor France wanted the alliances which Charles successively offered them. Powerlessness, combined with a busy diplomacy and grandiose pretensions, made England contemptible – a situation which recurred after 1660. Like his father, Charles II repeatedly pressed himself as an ally on European powers which distrusted his sincerity, and doubted if England had the ability or intention to fulfil her obligations, as can be seen in the lack of response to her pretended anti-French proposals of 1679–80. Charles's excessive demands led Louis to prefer a Dutch alliance in 1662, an important reverse which led to the dangerous isolation of 1665–6. In 1670 it was apparently worth France purchasing an English alliance, but experience proved otherwise. English historians have described with some satisfaction the speed with which Charles detached himself from the French alliance and the Third Dutch War in 1674, and the way in which the French ambassador was taken by surprise: in reality the lack of French reaction, the absence of a determined attempt to preserve the English alliance, was a true but unflattering estimate of how much it was worth. In terms of French diplomatic activity and expenditure, England mattered far less than Brandenburg or Sweden, and when Louis did later respond to Charles's appeals for money the amounts which were paid put him on the same level as a minor French pensioner like the Elector of Trier. In 1688 Louis, by his decision to proceed with his aggression in the Rhineland, judged England to be less important than Cologne or the Palatinate.

In their interventions in English politics foreign rulers naturally paid attention to ministers. Too much importance should not be attached to the influence which could be gained in this way. There were 'French' and 'Spanish' parties among the ministers before 1640, but this does not mean that they were under the control or even the permanent influence of the ambassadors. Similarly the influence of Gondomar over James has been exaggerated; it was probably no greater than that of Caron, the Dutch envoy.[1] In any case, foreign policy was far less important

[1] C. H. Carter, *The Secret Diplomacy of the Habsburgs* (New York–London, 1964).

for ministers than the internal struggle for power, position and influence, in which their relations with the king were naturally of the first importance. For example Danby, architect of William's marriage to Mary and the alliance of 1677–8, was aware of, and had to acquiesce in, Charles's negotiations with France in order to prevent this alliance having any effect. Arlington's participation in the secret treaty of Dover, after he had sponsored the Triple Alliance, reveals his sense of priorities. As his career shows, no minister could rise to supreme power through experience, ability or success in the conduct of foreign affairs. Foreign policy depended on royal solvency, and this in turn on parliamentary management, so that secretaries of state were often selected for their ability in Parliament as much as for their knowledge of Europe. It is significant that the three chief ministers who tried to consolidate their position by a successful foreign policy all wrecked themselves by doing so: Buckingham's reputation was finally shattered by his failures in 1625–7, Danby's anti-French moves in 1677–8 provoked Louis to destroy him, and Sunderland's francophile activities did not save him from dismissal in 1688.

Royal officials justified the King's refusal to allow Parliament a share in the formulation of foreign policy on practical as well as constitutional grounds. Few members had any direct knowledge or experience. It was pointed out that, like the States-General or the Venetian Senate, the Commons was too numerous an assembly effectively to discuss and decide foreign policy.[1] But the failure to give Parliament any real information had serious consequences. It gave opposition leaders an unanswerable case for obstruction and inaction when they were asked for supply, or occasionally (for tactical reasons) for advice. The pitiably low level of knowledge and understanding revealed in any study of debates was another direct consequence. Moreover this general ignorance, the survival of false assumptions and unchallenged prejudices, was almost complete in the country as a whole: to cite an extreme example, some staunch but woefully ill-informed people with Protestant prejudices welcomed the Turkish attack on Vienna in 1683 as a possibly mortal blow to Popery. Foreign affairs were a matter for a tiny minority. Taking active royal servants, former diplomats and educated and well-informed merchants, the number

[1] Anchitell Grey, *Debates of the House of Commons* (1769) IV 197.

cannot have been much more than a hundred. With such a small number directly involved, and given the insulation of the Court from the country as a whole, there was no regular or automatic way for pressure groups to operate in order to influence policy. Nor could the Court always explain its policies when it was necessary to ask for money or other support. For instance, in 1625, the refusal of seamen to man the ships that were to be transferred to France for use against Soubise's Huguenot privateers damaged the possibility of an alliance with France against Spain. Public opinion remained sceptical when Charles claimed that the levying of ship-money would enable him to assert English rights at sea.

Powerlessness was the crucial factor in the period before 1640. In relation to France and Spain, absorbed as they were in their diplomatic and military struggle, this was of comparatively minor importance. But in relation to the Dutch it was crucial. For the majority of Englishmen the Dutch were primarily fellow-Protestants, old friends, the outer bulwarks of our defences against Popery. The complaints of those whose interests were directly and adversely affected by Dutch conduct – in the East Indies, in the Mediterranean and Archangel trades, and by the blockade of Flanders – led to neither effective government action nor to a change in public opinion. The merchants and seamen concerned were socially and politically less influential than those who maintained close links with the United Provinces – the puritan clergy, and the nobility and gentry who served in the Dutch army.[1] The fact that both these classes were attached to the Orange cause helped to conceal the real clash of interests between the two countries. Such acts of aggression as the Amboina 'massacre' were explained away as the work of the traitorous elements which Oldenbarnevelt and his party had represented. For example, John Chamberlain described Coen as 'false to his masters, popishly affected or even Jesuited'.[2] Until the dynastic marriage of 1641, and again after 1660, the House of Orange and its supporters were generally regarded as friendly to England,

[1] This is a subject which would repay examination, both in itself and in assessing the influence of these men on developments in early Stuart England.

[2] N. E. McClure (ed.), *The Letters of John Chamberlain* (Philadelphia, 1939) II 398. On Coen, governor-general of the Dutch East Indies, see below, Ch. 3, and for the Amboina 'massacre', below, pp. 90–1.

while their Republican opponents were suspected as representatives of those mercantile elements who put profit before principle or religion. Only during the Civil War, as a result of Frederick Henry's and William II's efforts to assist the Stuarts, did any large group of Englishmen understand and share the regents' suspicions of possible Orangist absolutist ambitions.

English diplomats were, from a very early stage, aware of the need to protect English interests against Dutch encroachment. In 1618 Carleton advised that the Dutch 'must be roundly dealt with, and rather by way of intimidation than persuasion or inducement';[1] but James and Charles lacked the power to intimidate. They had to accept the 'good words' of successive embassies which successfully evaded demands for reparations – at the price of gradually accumulating unsatisfied grievances, which contributed directly to the outbreak of the First Dutch War. It would be wrong, however, to describe this first war as simply a commercial one, and as yet we know too little about the pressures which influenced the decisions of the Council of State in 1651–2. In general terms the crucial factor would seem to have been the power now at the disposal of the Commonweath. It should be remembered that this was not the only major war of that decade, although historically it may appear to be the most important because it was the first of a series. There were also the undeclared French War of 1649–55, from which the breach with the Dutch largely developed, the Spanish War of 1655–60, Blake's intimidation of Portugal, and in addition the naval interventions in the Mediterranean and Baltic. The common factor in each case was English naval power. English interests had been infringed and damaged with impunity, especially during the years of the Civil War, but now there was the power to enforce respect for them and reparations for past losses. In these wars naval power was nevertheless employed energetically rather than systematically, to satisfy specific demands rather than in the pursuit of national profit and economic advantage – the only important exception being the optimistic West Indian expedition. In a commercial sense the purpose was defensive, not aggressive – to guarantee equal access to the Baltic, to check French and Tunisian piracies, to stop Dutch aggression in the East Indies. Moreover, for Cromwell himself, besides the general concept of a

[1] Carleton, *Letters* 312–13.

Protestant foreign policy (which *partly* inspired the Spanish War), the main consideration was the security of the republican régime, as can be seen in his satisfaction at the Act of Seclusion. Just as the Commonwealth régime rested on the power of the army at home, so the strength and operations of the navy were the basis for its ability to survive in a hostile Europe.

Nevertheless, although the First Dutch War was not directly caused by commercial issues, considerable significance must be attached to the protests made against the treaty which ended it. Cromwell was charged with neglecting to obtain the commercial advantages which the naval victories had placed within his reach, of losing the peace when the war had been won. At the time these protests had no effect, but after 1660, as the rapid re-passage of a strengthened Navigation law showed, mercantile interests were eager to use the power of the state to exert pressure – if necessary to the point of war – against those Dutch interests which, as they believed, were impeding their own development and expansion. They found ministers and politicians willing to support them, though for reasons of their own. Like everything else in the political world of Restoration England, foreign policy was subordinated to the demands of the intense internal struggle for power, office and influence among ministers and aspiring politicians. Few could afford to be consistent; it was consistency that ruined Clifford and Sir William Coventry and damaged Sir William Temple's career. Internal instability, the constant uncertainty and continual changes at Court, and the tension between the King and Parliament naturally handicapped English representatives abroad and often nullified their efforts.

Apart from Temple, the ablest English diplomat employed abroad by Charles II was probably Sir George Downing. He has always been depicted by historians, particularly Dutch ones, as *the* enemy of the United Provinces, dedicated to the destruction of their political power and economic wealth.[1] I believe that to generalise in this fashion is to distort Downing's outlook and position. His aims were generally limited and specific and, despite the violent language to be found in his dispatches, he had no formed intention of annihilating the Dutch. Indeed in his own eyes he was following a defensive, not an offensive, policy. Like most of his contemporaries he felt overwhelmed by the trading wealth

---

[1] For example, P. Geyl, *Oranje en Stuart* (paperback edn, Zeist, 1963) 140.

and strength of the Dutch, so that the first task was to protect the comparatively small share of trade which England retained. For Downing, political instability and poor economic organisation outweighed England's advantages from her geographical position and natural resources. Such weaknesses must be remedied, but they had given the Dutch such a lead that the longer the *status quo* continued the more advantageous their situation would become. They would continue to refuse to respect English interests. This was the conclusion at which Downing arrived soon after his appointment to The Hague in 1658. He was instructed to secure the release of ships seized in the East and to obtain compensation for their owners, and he also tried to recover ships taken by Spanish privateers and sold with their cargoes in Dutch ports. Soon it became obvious to Downing that De Witt's failure to give justice in these cases was not accidental, or an isolated example of evasion; he concluded that it was consistent with a half-century's temporising, that it represented a continuation of the tactics of paying England with good words instead of good deeds.[1] He became convinced that even the conclusion of a treaty would not mean a satisfactory settlement, in view of the way in which the Dutch had skilfully exploited previous treaties, like that of 1619, to entangle the English and prevent action being taken. Downing did realise the difficulties of De Witt's position and the limits to his power, which meant that he could not control or override virtually independent entities such as the East and West India Companies, Amsterdam, or the States and Admiralty College of Zeeland.[2] These bodies were the source of nearly all English grievances. The East India Company, a state within the state, was continuing its expansionist and exclusionist policies in the East and could be brought to reason only by reprisals – which would have to be in European waters because of its massive superiority in the East. The role of the West India Company also needs emphasis; it was, from its foundation, an aggressive and semi-piratical body, resembling the unsuccessful English Providence Island Company. Its pretensions to a monopoly of the Brazilian trade helped to block a settlement with England in 1651-2, its offensive in West

[1] T. Birch (ed.), *Thurloe State Papers* (1742) VII 257, 275, 296, 333, 421, 430–1, 848.

[2] Ibid., VII 849; T. H. Lister, *Life and Administration of Edward, first Earl of Clarendon* (1837) III 287.

Africa led to the Second Anglo-Dutch War, and its behaviour in Surinam gave Charles II a pretext for the third war.[1]

The weakness of central authority, which had permitted the East and West India Companies to become virtually independent and to act to the detriment of English interests, could also be exploited. Downing found it easy to enlist spies, even in committees of the States-General, to play off the landward provinces against Holland and, after 1660, to encourage the Orangist faction. Unfortunately Zeeland, of all provinces the most effectively obstructionist and jealous of Holland, and a traditional centre of Orangist sentiment, was the worst offender against English interests – resisting claims for reparations, harbouring Ostend privateers, libelling the Duke of York, and refusing justice in its Admiralty Court. Downing also used diplomatic pressure, for example in obstructing the treaty between the Dutch and Portugal. But altogether, such was the predominance of Holland and the ability of De Witt, all these tactics could only embarrass the Dutch, they could never prove decisive. The same is true of the issue of the status and education of the Prince of Orange; although (as Japikse and Geyl noted) Downing brought up this issue in 1661–2, in fact he received very little support or encouragement from Charles in doing so, while for Clarendon England lacked the power to force the issue with De Witt.[2] The only method which, in Downing's view, would produce results was the resolute and systematic application of pressure. But it was the threat, rather than the actual use, of force that he advocated:

... let them know that if they will not do you right you can and will do yourself right, [then] you shall have right and they will love and esteem you the better for it, and be better friends and neighbours for the future.[3]

The assumption which is to be found in all Downing's dispatches is that the Dutch will give way before pressure, if only it is applied with obvious energy and determination. He believed that De

[1] *Thurloe*, VII 296, 547; N. Japikse, *De Verwikkelingen tusschen de Republiek en Engeland* (Leiden, 1900), p. li. For Charles II's comments see C. H. Hartmann, *Charles II and Madame* (1934) 111.

[2] Japikse, *Verwikkelingen*, pp. xix, xxiii–iv; Lister, *Life of Clarendon*, III 167, 169–70.

[3] B.M., Egerton MS. 2538, fos 10, 83, 92.

Witt was bluffing; the Dutch would continue 'to talk big, as if they feared nobody, yet at bottom they are sensible what a business it would be to grapple with his Majesty'.[1] So far from precipitating a war, the application of pressure would ensure the peaceful settlement of disputes: 'they will yield and knock under board, his Majesty will gain great honour, his subjects relief, trade thereby encouraged and increased.' This miscalculation is understandable. Downing knew that 'interest of trade' was the all-important consideration for Holland, and everyone remembered how close to collapse the Dutch economy had come during the final stages of the previous war. Impressed, like all contemporary English commentators, by the burden of taxation in the United Provinces, Downing believed that they (and not Charles) faced bankruptcy in the event of war, which would have to be

maintained by extraordinary means and borrowing and how possible that will be . . . if their trade be stopped (as it will be if a war with his Majestie), their credit will not be very great (as was plainly seen in their war with Cromwell), nor will their people be able to pay the taxes already upon them, much less new ones.[2]

More generally and, at least in the short run, equally erroneously, Downing thought that Dutch resources were insufficient for them to try to maintain the independent status of a European power. Instead, as he told De Witt in 1658, the Dutch should 'keep to their old maxim, which their first Prince of Orange left them, of continuing well with, and depending upon, England',[3] a state of dependence which, of course, was to exist throughout Queen Anne's reign. But in 1664 Downing could hardly have been more mistaken in his estimates of De Witt's resolution and of the financial resources which he could mobilise.

On the other hand, Downing was always acutely aware of English governmental weaknesses and of their political and economic effects. Above all, he always stressed the need for harmonious co-operation between King or Protector and Parliament, believing that the Dutch kept a close watch on its proceedings and varied their tactics according to whether supply was likely to be

---

[1] Ibid., 2537, fo 404, and 2538, fo 116; Lister, *Life of Clarendon*, III 300, 314.
[2] Japikse, *Verwikkelingen*, pp. l, liii.
[3] *Thurloe*, VII 245.

granted. Still more fundamental was the need for the government to foster economic development:

I find that the gardener doth not more contribute to the growing of his herbs and trees, than doth the Government of any country to the growth of its trade. Holland was Holland from the beginning of the world, but never a place of trade till within these fifty or sixty years that the Government did espouse that interest. And I do evidently see in all my experience here, that it is not the people puts on the Governours but the Governours by prudent orders and contrivances put on the people to all manner of trade.[1]

This, Downing believed, applied to all kinds of governments, and it is very important to note that he never thought that an absolute form of government was necessary for the expansion of either the power or the wealth of England. It was the Cabal, and especially Clifford and James, who shared Colbert's views of the essential interdependence of royal absolutism and commercial expansion.

The war of 1672 was largely a Court war. Compared with the situation in 1662–5, when there had been considerable commercial and mercantile, as well as political, pressures for direct action against the Dutch, only individual merchants now had outstanding claims. In 1665 there was spontaneous enthusiasm and, with some careful preparation, Parliament voted £2,500,000. In 1672 the Cabal dared not call a session and financed the first campaign by the gamble of the Stop of the Exchequer. Of the ministers both Clifford and Shaftesbury had some mercantile connections, but for them (as for Colbert) political power, not commercial wealth, was the ultimate objective. There was also an important element of ministerial self-aggrandisement; ten years earlier the author of *Het Interest van Holland* had emphasised the greed and acquisitiveness of the English Court. Clifford, the most dynamic and anti-Dutch member of the Cabal, was about to complete his climb from obscurity to the Lord Treasurership, but it was ambition for power rather than for riches that motivated him. He had fought in the second war and served as prize commissioner and diplomatic envoy in Scandinavia. He used the offices and influence which these services earned him to undermine Temple, wreck the Triple Alliance and provoke the third war. The conventional estimate,

[1] Japikse, *Verwikkelingen*, p. xlv.

that he was the least important member of the Cabal, is in my view the exact reverse of the truth. Admittedly his policies failed and he was himself ruined, but the Dutch War was the heart of the Cabal's policies, and Clifford was the inspirer of the war.[1] It was he, and not Arlington his former patron, who took a leading part in the negotiation of the secret treaty of Dover.

Like Louvois, Clifford despised the Dutch regent class as 'a company of rogues and rascals, not fit for his Majesty or any other Prince to have anything to do with', and in 1672 he pressed for their total submission or annihilation.[2] He wanted to put the Dutch into such a state of political dependence as to prevent them ever following any policy inimical to English interests. They must accept English sovereignty of the seas, symbolised by the demand for the salute. This was far more than a prestige matter. It would mean that all Dutch merchantmen would sail the 'British' seas on sufferance, that permission would be required for the passage of warships and that the fisheries would continue only on English terms. To enforce these demands England was to have, in addition to naval supremacy, direct control of strategic points on the Dutch coast, so that a close blockade could be established at will. By the treaty with France England was to have Brielle and Goeree, controlling the Maas, Cadzand and Walcheren – which would also mean reopening the Scheldt and the port of Antwerp. Further, while England established this ascendancy in the North Sea area, the Dutch were to concede a share of the trade of their areas of supremacy in the East Indies.

If these objectives could be achieved English commerce would have enormous advantages over competitors, who would be defenceless against arbitrary action. For the Dutch, for the Scandinavians and Hanse towns (and also, significantly, for the French), this would amount to the establishment of what contemporaries called a Universal Monarchy at sea. This prospect of a permanent condition of maritime tyranny was no more tolerable to them than Louis XIV's pretensions on the Continent.[3]

In practice the Cabal's foreign policy, because of its insecure

---

[1] M. Lee, Jr., *The Cabal* (Urbana, Ill., 1965) rightly emphasises Clifford's failings and failures both as a financial administrator and as a parliamentary manager, but tends to underestimate his influence on Charles and his part in foreign affairs.

[2] C. H. Hartmann, *Clifford of the Cabal* (1937) 157.

[3] Hartmann, *Charles II and Madame*, 145.

financial basis, was largely opportunist.[1] The Court, while professing to follow long-term and national policies, had no choice but to take short-term views and short cuts. In 1672, as in 1665, an attack on the returning Smyrna convoy preceded the declaration of war. Victory was to be exploited by exacting a large indemnity. In both wars close blockades were abandoned for unsuccessful attempts to intercept East Indiamen. After the failures of the second war the Court proposed to recoup its losses by an attack on defenceless Hamburg, although English trade with Hamburg was particularly favourable and profitable. The whole policy of the Cabal was a risky gamble, at home and abroad, with exposure to parliamentary resentment as the penalty of failure.

It was characteristic of the parliamentary opposition that its first attacks were directed against the domestic policies of the Cabal: only from October 1673 did it attack the war. Two aspects of the criticisms of the war deserve examination. Defending the Court, Secretary Coventry claimed that we had to ally with either the French or the Dutch, that the former had been chosen because they were the stronger, and that French military victories vindicated this choice.[2] Similar reasoning had led Cromwell to ally with France, not Spain, but by 1672 the existence of a formidable French navy had transformed the situation. The new fleet represented a direct challenge to English claims to sovereignty over the seas, and a potential threat to English security. Charles's attitude was inconsistent. Rejecting as insufficient Dutch offers of concessions on the salute, he acquiesced in the French refusals to acknowledge English rights. More serious, Charles failed to persist with diplomatic attempts to limit French naval strength. Although insisting that the expansion of French commerce and the size of the new fleet were impediments to an alliance, Charles concluded one without receiving French assurances.[3] Buckingham's claim, when questioned by the Commons, that Louis accepted English naval supremacy, was disproved by French naval strength, which threatened the plantations and Mediterranean trade, and might even

---

[1] There is a significant contrast between the opportunism of Clifford and the systematic work of Downing, both in their comments and action on foreign policy and in their conduct at the Treasury, the former as commissioner and later Lord Treasurer, the latter as secretary.

[2] Grey, *Debates*, II 10.

[3] Hartmann, *Charles II and Madame*, 36–7, 223, 291.

enable Louis to invade Ireland or England.[1] It could not be justified by the needs of trade protection, since France had so little overseas trade; therefore, as Downing concluded, the French navy must be expressly intended against us.[2]

A second argument used by opposition members was to question the idea that offensive wars could produce commercial advantages. Leading the way, Sir William Coventry argued that trade could be obtained by war and conquest only in barbarous parts of the world, not in Europe. Claiming that we had gained on the Dutch since the Navigation Act he asked, 'what probability is there, if we beat the Hollander, that we shall get all trade?' Prosperity, based on 'industry and parsimony and by under-selling us', could not simply be annexed. He refuted the belief (which Downing had often asserted) that naval and military defeat would produce large-scale emigration of merchants, capital, artisans and trades from Holland into England. If they did have to leave, there was no obvious reason why they should come to England.[3] Other members stressed the cost of the Dutch wars: it was estimated that the first had cost £3,700,000 – was it worth the money? Clifford's facile promises were recalled, that victory over the Dutch would mean no more land tax or excise. Anticipating arguments that were to be so prevalent in Anne's reign, members attacked the bankers who made excessive profits out of the King's necessities, and compared them with the financiers in France. Arguments were produced to show how war enhanced the cost of coal and corn, and forced merchants to hire foreign ships at a cost of £300,000 a year, undoing the benefits of the Navigation Act. The pressing of seamen caused paralysis of shipping, and still more serious damage might be done by the closing to us of foreign markets, especially Spain, which once lost might never be regained.[4] But it should be added that, with the increasing importance of colonial and especially West Indies trade, the thesis that war could be profitable, both immediately in the form of prizes and colonial conquests and in the long run by diversion of trade, was to revive after 1688.

However justified its criticisms of the Cabal, it is not to Parliament that one must look for a clear appreciation of the problems which England faced, either before or after 1688, as a result of

[1] Ibid., 338–43; Grey, *Debates*, II 261.   [2] Ibid., IV 125.
[3] Ibid., II 203.   [4] Ibid., II 211, 231, 332; III 5, 7.

French policies and strength. In reading debates in the Cavalier parliament, particularly those of 1675 and 1677–8, the same individuals and the same prejudices and attitudes are encountered that were to prove such an embarrassment to William III. Apart from a few actual traitors – men like Harbord and Montagu who worked with the French ambassador in 1678 and maintained the association throughout the Exclusion crisis – or crypto-Jacobites after 1688, everyone feared Louis XIV as a threat to all Europe. As a general principle, it was considered that a balance could be established in Europe only by forcing France back to the frontiers of 1659. But both parliamentary and general opinion constantly and grossly under-estimated the investment of men, money and effort that this would necessitate. Members not only wanted, they actually thought they could have, an effective foreign policy on the cheap. To take an important example, the only real action taken by Parliament in the crisis of 1678 was to prohibit the import of French commodities, and on this the most exaggerated expectations were placed. France's ability to continue the war against most of Europe was attributed to her favourable balance of trade with Spain, Germany, Holland and especially England. Following the estimate contained in the 'Scheme of Trade', it was claimed that England lost nearly £1,000,000 annually through the import of French commodities (mostly non-essentials), and through the decline of exports to France as a result of Colbert's regulations, prohibitions and tariffs. By excluding all French commodities England would be strengthened, France weakened and her commercial competitiveness in peace-time impaired. It was even suggested that these measures would provoke rebellions against Louis.[1] After 1689, in the same facile way, greatly inflated hopes were placed on the blockade of France, and these account for the bitter recriminations directed against the Dutch practice of trading with the enemy, which was blamed for enabling Louis to prolong the wars. In the debates of 1678, when the question of war against France was under discussion, both Court and opposition speakers displayed complete ignorance and a baseless optimism about the damage which French privateers might inflict on English shipping.[2] After 1689, when losses began to mount, there was a similar lack of understanding

[1] Ibid., III 8, 127, 133, 327; IV 190, 388.   [2] Ibid., V 99–101.

of the strategic advantages which France possessed, and failures to protect English trade were attributed to corruption, cowardice and treachery.

If in general the need was to balance France, the most urgent and difficult task was to preserve the Spanish Netherlands from Louis XIV. During the whole period, from the French offensive of March 1677 until Marlborough's victory at Ramillies, this area lay at the mercy of France. Its loss would have crippling effects, for not only would it give Louis permanent and perhaps decisive strategic advantages over England and the United Provinces, but the possession of Antwerp would in the view of contemporaries give France the major share of world trade. Yet Parliament consistently refused to face the practical implications of this threat. For instance Sir Thomas Clarges, a long-lived and representative exponent of 'country' views, in 1678 denounced as unnecessary the raising of 30,000 men for the preservation of Flanders, and in 1690 he denied that England was obliged by her treaties to act as a principal in the continental campaigns.[1] The debates of 1678, and the furious controversies of 1697-1700, showed that an army was feared as the instrument for the establishment of absolutism, rather than seen as an essential element in English security. In the critical year 1691 a member could say that war against France was but a colour for a standing army.[2] Ministers were depicted as *the* danger to English liberties. In 1678 Clarges declared that he feared Lauderdale, Charles's minister in Scotland, more than Louis; and after 1697 the country opposition showed more enthusiasm for the impeachment of the Junto ministers than for the impending crisis over the Spanish succession.

Parliamentary ignorance and irresponsibility are seen in their most extreme form in the reluctance to accept as necessary the need for taxes on an unprecedented scale, and the need for allies. Usually the assistance provided by the allies was deliberately disparaged, and they were accused of dragging England into war, obstructing moves towards peace, and exploiting English resources for their own advantage. But at other times the same members expressed fears that the allies would make a separate peace, leaving England as isolated against the power of France as Brandenburg had been in 1678-9, thus assuming that English

[1] Ibid., IX 108, 388-9, 412; X 264, 332, 359.
[2] Ibid., X 176-7. The member was Sir John Thompson.

security did at least partly depend on allied powers. Attitudes displayed towards the Dutch were particularly inconsistent. On the one hand it was argued that, from motives of self-preservation, they were bound to defend Flanders as their 'barrier' and to maintain a balance in Europe, so that England need not concentrate her own energies on either task. Yet self-interest, in terms of commercial advantage and financial retrenchment, and the internal struggle between William and Amsterdam, might lead them to conclude a separate peace (as in 1678), or even to renew the old alliance with France.[1]

There is a close parallel between the opposition of the Dutch republicans to William in the years 1677–85 and the conduct and attitudes of the first Whigs during the Exclusion crisis. Both groups concentrated almost exclusively on domestic issues, and particularly on the danger to constitutional liberties from the absolutist ambitions of their rulers. The republicans wrecked the Confederation in 1678; the Whigs wilfully ignored Temple's warnings on the dangers from France, and virtually forced Charles to evacuate Tangier. In both countries the leaders of the opposition factions were ready to use French assistance in order to ruin their rivals and achieve their immediate objectives, shortsightedly ignoring the advantages which they were conferring upon Louis. Barrillon in London, d'Avaux at The Hague, were able to paralyse English and Dutch foreign policy, and give Louis the freedom of manœuvre which enabled him to seize Strassburg, Luxemburg and parts of the Spanish Netherlands. It is not surprising, then, that William's equation of the Whigs with Dutch republicans, and his experienced knowledge that all but one or two English politicians gave priority to the internal faction-fight over foreign affairs, determined him to keep the conduct of foreign policy in his own hands. Despite his royal title his position in England did not differ essentially from that to which he was accustomed. With limited powers, financially dependent on slow-moving and corrupt representative institutions which were infiltrated by his enemies, served by men whose loyalty he often suspected, and beset by pressure-groups whose perspectives were narrow and selfish, he could not simply give up and retire into inert isolation, like Charles II. With, or without, the understanding and assistance of his subjects he must persist with his mission to save Europe and

[1] Ibid., III 334; IV 371–2; V 299, 322; VI 4–5, 79.

England from Louis. He has been criticised for not educating his new subjects in the realities, principles and techniques of foreign affairs, but this failure is intelligible when one appreciates the ignorance, prejudice, self-interest and treachery which he encountered, and the immensity and urgency of the problems with which he had to deal. Yet it is not certain that he did fail in this task of education. Although William was right in suspecting some of their motives and much of their conduct, the new generation of Whigs who came into office under him were to understand, inherit and carry to success the policies which he brought with him to England.

FURTHER READING

1. *Documents*
   There is no single convenient volume of documents which deals adequately with English attitudes to Europe, including foreign and commercial policies, and these subjects receive little attention in the well-known collections by Gardiner, Tanner, Grant Robertson and Kenyon. The best selection is in David Douglas, *English Historical Documents* VIII, ed. A. BROWNING (1953). Also useful are the volumes of the Navy Records Society, especially *Letters and Papers relating to the First Dutch War*, ed. S. R. GARDINER and C. T. ATKINSON, 6 vols (1899–1930). See also J. R. McCULLOCH (ed.), *Early English Tracts on Commerce* (reprinted, Cambridge, 1952).

2. *Secondary Works*
CLARK, SIR GEORGE: *The Seventeenth Century*, 3rd ed. (Oxford, 1960). Still the best survey of general aspects of seventeenth-century Europe.
STOYE, J. W.: *English Travellers Abroad, 1604–1667* (1952). An admirable account of the connections between England and Europe, on general cultural as well as on personal levels.
WILSON, CHARLES: *Profit and Power* (1957). Stops short of the third Anglo-Dutch War. The same extremely rewarding approach could be used to interpret the commercial and foreign policies of the English Court after 1667.
BERESFORD, JOHN: *The Godfather of Downing Street* (1925). The only biography of Downing; a new one is overdue.
WOODBRIDGE, H. E.: *Sir William Temple, the Man and his Work* (New York, 1940). Concentrates on the literary side.

FEILING, SIR KEITH: *British Foreign Policy, 1660–1672* (1930). Detailed and well documented.

DAVIES, GODFREY: 'The Control of British Foreign Policy by William III', in *Essays on the Later Stuarts* (San Marino, 1958).

HARTMANN, C. H.: *Charles II and Madame* (1934) and *Clifford of the Cabal* (1937) are both documented, but the interpretation requires revision.

FRANCIS, A. D.: *The Methuens and Portugal* (1966). An important monograph based on much fresh research.

BACHRACH, A. G. H.: *Sir Constantine Huygens and Britain* (Leiden, 1962). The first volume of a definitive biography.

FULTON, T. W.: *The Sovereignty of the Seas* (Edinburgh, 1911). Still authoritative on Anglo-Dutch disputes about territorial waters, the salute and fishery rights in the North Sea.

JONES, J. R: *Britain and Europe in the Seventeenth Century* (1966). A brief survey.

Many major subjects need either adequate treatment or fundamental revision and reinterpretation. Examples are the careers of Winwood, Carleton, Thurloe, Downing, Clifford, Melfort, the 3rd Earl of Sunderland, and Bolingbroke. We need studies of English policy towards Spain before 1640, which C. H. Carter (above, p. 39, note) has only touched in part; of Buckingham's foreign policies (as indeed of his whole career); and of the Long Parliament's relations with Europe. Studies of English (and also Scottish and Irish) attitudes to individual countries – on the model of G. ASCOLI, *La Grande Bretagne devant l'opinion française* (2 vols, Paris, 1930) and R. MURRIS, *La Hollande et les Hollandais au XVIIᵉ et au XVIIIᵉ siècles vus par les Français* (Paris, 1925) – would be illuminating. There is no adequate study of the army to compare with J. EHRMAN'S *The Navy in the War of William III* (Cambridge, 1953). In naval history the whole question of the *guerre de course* has been neglected, apart from J. S. BROMLEY's penetrating study, 'The French Privateering War, 1702–13', in *Historical Essays 1600–1750 presented to David Ogg*, ed. H. E. BELL and R. L. OLLARD (1963), and his other articles.

3 Aspects of Dutch Colonial Development in Asia in the Seventeenth Century

M. A. P. MEILINK-ROELOFSZ

IN recent years, foreign scholars have shown an increasing interest in the history of Dutch expansion. Down to the Second World War this field of study was investigated almost exclusively by Dutch colonial historians, who placed greatest emphasis on the history of the colonial administration in Indonesia, the former Dutch East Indies. Only a few historians occupied themselves with the territories lost by the Dutch in the past or still possessed in the West Indies.

With regard to the history of the Dutch settlements on the coast of India, special mention should be made of the pioneer work done by Dr Terpstra.[1] Unfortunately, his studies have not been translated into English, and so are not as well known outside the Dutch-speaking countries as they deserve to be. His first study, on the Dutch settlements along the Coromandel coast, appeared as early as 1911; and yet the Dutch factories on the Indian coast were quite inadequately dealt with in the well-known handbook of colonial history published in 1925 by Colenbrander, then professor of that subject at Leiden University, who dispatched the history of these settlements in a most offhand manner, as the defunct history of regions no longer of the slightest significance for the history of the Netherlands.[2] This very short-sighted attitude was undoubtedly due to the fact that colonial history was not taught at the University for its own sake, but only as part of the syllabus of studies for the East Indian Civil Service, of which the oldest centre was in Leiden and the later, more conservative one in Utrecht. After Indonesia gained its independence, the courses for this Service at both universities were discontinued. The University of Leiden did away with the

[1] For the works of H. Terpstra, see Further Reading below, p. 82.
[2] H. T. Colenbrander, *Koloniale Geschiedenis*, II 292.

Chair of Colonial History altogether; it had been combined with that of Maritime History for a short period after the war, and the latter subject received by far the greatest emphasis. Colonial history continued to be taught in Utrecht, under the less provocative title of History of Overseas Relations. The secession of Indonesia and the decline of the Netherlands to its rank as a small European power apparently gave rise to a sort of trauma. The colonial past was over and done with; people evidently wanted to hear as little about it as possible and seemed not to realise that another approach was also feasible. The slight interest in Dutch expansion that remained was primarily focused on the recent past of Dutch-Indonesian relations. Undoubtedly this was partly owing to the desire to justify Dutch policy there, but this reason, unfortunately, cannot hold good for the history of the East India Company. The concept of colonialism is too closely associated with that of the Company, and the Dutch historians kept well away from it. Only the odd sociologist or agricultural historian found his way to the Company's archives and enthusiastically discovered these fine sources.

Outside the Dutch-speaking countries, however, historians began to work on these treasure-hoards of material; and whereas hardly any Dutch historians ever appear there, the section of the Company's archives in the Algemeen Rijksarchief (General State Archives), at The Hague, is swamped with oral and written requests for information from foreigners. Several of them, both from Anglo-Saxon countries and the Asian world, go to the trouble of learning the old Dutch language and handwriting, so that they can read and understand the documents at first hand. The Asians in particular can consult here unique material for their history which cannot be found in their own countries. Some of these research workers have already produced remarkable results.[1] At the order of Asian governments, moreover, certain large-scale microfilm projects have been carried out: for example, India and Japan have filmed a large proportion of the material relevant to their history.[2] Whereas, furthermore, the Dutch

[1] See H. Terpstra, 'Inheemse stemmen over het Compagniesbeleid in Voor-Indië en Ceylon', *Tijdschrift voor Geschiedenis*, LXXVII (1964) 288–306. Cf. Further Reading below, p. 82.

[2] Since 1963 the Historiographical Institute of the University of Tokyo has been publishing a list in *Historical documents relating to Japan in foreign countries: an*

colonial historians of the period before the Second World War based their studies exclusively on Dutch material, foreign historians include in their scope the archives of other European trading companies and hence place the Dutch data in a broader frame of reference.

In addition to these studies based on manuscript sources, there have appeared in recent years summaries of the history of Dutch expansion, written in English and intended for a larger public than one of fellow-historians only. I should like particularly to mention the excellent book by Professor C. R. Boxer, *The Dutch Seaborne Empire* (1965), which commands our deepest admiration for the extensive acquaintance with Dutch historical writings revealed in it, and for the way its author sets the history of the Dutch overseas in the seventeenth and eighteenth centuries within the broad framework of Dutch history as a whole; no facet of our historical evolution is omitted, and ever and again its connection with the sea and with the overseas settlements is demonstrated. Even though the picture turns out to be rather too kaleidoscopic on occasion, the light sometimes falls on unexpected spots and leads to further investigation. Since Boxer bases his work purely on printed matter, it is inevitable that occasionally his conclusions should be drawn from insufficiently sound data. Thus, for example, there are many familiar published documentary sources which deal with the Company's employees, whereas exact statistical data since the end of the seventeenth century can be obtained from the Company's meticulously recorded wage accounts, though a computer would be a great aid in processing them. Boxer devotes a great deal of attention to the human element, the seagoing personnel and the Company's employees in the outposts. As he had already demonstrated with regard to Portuguese expansion, in the Netherlands empire the people were certainly not of lesser importance than the maritime-technical, political, military and commercial factors: it is characteristic that Boxer considers one of the main factors of the Company's decline to have been the widespread corruption among its employees, in other words the human failure. Boxer's summary is, in my opinion, of much higher merit than the nevertheless readable work of the American Dutchman George Masselman, *The Cradle*

---

inventory of microfilm acquisitions in the library of the Historiographical Institute: for the Netherlands see I pt 1; II pt 2; III pt 3; IV pt 4; V pt 5.

of Colonialism,[1] a best-seller in America. This is a pragmatical historical account based on a not very critical use of printed works dealing with the age of Governor-General Jan Pietersz. Coen (1587–1629; Governor-General 1619–23, 1627–9).

Having digressed on the large amount of interest shown abroad and the lack of it in the Netherlands, I should like to touch on certain main aspects of Dutch policy in Asia in the seventeenth century. These are, in particular, the monopoly which determined that policy, the conceptions of it entertained by the directors in the Netherlands and by the Hoge Regering (High Government) in Batavia, the repercussions of the monopoly on the trade and shipping of the Asians, and the beginnings of the growth from a maritime trading empire into a territorial power.

I have already mentioned the archives of the United East India Company (VOC) as a primary source from which we may follow its management by the directors in the Netherlands. As a summary, however, the work which the Company's lawyer Pieter van Dam (1621–1706) wrote in 1693–1701 at the request of the directors is of very great value: *Beschryvinge van de Oostindische Compagnie*. The original manuscript bearing his signature is in the keeping of the Algemeen Rijksarchief, but today this work is available in an excellent edition by Dr F. W. Stapel:[2] it is to be hoped that an English translation, in whole or part, will become available one day. As the Company's most important permanent official, Van Dam, who acted less as legal adviser than as general secretary to the directors, was conversant with Company affairs during a term of office lasting more than forty years. He attended the meetings of the seventeen directors known as the 'Heren XVII', drew up their resolutions, read their correspondence and drafted their replies. He was on most of the committees appointed by the Heren XVII, exercising an advisory vote. He held a seat in the Amsterdam chamber of the Company, sitting in an advisory capacity also towards the directors of that chamber. Since Van Dam identifies himself largely with the standpoint of his superiors, it is no use expecting to find him critical of Company activities. His primary concern is with the preservation of the established organisation, and he attributes any defect to human failing, rather

[1] New Haven, Yale U.P., 1963.
[2] See Further Reading below, p. 80.

than to the system, and does not hesitate to criticise those whom he considers culpable. Since his 'Description' was meant to be read only by the inner circle of the Heren XVII, nothing is suppressed or glossed over. Fear of competition caused the directors to maintain as much reserve as possible about the administration of their business, and they did not fail to surround Van Dam's work with all appropriate secrecy; the very existence of his manuscript was concealed from outsiders.

Van Dam's work is not primarily a description of a historical phenomenon, but a practical handbook for the use of the directors, illustrated with reference to history. As his modern editor remarks with good reason, 'we must not expect appreciation from Van Dam, but rather an explanation of the mechanism'; and the explanation he gives is excellent. Yet there is practically no indication of any development taking place in the Company's institutions or in its monopoly system, no sign of adaptation to the exigencies of changing circumstances. This quality of immutability means that Van Dam's 'Description' retains some validity for the history of the Company's organisation in the eighteenth century. His knowledge of Asia was confined to what he could learn from the letters and papers sent over to the Netherlands, and that part of his work which deals with management and property in Asia is clearly not based on personal observation. This is in contrast to the Dutch part, where the expert holds the floor. But enough of Van Dam, whose importance should be stressed here because he deserves to be better known outside the Netherlands than he is at present. There is another and a special reason why I have invited your attention to him. His manuscript has not been handed down intact to us. Precisely that portion which deals with Anglo–Dutch relations has been lost – at least all attempts to trace the missing part in the Netherlands have been in vain. I wonder if it could possibly have found its way to England, and if it is now lying forgotten in some library or private collection here?

At the outset, Dutch trade in Asia was pursued on a footing of equality with the Asians, though there was, even then, an endeavour to exclude others. Jacob van Neck, leader of the most profitable voyage made by the so-called Fore-Companies (Voor-Compagniën), could proudly claim on his return in 1599 that the great profits yielded by his voyage had not been made by injustice or oppression, but by honest trading.[1] Van Neck was certainly not the only one to uphold such a principle in this early period. On the other hand, the keen rivalry between the pioneer companies in the East led to a very rapid rise in the buying price of spices, and it was mainly for spices that the voyages to Asia were made. In Europe the opposite effect was revealed in competitive price-cutting.[2] Co-operation was necessary if, as contemporaries expressed it, they were not to end up by 'trading the shoes off their feet and the money out of their purse'. With their relatively limited resources of power, the Dutch could only maintain their position in Asia by consolidating their efforts. Although the Fore-Companies were not aggressive in purpose, since the States-General had explicitly forbidden them to use force, their mutual rivalry paralysed every attempt at co-operation against the Portuguese-Spanish enemy.

The States-General's policy with regard to the Fore-Companies was abstention from direct participation, a policy continued with regard to the United Company formed in 1602. The result was a trading company that differed completely from the Portuguese type. In Portugal this was a state enterprise in certain monopoly products only. Apart from them private trading was conducted on an extensive scale, mainly by Portuguese of Eurasian origin, whose business worked entirely along the lines of the existing Asian trade. Moreover, Portuguese merchants could participate directly in the government trade by means of investments.[3] For the United East India Company, which was founded against the resistance of local interests in the Republic, the basis of existence really was a rigid monopoly. This monopoly was originally obtained exclusively with regard to other groups and individuals in the Republic, but the natural line of development was that the Company tried to secure a monopolistic position in Asia as well, against both other Europeans and the Asians.

The charter granted to the Company by the States-General gave it a singularly autonomous position *vis-à-vis* the state. It conferred on the Company the right to conduct war, since now the

[1] H. Terpstra, *Jacob van Neck, Admiraal en Regent* (Amsterdam, 1950) 73.

[2] J.A. van der Chijs, *Geschiedenis der stichting van de Vereenigde O.I. Compagnie* (Leiden, 1857) 63 ff., 87–90; M. A. P. Meilink-Roelofsz, *Asian Trade and European Influence in the Indonesian Archipelago* (The Hague, 1962) 173–4.

[3] Ibid., 120, 174, 176–9; Van der Chijs, *Geschiedenis*, 104, 108, 113.

emphasis was very definitely placed on the aggressive character of the United Company, in contrast with the Fore-Companies. The state provided military forces in order to extend the European war to Asia, and at the same time an economic offensive was to be undertaken. In addition, the United Company was granted the right to sign treaties with native monarchs, to build forts and to appoint administrators – in other words, sovereign rights which made it a state outside the state. But the dual nature of a commercial body endowed with sovereign rights bore within itself the seeds of great problems. The incompatible qualities of merchant and sovereign made for a rather ineffectual policy on the part of the directors, who considered themselves first and foremost leaders of a trading concern, whereas their subordinates in Asia considered the sovereign aspect of the United Company as of greater importance.

At first the directors' conception of their Company's influence in the politico-military field accorded with the ideas of the Portuguese: that is, a system of ruling through maritime trading channels, with a few fortified bases, was to suffice. It was quite beyond their powers of imagination, certainly at the beginning of the seventeenth century, to conceive of a territorial empire growing out of this policy. Even the 'lofty projects' of J. P. Coen, which the Directors criticised, did not go as far as that, although Coen wanted to extend his trading supply-lines to the coasts of China. He was certainly, however, less scrupulous in his choice of means than the directors deemed permissible; to judge by the results of his actions, they allowed him a great deal of scope, in spite of their never-ending complaints about his poor financial returns. The decision whether to attain the aim of enforcing the spice monopoly throughout the Indonesian archipelago by purely commercial means, with only an incidental use of force, or to attain it entirely by force, was determined in practice by Coen. There was indeed a strong trend against a policy of violence among both the administrators of the United Company in Asia and the directors in the Netherlands, so that Coen had to overcome very stiff opposition before he pushed his policy through. In the long run, nevertheless, the pacific trend regained ground among the directors, especially after the position of the United Company had become more or less consolidated in the East. It acquired an ascendancy over the Portuguese thanks to its superior naval techniques and strategy and to a more efficient organisation of business. The Portuguese, in fact, held their own in Asia for much longer than is often supposed, largely because of their relatively strong position on the coast of India and their possession of Macao in the Far East. It was the loss of Malacca in 1641 which disrupted their network of trade routes. Its capture gave the Dutch the upper hand in the Archipelago. Even so, Portuguese private traders continued to operate in this region until after the fall of Macassar in 1667, thanks largely to their connexions with Macao.[1]

The Dutch made more strenuous efforts than the Portuguese and Spaniards to extend their monopoly in Asia. Their efforts were concentrated on excluding all rivalry whatsoever, in order to be able to buy products there as cheaply as possible, by means of treaties or even violence if need be, and then to sell them for as high a price as possible. The spice monopoly was disastrous for the population of the Spice Islands.[2] The trading and shipping formerly carried on there were wiped out. Indeed, the majority of the Bandanese were annihilated or expelled from their islands.[2] The population of the Spice Islands became entirely dependent for food and clothing on the much too scarce and expensive imports of the United Company. And yet the enforcement by violence of the spice monopoly only succeeded for one product, nutmegs. As cloves were produced over a very widespread area, the production had to be regulated in such a way that the amount produced was exactly what the European and Asian markets could absorb, at the prices fixed by the Company. Efforts were made to find new markets, but the nature of the product made it difficult to stimulate consumption. Besides, the trading policy followed by the Company did not generally include such stimulation.[3] The Company tried to restrict the culture of cloves

[1] See C. R. Boxer, 'Francisco Vieira de Figueiredo: a Portuguese merchant-adventurer in South East Asia, 1624–1667', *VKI*, LII (The Hague, 1967). For the relations of the Dutch with Macassar, cf. F. W. Stapel, *Het Bongaais Verdrag: de vestiging der Nederlanders op Makassar* (The Hague, 1922).

[2] See J. A. van der Chijs, *De vestiging van het Nederlandsche gezag over de Banda-eilanden, 1599–1621* (Batavia, 1886); L. Kiers, *Coen op Banda, de conqueste getoetst aan het recht van den tijd* (Utrecht, 1943); C. Gerretson, *Coen's eerherstel* (Amsterdam, 1944).

[3] Meilink-Roelofsz, *Asian Trade*, 94–5, 219–20, 226; K. Glamann, *Dutch-Asiatic Trade, 1620–1740* (Copenhagen–The Hague, 1958) 92–3.

to a small area, whilst the rest of the Islands were subjected to strict control. In spite of the notorious annual expeditions to destroy the clove trees, however, smuggling continued on a large scale as long as there were free ports in the Archipelago like Macassar, Bantam and the seaports of northern Java. With its limited naval power, it was impossible for the Company to inspect all these islands, with their innumerable bays and creeks.

The Company was always careful to observe the legal forms. It believed that its policy was in part sufficiently justified by the rights of sovereignty it had acquired by its conquests at the expense of the Portuguese; wars against the natives were waged because of the alleged violation of contracts, although these had themselves usually been extracted by force. In this respect, the Company displayed a complete lack of understanding of the psyche of the indigenous peoples, who are so very different from Europeans, and of their different customs of trade and law, which rendered contracts in particular much less binding in Asian minds than in those of the Dutch.[1] In this matter the native populations could expect no support at all from their monarchs and notables. Once the monarchs had granted exclusive contracts to the Company, their further co-operation would be bought for annual monetary subsidies and gifts. The Sultan of Ternate appointed a Company employee as his stadholder in the clove district.[2]

Before the Company adopted this line of action, the monarchs and notables had been accustomed to enjoying the largest share of the profits from the spice trade, but enough scope had been left to the people for their own trading activities, and so prosperity increased for all. The rigorous monopoly of the Dutch put an end to this. The Portuguese had never tried to gain such comprehensive control over the spices. The decline of the native economy was pointed out by practically every Company official in his reports.[3] The Company's system was inhuman, though some of its servants had a real understanding of native conditions. There is no better description of native society than the memoir on Macassar by Cornelis Speelman, who was both

[1] B. H. M. Vlekke, *Geschiedenis van den Indischen Archipel* (Roermond, 1947) 171; Meilink-Roelofsz, *Asian Trade*, 211–13, 215.

[2] J. K. J. de Jonge, *Opkomst van het Nederlandsch gezag in Oost-Indië*, VI p. lxxiv; J. E. Heeres and F. W. Stapel, *Corpus Diplomaticum*, II 37–42, 102–4.

[3] Meilink-Roelofsz, *Asian Trade*, 155–6, 159 ff., 217–21.

commander-in-chief against Macassar and executor of the war policy in Java.[1]

Heavy expenses were involved in acquiring the spice monopoly. Repeated rebellions in the Spice Islands and the war against Macassar necessitated the maintenance of a larger military force and many forts. When the final accounts were made up, they generally showed a large deficit both in the Moluccas and in Amboina. And yet, of course, the United Company made large profits on spices in Europe and elsewhere. Its bookkeeping was so very inadequate that it is impossible to determine the ratio between the enormous deficits in the islands and the gains in the spice trade, but I think it is important to note the very expensive way in which cloves and nutmegs were acquired.[2] In the eighteenth century the accounts of the spice-producing settlements of the Company always showed a deficit, in spite of the big profits still being made on spices in both Europe and Asia. Moreover, one gets the impression that the Company invested a great deal of its energy and resources in the acquisition of products which were losing their relative importance in international trade.[3] By the time that spices had come almost entirely into Dutch hands in the second half of the seventeenth century, they had already largely lost their market appeal.[4]

In the long run the United Company controlled most of the trade in nutmegs and cloves, and moreover got hold of practically all the cinnamon after the Portuguese were driven out of Ceylon, but it never enjoyed a comparably large share of pepper. Many pepper-producing areas never fell within its control, although it did eventually succeed in cornering a very considerable share of the pepper trade, particularly during the struggle with the Portuguese along the Malabar coast[5] and also by concluding exclusive contracts in Sumatra and Java, notably with Achin,

[1] F. W. Stapel, *Cornelis Janszoon Speelman* (The Hague, 1936) 72, 102. Speelman's 'Notitie' is preserved in ARA, Inventory of acquisitions 1926, I (10) : a publication by J. Noorduyn is in course of preparation.

[2] W. M. F. Mansvelt, *Rechtsvorm en geldelijk beheer bij de Oost-Indische Compagnie* (Amsterdam, 1922) 93–4.

[3] D. G. E. Hall, *A History of South-East Asia* (1955) 250.

[4] T. Raychaudhuri, *Jan Company in Coromandel* 156; Meilink-Roelofsz, *Asian Trade*, 212–27.

[5] See M. A. P. Roelofsz, *De vestiging der Nederlanders ter kuste Malabar* (The Hague, 1943).

Bantam and the other Sumatran states. But the European market could only absorb a limited amount of this product too, and so markets for it had to be found in the Asian countries.[1]

In Asia outside the Archipelago, however, the Company could no more lay down the law than it could control the sales market in Europe. It is true that big profits could be made, but only in competition with other Europeans and Asians, and here all depended on the sometimes very arbitrary decisions of the Asian rulers. Barter goods in exchange for the spices also had to be obtained in Asia on the open market. There was hardly any demand for European products in Asia, and so the only alternative to shipping large consignments of money from Europe, which was contrary to the prevailing economic principles, was to purchase Asian products. For that matter, the Company aimed at establishing an inter-Asian trade which would not only pay its own way, but could also be used for the purchase of return freight in the Netherlands and for covering the costs of the Company's organisation in Asia – an ideal never realised.[2] The main barter product for spices was cottons from the coast of India, the 'left arm' of the Company's trade in the Archipelago. Very early on the Company established factories on the Indian coast, where it met with the competition of the Portuguese and, as in the Archipelago, that of the English.

The English were cut out of the Spice Islands. A brief period of co-operation with them proved a failure, both in the Archipelago and in India. Politically the situation was certainly unfavourable for such co-operation, largely because of the almost pathologically anti-English attitude of Governor-General Coen. Events on Amboina marked the nadir in Anglo–Dutch relations.[3] The Coen period was followed by latent mistrust on both sides, though with repeated warnings from the Dutch directors to their employees in Asia to preserve the peace with the 'seeming friends' and to avoid all 'disputes' and 'incivilities'. Less sympathetic was the recommendation to lend as little help as possible to the English, and

[1] Glamann, *Dutch-Asiatic Trade*, 73 ff.

[2] Pieter van Dam, *Beschryvinge van de Oostindische Compagnie*, ed. F. W. Stapel, 7 vols (The Hague, 1927–54) I (1), 451; Meilink-Roelofsz, *Asian Trade*, 378, n. 149.

[3] See below, pp. 90–1. Cf. F. W. Stapel, 'De Ambonsche moord', *Tijdschrift Bataviaasch Genootschap* LXII (1923) 209–26; W. Ph. Coolhaas, 'Aantekeningen en opmerkingen over den zoogenaamden Ambonschen moord', *BKI*, CI (1942) 49–93.

indeed to other foreigners as well, in providing 'accommodation'. To use their own terms, the directors preferred 'to let them fend for themselves'.[1] The Dutch were annoyed beyond measure if the English profited from the peace maintained in any region by expensive Dutch fortifications. They got particularly angry if, to make matters worse, the English spread the rumour among Indian merchants that the Dutch did no more than pick the spices they sold at such exorbitant profits.[2]

In the beginning the Dutch on the Indian coasts owed their superiority to greater capital reserves and a better integrated organisation.[3] The English were cut off from the greater part of the spice supplies and so forced to turn to other products, thus increasing their commercial opportunities. Unlike the Dutch, they had no objection to renting tonnage to the Indian merchants. It was only when this transport business proved profitable that the Dutch followed the English example, though hesitatingly and against their will, for they were afraid this would be to the advantage of their Asian rivals.[4] Gradually the English built up larger reserves of capital; and since they were not as afraid as the Dutch of investing larger sums in their overseas trade, that capital increased. Moreover, the English were never so dependent as the Dutch on the South-East Asian markets for the sale of textiles; they found an increasing outlet in Europe, in spite of the fact that the textile industry in their own country was protected. For the Dutch, the export of textiles remained limited mainly to South-East Asia. It was only at the end of the seventeenth century, when spices began to be less important for the European market and when the sale of textiles in the Archipelago was unfavourably influenced by keen competition, that the United Company began to increase its textile exports to Europe.[5]

The Dutch met competition even more dangerous than that of

[1] P. Mijer (ed.), *Verzameling van instructiën, ordonnanciën en reglementen voor de regeering van Nederlandsch Indië* 115; P. A. Tiele and J. E. Heeres, *Bouwstoffen voor de geschiedenis der Nederlanders in den Maleischen Archipel* III p. lx.

[2] Meilink-Roelofsz, *Asian Trade*, 204.

[3] W. H. Moreland, *From Akbar to Aurangzeb: a Study in Indian Economic History* (1923) 30 ff.

[4] Meilink-Roelofsz, *Asian Trade*, 204; ARA, VOC 452 and 453, Heren XVII to Gov.-Gen. and Council, 8 Dec 1625 and 27 Aug 1630; Raychaudhuri, *Jan Company*, 110–12, 139, 156, 162.

[5] Ibid., 139, 156.

the English company from the English interlopers, who spent much less on equipment and could therefore force down prices.[1] As long as Macassar, Bantam and the towns of north Java were not subjected to the United Company, the competition from the English in the Archipelago continued to be troublesome for the Dutch, especially since it stimulated trade in Bantam as a rival port of Batavia: in the second half of the seventeenth century Bantam was even called the port of Batavia! It was only after the subordination of the sultanate of Bantam in 1684 that an end was put to this economic threat and the English restricted to Benkulen, their new Sumatran base.[2]

No matter how strained relations were between English and Dutch at times, particularly when the two countries were at war with each other in Europe, there were often individual instances of good understanding between the staffs of the Dutch and English factories, though this is not surprising in itself when one considers the isolated position of these little groups of Europeans living in completely alien and sometimes hostile Asian surroundings. Far from every form of European protection, they had to depend on each other. They helped each other by delivering mail and lending money. Eventually they even transferred money made in private trade at the expense of their own superiors, either to accounts in England for the Dutch, or in the Netherlands for the English.[3] They sought each other's company in feasts and especially drinking-parties, where rows were apt to break out when the gentlemen had drunk too deep and too long. And then they were quick to outsmart each other. The natives undoubtedly profited from this European rivalry, which enabled them to retain the remnants of their old trade and even to increase it.

In spite of the great naval power of the Dutch in the Indian Ocean, demonstrated in their victories over the Portuguese, French and English, the natives continued to ply their trade and found means of smuggling even in the Archipelago. There can be no doubt, however, that European activities exercised a tremendous influence on Asian trade and shipping. Very valuable products passed into the hands of the Dutch. They and other Europeans

[1] Glamann, *Dutch-Asiatic Trade*, 9–10; M. A. P. Roelofsz, 'Een Nederlander in Engelschen dienst op de Voor-Indische kust', *Tijdschrift voor Geschiedenis*, LVII (1942) 263–73.
[2] See below, p. 104.   [3] Boxer, *Seaborne Empire*, 202.

could influence to some extent the consumption and the production of certain goods, particularly textiles. The European barter trade brought into contact with each other regions in Asia between which there had never previously been any relations. For example, precious metals poured into western Asia from the Far East. This probably stimulated indigenous trade to a certain degree, but the native merchants lacked good organisation. There was no consolidation of capital for investment in trade and industry comparable to that of the European trading companies. Nor was there continuity in Asian commerce. It appears that the Indian merchants exercised only a very slight influence on Asian production, while their maritime techniques could not measure up to those of the Europeans. There is ample proof of this. It is clear enough in the fact that they offered no resistance to using the passes issued by the European nations to guarantee freedom from molestation at sea and confiscation. Here again, however, the mutual European rivalries permitted the Asians a certain freedom of movement. Thus the directors of the United Company took great care not to forfeit goodwill in regions where they could not assert their authority – and where they did not dare refuse the Asians their passes. They even found themselves forced to issue passes for places in the Archipelago, in an area where they did enjoy a monopoly. In the second half of the seventeenth century this development indeed began to build up into an economic threat, accompanied as it then was by increased European competition.[1] But the fact that the United Company continued to look upon the Europeans as its greatest and most dangerous rivals cautions us against overestimating the scope and influence of Asian shipping as a rival of the Dutch.

On the other hand, it appears that the Dutch found it difficult to parry that competition whenever they could not make use of their superior naval technique and had to compete with the Asians on equal terms, as for example in the case of Bantam or the Malayan tin quarters – the region of the tin mines.[2] The Asians had the great

[1] Raychaudhuri, *Jan Company*, 125 ff., 145 ff.
[2] F. de Haan, *Priangan*, 4 vols (Batavia–The Hague, 1910–12) III 238; W. Fruin-Mees, 'Een Bantamsch gezantschap naar Engeland in 1682', *Tijdschrift voor Indische Taal-, Land- en Volkenkunde van het Bataviaasch Genootschap*, LXIV (1924) 207–26; Heeres, *Bouwstoffen* III p. lviii; Mijer, *Instructiën*, 83. Cf. ARA, VOC 455, fos 111ᵛ–12 (Heren XVII to Gov.-Gen. and Council, 22 Sep 1648).

advantages of cheaper shipping, lower administrative costs and a better knowledge of local conditions. The United Company's power-machine cost too much to run and made competition on an equal level impossible. This tempted it to use violence against the weaker, which in turn involved a greal deal of expenditure. The ultimate result was a vicious circle from which there was no longer any way out. When dealing with powerful Asian states against which violence could not be applied, trading had to be done in competition with others. Even in a country like Japan, where the Dutch for long occupied a particularly favourable position, they had to take account of strong Chinese competition.[1]

Nevertheless, when in 1650 a famous Instruction was drafted to regulate the Company's policy and administrative organisation for the years ahead,[2] the Company had attained a powerful position in Asia. As yet, however, it ruled what was principally a maritime trading empire. It was only in the following years that development in the direction of territorial possession began, and even then it was gradual and contrary to the will and intention of the directors in the Netherlands. The pacific tone of this Instruction has surprised some writers,[3] but the directors followed in it their traditional policy, which can be discerned in their letters from the beginning. They were merchants or regents closely associated with merchant circles in the Republic.[4] A remarkable illustration of what those circles thought about colonial affairs is an Instruction drafted in 1599 by the delegates of the Colleges of Admiralty – in other words by members of the same circles as those to which the Company directors belonged. This draft Instruction[5] deals with merchant shipping in the East and West Indies. It states that no damage may be done to native traders, no hindrance caused to their free trade with other people, whether Spanish or Portuguese, and no embargo laid on goods in their

---

[1] O. Nachod, *Die Beziehungen der Niederländischen Ostindischen Kompagnie zu Japan im 17. Jahrhundert* (Leipzig, 1897) 389 ff.; M. P. H. Roessingh, *Het archief van de Nederlandse factorij in Japan* (The Hague, 1964) p. xiii.

[2] Mijer, *Instructiën*, 71–116; ARA, VOC 755, fos 168ᵛ–185 (26 Apr 1650).

[3] Cf. Boxer, *Seaborne Empire*, 95.

[4] Johan E. Elias, *De vroedschap van Amsterdam, 1578–1795*, 2 vols (Amsterdam, 1903–5): from Elias's biographies of members of the Amsterdam magistracy it is evident that these magisterial functions were combined with functions in the East and West India Companies.

[5] De Jonge, *Opkomst*, I 134–5, 249–53 (22 Dec 1599).

ships outside the territory of the Spanish king. It was undoubtedly owing to the plans for granting a charter to the United Company that the States-General did not accept the Instruction, but the ideas embodied in it were supported by many in the Republic. Long after the Company was founded, traces of them could be found in the resolutions and letters of its administrators, who evidently found it difficult to reconcile the *mare liberum* in Europe with the *mare clausum* in Asia.[1] The methods they used as merchants in Europe differed vastly from the violent ones sometimes applied by their subordinates in Asia. They repeatedly expressed their scruples about the use of piratical trading practices in Asia.

Of course, the directors were often confronted with accomplished facts by their servants in the distant outposts, and they were even somewhat impressed by the successes so gained, especially when these produced substantial economic advantages. That is why Van Diemen usually managed to get the approval of the directors, in spite of sharp reprimands on occasion.[2] In contrast with the poor financial results recorded during Coen's time as governor-general, those of Van Diemen were successful. Moreover, Van Diemen observed the legal forms, adhering for instance, strictly, to the terms of the contracts with the native princes. His war policy was aimed mainly against the Portuguese and Spanish national enemies, whereas his operations in the Moluccas could be justified as a fight against breakers of contracts, at least in the eyes of the directors. First and foremost, however, peace had to be maintained with countries outside the sovereignty of the United Company, certainly if they were powerful Asian states. The little Dutch factories along the periphery of those regions depended entirely on the local potentates for supplies of merchandise and food. There was no question of laying down the law there.

Nevertheless, the directors' many expressions of apprehension about violating local laws, in regions where the Company possessed no sovereign right, must not be seen as inspired only by hypocrisy, self-interest and fear of reprisals. On grounds both of international law and of Christian ethics, they forbade their officials in Asia to use such 'strange and unheard-of trading methods', which would call down on their heads the anathema of

[1] Boxer, *Seaborne Empire*, 84 ff.   [2] Heeres, *Bouwstoffen*, III p. lxiii.

all Asian peoples. They considered this the line of least resistance; it was better to try all possible means of trading before resorting to war. Asia was big enough to offer such possibilities.[1] The High Government at Batavia probably thought this admonition excessively theoretical, for their task was to defend the power position already gained, and often they had no option but to extend the power of the Company in places which were of strategic but no trading value, and whose possession was not even desired for strategic reasons.

Such enlargements of power, when they failed to produce favourable economic results, led in turn to tensions between the directors and the High Government. Although the Heren XVII sometimes showed a certain lack of understanding about Asian relations, their knowledge of them should not be underestimated. All reports reaching the Netherlands from India were meticulously studied. In the early years this was a lawyer's duty, but in 1653 a special committee of the directors took it over.[2] Just how thoroughly these directors studied the state of affairs can be discerned in their private archives: for example, those of Johannes Hudde for the seventeenth century and of De Vrij Temminck for the eighteenth century.[3] The directors themselves thought it an advantage that only they could weigh the interests of the Company in Europe against those in Asia, since they were cognisant of both, whereas the High Government in Batavia was acquainted only with Asian aspects. Even though the directors were often compelled to accept the decisions taken by their governor-general and council in Batavia, they did not hesitate on occasion to declare them invalid.[4] When certain undertakings failed to produce economic results, as with Van Diemen's voyages of discovery, they were dropped, though in this case only after his death in 1645. The gradual development of the Company from a maritime trading empire into a territorial power began, *mirabile dictu*, when the office of governor-general was filled (1653–78) by Johannes

[1] Ibid., III pp. lvi–lvii, lx, lxv; Mijer, *Instructiën*, 87. Cf. ARA, VOC 455, fos 30, 61ᵛ, 111ᵛ–12.

[2] Van Dam, *Beschrijvinge*, ed. Stapel, I (1) 309 ff.

[3] *Verslagen's Rijks Oude Archieven*, I (1925) 225 ff.; *Inventarissen 's Rijks Oude Archieven*, III (1930) 270 ff.

[4] See (e.g.) F. W. Stapel (ed.), *Geschiedenis van Nederlandsch Indië*, 5 vols (Amsterdam, 1938–40) III 292–3 (Persia) and 382 (Cambodia); cf. Mijer, *Instructiën*, 88–9.

Maetsuycker, a supporter of the pacific policy of the directors in the Netherlands.

The older nineteenth-century Dutch colonial historians were certainly aware of this dual nature of the United Company's policy.[1] These historians, several of whom were greatly influenced by contemporary liberalism, have even been called its severest critics.[2] It is true that very critical commentaries indeed are to be found in the works of De Jonge, Van der Chijs and Heeres, to mention the most prominent authors. Yet they wrote at a time when the Dutch colonial empire was still in its prime, and their criticism came second to their admiration for the seventeenth-century mercantile empire, so that duality was as inherent in it as in the old Company's policy.

In the first part of the seventeenth century the Company's territory was very limited: Banda, Amboina, a very precarious area around Batavia and for a short while Formosa, occupation of which was a consequence of Coen's policy towards China. Here, for the first time, the United Company devoted some care to the natives.[3] In Formosa the population proved the more susceptible to Christianity because here it had not to compete with Islam, completely inaccessible to the Christian mission, or with Hinduism and Buddhism. The result was that Formosa got schools, churches and preachers. An attempt was also made to educate its people in the cultivation of edible crops and of trade products useful to the Company – in this case the raw silk urgently needed for trade with Japan. Only the Chinese, however, could teach silk culture to the people of Formosa, and the directors correctly estimated the danger to the indigenous population that would follow from Chinese colonisation of the island. It is in the celebrated Instruction of 1650, whose pacific tone I have already mentioned, that there occurs one of the rare pronouncements from the Company directors expressing any sympathy with any group of the indigenous population. They are to be treated well, not taxed too heavily, certainly not to be exploited by others, on this occasion by the Chinese.

In Ceylon, the main purpose of the Company's settlements was

[1] Cf. De Jonge, *Opkomst*, VI pp. vi, vii, lxxiv–vi.

[2] Vlekke, *Geschiedenis*, 135.

[3] Mijer, *Instructiën*, 94–5. Cf. William Campbell, *Formosa under the Dutch Described from Contemporary Records* (1903).

to control the monopoly of cinnamon, again a product for a limited market, cultivated in a small region. In Ceylon as in Formosa, care for the welfare of the population was related mainly to their christianisation. Here the Company took over the task of the Portuguese, and here, for the first time, the Dutch had to cope with the administration of a highly organised native territory and a population with its own centuries-old civilisation. This is what makes the Dutch relationship with the island so fascinating.[1] Stress should be laid on the efforts made by the Dutch to promote education, both in the villages and in the institutes for training the Ceylonese to be preachers and teachers, to promote agriculture by improving the ancient irrigation works and by introducing the cultivation of new commercial crops.[2] Of great importance, too, was the registration of landed property in part of the island, as a result of which Ceylon was practically the only country in Asia to have at its disposal a land-survey register. For the purposes of legal security, one of the indigenous legal systems was codified as early as the beginning of the eighteenth century.[3]

It is significant also that the far-reaching projects of Rijklof van Goens, governor of the island and commander-in-chief (1659–72), were related to Ceylon. These were truly imperial plans, such as no official of the United Company had ever entertained in the seventeenth century. Once the entire state of Kandy had been captured, Ceylon was to take the place of Batavia as hub of a great empire colonised by the Dutch. Strangely enough, Van Goens managed to win over to this conception some of the normally circumspect directors, though not for long: the majority opinion is probably reflected in the critical inside information which Van Dam gives us,[4] dismissing these flights of

[1] For a short bibliography see M. A. P. Meilink-Roelofsz, 'Een tentoonstelling Ceylon-Nederland in het verleden, 1602–1796', *Bulletin van de Oudheidkundige Bond*, LXV (1966) 48–55.

[2] H. Terpstra, 'Compagniesonderwijs op Ceylon', *Tijdschrift voor Geschiedenis*, LXXI (1958) 26–50. Cf. ARA, collection of foreign maps and plans, 929 and VOC 2416, OB 1742 XII (report on irrigation works in connection with the big tank of Cattoe Carrie, 1741).

[3] M. W. Jurriaanse, 'The compilation of the customary law of Jaffna (Thesawa-lamai) in 1707', *Bijdragen tot de Taal-, Land- en Volkenkunde van Nederlandsch Indië*, CX (1954) 293–304.

[4] *Beschryvinge*, ed. Stapel, II (2) 247 ff.

fancy as the plans of an ambitious king, not of merchants who have to see to their profits. The peace-loving Maetsuycker, who occasionally came into conflict with his more go-ahead council, could count on the co-operation of the directors' full support when it came to rejecting Van Goens's proposals. For that matter, when Van Goens himself occupied the high office some time later (1678–81), he showed himself an opponent of Dutch colonisation:[1] yet what possibilities had not opened up by then in Java, the real centre of the Company's power in Asia!

On this island, as in Ceylon, territorial expansion was connected with the monopoly, in the shape of exclusive rights for the Company to import textiles and opium. Other factors were also involved, not least of them being the exposed location of Batavia, lying between the two Javanese kingdoms of Bantam and Mataram. True, the one state was played off against the other, they were kept 'in balance', as was said; but always there was the danger that they would combine to surround the Company and attack it on two fronts. Batavia depended on Mataram for its food supplies, the deliveries of rice which were also needed for the Spice Islands: any stoppage in the transport of rice to these islands would cause famine there and so react disastrously on the collecting of spices.[2] In the case of Bantam, by contrast, the Company was primarily afraid of the acute commercial threat constituted by the busy traffic of both Europeans and Asians with this port.

During the second half of the seventeenth century, disputed successions and rebellions in the two Javanese kingdoms gave the Company the opportunity of safeguarding its position. There is probably some connection between this disintegration of the native states and the activities of the United Company in the Archipelago. In the static indigenous society there had appeared a new dynamic element which disrupted the existing economy. Spiritual forces were evoked, since the material means of native society were inadequate to protect it. In the second half of the seventeenth century the growth of the Company's influence was accompanied by a revival of the Islamic religion. A fanatical movement developed against the existing order and the infidel foreigners alike. In this way the rebellion against the lawful reigning family in Mataram assumed a strongly religious charac-

[1] De Jonge, *Opkomst*, VII 1–3.
[2] Ibid., VI pp. lv, lxvi–viii, lxxvii–viii, lxxxvii–ix; VII pp. cxii–clxxi.

ter; indeed one of its foremost leaders was the spiritual head of Islam in Indonesia.

The United Company was fully alive to the menace of an excited mass of people, especially as the movement was not restricted to Mataram but found supporters in Bantam and in the other islands of the Archipelago.[1] Nevertheless, to begin with, there was no unanimity among members of the High Government as to the extent of the support to be lent to the threatened sultans of Mataram, Amangkurat I and II. It was Speelman who, against the wishes of Maetsuycker and in particular after the latter's death (1678), carried out successfully the military expeditions to the interior of Java of which Maetsuycker had been so apprehensive.[2]

By the peace of 1677–8 the Company succeeded in obtaining all its demands, the sultan becoming its mere willing tool.[3] Rice supplies were safeguarded, exclusive rights to the import of textiles and opium guaranteed. The territory behind Batavia was now considerably enlarged. In addition the Company acquired the region around the north Javanese port of Semarang, where a great deal of sugar-cane was grown. When Bantam was also forced to accept peace in 1684,[4] the Company gained possession of an area in the Preanger, the mountainous district south of Batavia which was excellently suited to the cultivation of cash crops, although its exploitation did not take place until the next century. In the seventeenth century only a few tentative experiments were made with new crops which might be suitable for export.[5] In any case, in the years immediately following its successes in Java, the Company was burdened with heavy financial commitments resulting from the wars it had waged. It now followed a very cautious and pacific line, putting its affairs in order, so much so that the recovery which started in the 'eighties was the beginning of a profitable period for its business. This prosperity lasted with a few interruptions down to 1736, perhaps owing much to the development of new export products, notably

[1] Vlekke, *Geschiedenis*, 191, 196–8; Stapel, *Nederlandsch Indië*, III 394 ff.
[2] Stapel, *Speelman*, 84 ff.
[3] Heeres, *Corpus Diplomaticum*, III 39–51, 70–83, 98–101, 121–5, 165–7, 191–6, 223–5.
[4] Ibid., III 336–50.
[5] Vlekke, *Geschiedenis*, 220–3; Stapel, *Nederlandsch Indië*, III 450.

coffee and tea, at the beginning of the eighteenth century.

The acquisition of territory should have been accompanied by Dutch colonisation. In spite of the numerous plans made for this in the seventeenth century, the results attained were extremely meagre. A great deal has been written, in particular, about the earliest and most ambitious plans of Coen.[1] These, however, were not at all well correlated with the real situation in Asia. They abounded in contradictions, taking no account of the quantity or quality of the Dutch colonists, the so-called 'free burghers', who were dismissed Company employees and the only Dutchmen with any desire to settle down permanently in Asia. In effect, therefore, Coen's plans proved quite impracticable. More realistic were those of Philip Lucaszoon and of Maetsuycker,[2] who wisely followed the Portuguese example. But they likewise had to try to combine the strict Company monopoly with the trading activities of the individual. There was no scope for private enterprise on any considerable scale; a limited field of shipping and trade existed, but there the colonist had to face the competition of other Europeans and Asians. Attempts to provide him with a means of living by agriculture were equally without result.

In practice every colonising initiative failed. Dutch society in Asia became one of civil servants with their own standards, their own justice[3] and their own morals. It was strongly influenced by its Asian surroundings, especially because of the lack of Dutch women and the consequent miscegenation. In Batavia itself, the largest centre of Dutch population in Asia, there sprang up a remarkable society: not particularly attractive perhaps, but certainly not sufficiently studied, even though we possess the pioneering, amusing and lively work of De Haan, trustee of the former government archives in Batavia.[4] It is to be hoped that the Indonesian government will find ways of making the treasures of their archives accessible once more for research. These unique

[1] W. Ph. Coolhaas, *Verloren kansen* (Groningen, 1955) 12 ff.; Meilink-Roelofsz, *Asian Trade*, 227–30.

[2] Ibid., 234–6; De Jonge, *Opkomst*, VI pp. xiv–xx, lxxi–iii.

[3] S. Keyzer (ed.), 'Statuten van Batavia (1642)', *BKI*, new ser., II (1863) 397–518. An incomplete publication in J. A. van der Chijs, *Nederlandsch Indisch Plakkaatboek. 1602–1811*, 17 vols (Batavia, 1885–1900) I 472–594.

[4] See Further Reading, p. 81 below.

materials for a social, economic and demographic history are entirely lacking in the Company archives at The Hague, since they were made in Asia and have therefore remained there.[1]

In view of the great financial importance of good wage administration for the United Company's extensive and widely scattered personnel, even in those days every attention was given to that section of the archives; although in the nineteenth century many documents were destroyed, the more important registers have fortunately been preserved. These illustrate how conscientiously the Company carried out this part of its task. From the moment he stepped aboard a Company ship, every Company servant was followed up step by step; not a penny too much was ever spent upon him, and all the time he remained in Company service no fact about his career which affected the Company financially was left unrecorded. An organisation like this, which at the end of the seventeenth century employed a total of some 17,000 to 18,000 men in Asia (not 30,000, as is stated in narrative sources), about a fifth of whom were serving in the fleet there, should certainly not be taken too lightly.

Historical literature frequently takes an exceedingly poor view of the men who worked for the United Company.[2] They have been called 'the scum of the nations'. Many foreigners indeed did take service with the Company. In the middle of the eighteenth century, Germans alone accounted for a quarter of the entire labour force.[3] They made up the lion's share, but there were also men from other European countries. Undoubtedly foreigners and Dutch alike included many prodigal sons, some of whom had to turn their backs on Europe for reasons which might not bear close investigation; for many of them, incidentally, service with the

[1] J. A. van der Chijs, *Inventaris van 's Landsarchief te Batavia, 1602-1816* (Batavia, 1882).

[2] In his *Dutch Seaborne Empire* Boxer gives a more favourable picture. See also the following articles by J. de Hullu: 'Het gehalte van de dienaren der Oost-Indische Compagnie tijdens het Gouverneur-Generaalschap van Pieter Both, 1610-1614', *De Indische Gids* (1913) 54-66; 'De voeding op de schepen der Oost-Indische Compagnie', *BKI*, LXVII (1913) 541-62; 'De handhaving der orde en tucht op de schepen der Oost-Indische Compagnie', ibid., 516-40; and 'Ziekten en dokters op de schepen der Oost-Indische Compagnie', ibid., 245-72.

[3] Result of provisional statistical examination of the General Muster Rolls in Algemeen Rijksarchief, VOC.

Company meant a speedy end to their lives. But among the thousands who went out to Asia there were also many able and energetic men who started at the bottom and worked their way up, frequently under circumstances of unimaginable difficulty. Sometimes they succeeded in attaining the highest positions. An extremely high standard of efficiency was demanded of the senior officials. They had to be conversant with all sorts of commercial matters, for, as their titles of junior merchant, merchant and senior merchant indicate, trade was their first and foremost task. At the same time, they needed political insight and had to exert real diplomatic talent in their dealings with a variety of Asian rulers, whose own circumstances were often extremely complicated and difficult to grasp. Even military skills were required of the merchants, for the Company had no supreme military command of its own. They had to take responsible decisions. Besides these top figures, the Company had also numerous experts in its service for whom high standards of professional skill were mandatory: in this connection I need only mention the medical men, who were such an important factor in the advance of Japanese science. But the Company also employed a great many simple artisans, and these no less certainly played their part in the introduction of Western techniques into Asia, most obviously as shipbuilders.[1]

Evasion of the elaborate regulations was strictly forbidden to all Company officials, high and low. On the other hand, the margin between precept and practice was wide. As we have seen, private trading was severely restricted, but the further one was from the centre of government at Batavia, the easier smuggling became. Bengal, for instance, was a country where vast riches could be gathered in a short time. On a smaller scale, too, there was plenty of black-market trading. This is not so surprising, really, in view of the extremely low wages which the Company paid its servants. The paralysing effect of the monopoly, which excluded these men as well as other compatriots, contributed in no small degree to the United Company's ultimate decline. Therein, also, lies the fundamental reason why the Company had relatively so little effect on the welfare of the Netherlands Republic in general.

[1] The General Muster Rolls, which mention the occupations of the Company's servants, give a good impression of their great variety.

79

FURTHER READING

1. *Collections of Documents*

De opkomst van het Nederlansch gezag in Oost-Indië, ed. J. K. J. DE JONGE, M. L. VAN DEVENTER and L. W. G. DE ROO, 17 vols (The Hague-Amsterdam, 1862–1909) contains the most important documents relating to the establishment of Dutch power in Java, from the archives of the Dutch East India Company preserved in the Algemeen Rijksarchief at The Hague.

Bouwstoffen voor de geschiedenis der Nederlanders in den Maleischen Archipel, ed. P. A. TIELE and J. E. HEERES, 3 vols (The Hague, 1886–1895) complements the preceding work in so far as it is mainly concerned with the Archipelago outside Java.

Corpus diplomaticum Neerlando-Indicum: Verzameling van politieke contracten en verdere verdragen door de Nederlanders in het Oosten gesloten en van privilegebrieven aan hen verleend, ed. J. E. HEERES and F. W. STAPEL, 6 vols (*Bijdragen tot de Taal-, Land- en Volkenkunde van het Koninklijk Instituut*, The Hague, 1907–55). Fundamental for the relations of the Dutch with the Eastern princes, 1596–1799.

PIETER VAN DAM, *Beschryvinge van de Oostindische Compagnie*, ed. F. W. STAPEL, 7 vols: Rijks Geschiedkundige Publicatiën, nos. 63, 68, 74, 76, 83, 87, 96 (The Hague, 1927–54). Magnificent edition of the indispensable work of Van Dam; the editing of the last volume was completed by C. W. TH. Baron VAN BOETZELAER VAN ASPEREN.

Daghregister gehouden int Casteel Batavia vant passerende daer ter plaetse als over geheel Nederlandts India, 31 vols (Batavia–The Hague, 1888–1931). Apart from the last two volumes it is indifferently edited, but is an extremely full chronicle of events throughout Netherlands India from 1628 to 1682.

Verzameling van instructiën, ordonnanciën en reglementen voor de regeering van Nederlandsch Indië, vastgesteld in de jaren 1609–1836. Met de ontwerpen der staatscommissie van 1803 en historische aanteekeningen, ed. P. MIJER (Batavia, 1848) contains the instructions, ordinances and regulations for the East Indian government from 1609 to 1836.

Generale Missiven van gouverneurs-generaal en raden aan Heren XVII der Verenigde Oostindische Compagnie, ed. W. PH. COOLHAAS, 2 vols: Rijks Geschiedkundige Publicatiën, nos. 104, 112 (The Hague, 1960–4), brings together the annual dispatches from Batavia to the directors, arranged according to the different Asian regions from which Batavia obtained its own information: valuable series still in progress.

Jan Pietersz. Coen: Bescheiden omtrent zijn bedrijf in Indië, ed. H. T.
COLENBRANDER and W. PH. COOLHAAS, 7 vols (The Hague, 1919–53).
Valuable collection, unfortunately still the only one covering the
whole career of a governor-general in the East Indies.

2. *Secondary Works*

COOLHAAS, W. PH.: *A Critical Survey of Studies on Dutch Colonial
History* (The Hague, 1960). Comprehensive and trustworthy.

VLEKKE, B. H. M.: *Nusantara: a History of the East Indian Archipelago*
(Cambridge, Mass., 1943). Although not written by an expert in
colonial history nor based on original research, this book remains
valuable as an attempt to rewrite Indonesian history from an Asiatic
point of view.

BOXER, C. R.: *The Dutch Seaborne Empire, 1600–1800* (1965). A rich
and penetrating study of connections between Dutch domestic and
colonial history, especially on the social side.

STAPEL, F. W. (ed.): *Geschiedenis van Nederlandsch Indië*, 5 vols (Amsterdam, 1938–40) remains useful, but shows all the disadvantages of
such a collective enterprise: it is the story of Dutch activities in
Indonesia, rather than Indonesian history.

CHIJS, J. A. VAN DER: *Geschiedenis der Stichting van de Vereenigde O. I.
Compagnie* (Leiden, 1857) may still be recommended as a short history
of the Company's origins.

——*De vestiging van het Nederlandsche gezag over de Banda-eilanden,
1599–1621* (Batavia, 1886) describes the extermination of the
population of the Banda islands following the arrival of the Dutch.

MANSVELT, W. M. F.: *Rechtsvorm en geldelijk beheer bij de Oost-Indische
Compagnie* (Amsterdam, 1922) studies the Company's complicated
book-keeping and arrives at the unconventional conclusion that the
Company was a business on joint account.

MEILINK-ROELOFSZ, M. A. P.: *Asian Trade and European Influence in the
Indonesian Archipelago between 1500 and about 1630* (The Hague, 1962)
is a study of Indonesian trade and the effect of both Asian and
European penetration on it; contains much new information.

GLAMANN, KRISTOF: *Dutch-Asiatic Trade, 1620–1740* (Copenhagen–The
Hague, 1958) examines the trade between the Dutch factories in Asia
and the motherland: important.

HAAN, F. DE: *Priangan. De Preanger regentschappen onder het Nederlandsch
bestuur tot 1811*, 4 vols (Batavia–The Hague, 1910–12). Despite its
title, important for the history not only of the area south of Batavia
but also that of the Company generally.

——*Oud-Batavia*, 2 vols and 1 album of plates (Batavia, 1922–3). A
lively picture of seventeenth- and eighteenth-century Batavian society.

GOONEWARDENA, K. W.: *The Foundation of Dutch Power in Ceylon, 1638–1658* (Amsterdam, 1958). Highly critical of Dutch policies.

ARASARATAM, S.: *Dutch Power in Ceylon, 1658–1687* (Amsterdam, 1958) is equally based on the archives of the Company at The Hague, but on the whole less critical.

TERPSTRA, H.: *De vestiging van de Nederlanders aan de kust van Koromandel* (Groningen, 1911). Exhaustive study of the earliest period of Dutch establishment on the Coromandel coast.

——*De opkomst der Westerkwartieren van de Oost-Indische Compagnie: Suratte, Arabië, Perzië* (The Hague, 1918) is detailed and excellent, but does not go beyond 1624.

—— *De Nederlanders in Voor-Indië* (Amsterdam, 1947). Concise description of the factories in India proper.

RAYCHAUDURI, T.: *Jan Company in Coromandel* (The Hague, 1962) concentrates on economic activities: interesting new material, particularly in the first part of the book.

ROELOFSZ, M. A. P.: 'De vestiging der Nederlanders ter kuste Malabar', *Verhandelingen van het Koninklijk Instituut voor Taal-, Land- en Volkenkunde*, IV (The Hague, 1943) is the first study of early Dutch settlement on the Malabar coast.

NACHOD, OSKAR: *Die Beziehungen der Niederländischen Ostindischen Kompagnie zu Japan im siebzehnten Jahrhundert* (Leipzig, 1897) remains authoritative.

4 Early English Trade and Settlement in Asia, 1602–1690

D. K. BASSETT

THE English colonies of the seventeenth century were founded by a variety of agencies and assumed many forms. There was, however, a basic distinction between the plantation colonies of the North American seaboard and those of the West Indies, on the one hand, whether deriving from proprietary grants to noblemen or from company charters, and on the other hand, the system of forts and factories adopted by the London merchant companies which enjoyed the national monopoly of trade with West Africa and Asia. The scale of settlement was totally different, and so was the economic function. The white population of Barbados, for example, was about 37,000 by 1643, although it fell to 20,000 later in the century as land came to be concentrated in the hands of a planter oligarchy.[1] The Royal African Company's merchants and soldiers in West Africa did not exceed 330 at any time during the century,[2] while the East India Company's establishment in Asia was probably about one thousand men in 1668–90. The difference was not only numerical. The presence of Englishmen in Barbados, Maryland or Virginia was proof *per se* of local English sovereignty and colonisation. The opening of simple factories or trading posts in Asia did not confer local sovereignty upon the East India Company, nor were the factors who resided there colonists. English colonisation in Asia can be equated only with the acquisition of forts wholly under English control. Madras, acquired by the Company in 1639, only partially met these requirements, because the Indian state of Golconda retained certain rights over the revenue as late as 1680–1. In this sense a proper English colony existed in Asia only after Portuguese Bombay was transferred to

[1] V. T. Harlow, *A History of Barbados* (Oxford, 1926) 338–40.
[2] K. G. Davies, *The Royal African Company* (1957) 241–52.

Charles II in 1665. The slow transition of the Company from a commercial to a limited imperial role is examined in this paper.

The East India Company's monopoly of English trade with Asia, with only minor exceptions,[1] was of paramount importance throughout the seventeenth century. English ambitions in Asia rarely transcended those of the Company. Since the Company's possessions in Asia were limited to a few city-ports with a predominantly alien population, there was neither scope nor incentive for the Crown to assert its own authority as it did in the white settler colonies of North America and the West Indies. The Commonwealth's expedition against pro-royalist Barbados in 1652, the capture of Spanish Jamaica in 1655 and the resumption of royal rights in Barbados and the Leeward Islands by Charles II in 1663 were the prelude to stronger metropolitan control in America, through royal governors subordinate to the Committee of Plantations.[2] The only parallel in Asia was the brief royal administration of Bombay in 1665-8, but this did not infringe the Company's privileges. The Company was already well suited to the imperial trade system. Its imports and exports were carried to and from London on English ships with English crews, so that the Navigation Acts, which imposed similar restrictions on the trade of the North American and Caribbean colonies, were irrelevant.

The development of royal government in the North American and Caribbean colonies, together with their acknowledged importance in the imperial trade system, won them a certain measure of national protection, admittedly inadequate, in European wars.[3] Even the Royal Adventurers trading to Africa (1663) and the Royal African Company (1672) enjoyed occasional support

[1] The Company's monopoly was broken by Courteen's Association in 1635-49, with Charles I's connivance, and by individual interlopers in 1654-7, before Cromwell granted a new charter to the Company. Interlopers were active again after 1680, and a rival East India Company existed from 1698 to 1708. But the newcomers added little to the old Company's existing establishment in Asia, unless one includes two short-lived colonies in Madagascar in 1645-6 and 1649-50.

[2] A. P. Thornton, *West-India Policy under the Restoration* (Oxford, 1956) passim; Harlow, 61 ff.

[3] Thornton, 94-5, 126, 129, 238-52; A. P. Newton, *The European Nations in the West Indies, 1493-1688* (1933) 237, 247-50.

from the Royal Navy against rival European states and domestic interlopers, because of the repercussions of Stuart foreign policy, the importance of slaves to the West Indian sugar economy, and the personal connection of James, Duke of York, with the Royal African Company.[1] The only occasion before 1683 on which Royal Navy ships appeared in Asian waters was in 1662–3, when the Earl of Marlborough was sent to Bombay to effect the formal transfer of the island to the English Crown.[2] Because of the different pattern of English settlement in Asia, there was also no local counterpart of the buccaneers of Jamaica, who were a semi-official substitute for the Royal Navy in the Caribbean until the Anglo–Spanish treaty of Madrid in 1670.[3] Anglo–Dutch and Anglo–Portuguese controversies in Asia were certainly matters for European diplomacy, but the East India Company was expected to fend for itself in Asia.

The primary function of the East India Company was to obtain Asian commodities and sell English manufactures,[4] not to promote colonisation, but in terms of policy the two roles need not have been mutually exclusive. The Portuguese, who established a chain of forts around the Arabian Sea, in Ceylon, Malacca and the Spice Islands early in the sixteenth century, regarded trade and political power as complementary. The Dutch, who had forts in the Spice Islands by 1605 and a headquarters in Batavia by 1619, soon reached the same conclusion. The English company, however, was not motivated by the crusading tradition of early Portuguese expansion or by Dutch belligerency against Spain and Portugal; nor did it aspire to that monopoly of valuable Asian commodities which underlay Portuguese and Dutch actions, and which ultimately led the Dutch to extend their warlike methods to specific Asian states. English restraint was dictated by circumstances rather than by any superior morality. The factory system

[1] Davies, 42, 103, 106, 107 n. 5, 114–15, 156.

[2] The Portuguese governor of Goa evaded delivery of Bombay until February 1665: S. A. Khan, 'The Anglo-Portuguese Negotiations Relating to Bombay, 1660–1677', *J. Indian History*, I (1921–2) 442–66.

[3] Thornton, 76–123; Newton, 232–3, 256–77.

[4] K. N. Chaudhuri, *The English East India Company* (1965) 13, argues that imports from Asia were far more important to the Company than exports of English cloth. This was so in practice, but the Company's anxiety to sell English cloth in Japan in 1613–23 and 1673, in Siam in 1674–84, and even at a loss in Indonesia in the 1660s, certainly influenced policy.

was the cheapest method of carrying on overseas trade: in the early days shareholders even in the Dutch company deplored the drain on dividends involved in maintaining forts and warships.[1] The English company, with inferior organisation and capital, was unlikely to favour the building of forts unless the factory system was palpably unsuitable and unless it had the resources and opportunity for building forts.

A highly complex international commerce already existed in Asia in which, with minor exceptions, the English could participate freely. They were not denied access to the important traditional coastal entrepôts, so long as these remained under indigenous government. The accessibility of inland production areas of calicoes, indigo, silk or pepper varied, but the method of purchase adopted by the English was determined as much by convenience as by restrictions on movement imposed by an Asian government. The direct buying of calicoes and indigo in Ahmadabad, Broach, Burhanpur or Lahore for transport to Surat, for example, was much easier than boating a hundred miles up a Sumatran river to buy pepper in the hills – for which Chinese middlemen were usually employed. In any case, after a period of scarcity, the supply of most of the commodities sought by the English and Dutch responded to the increased demand. Initially, therefore, the factory system was well suited to English needs. It was unnecessary to foster a new plantation economy like the West Indian, based ultimately on sugar and imported slave labour; nor was it necessary, as in West Africa, to build forts for protection against rival Europeans and as stable markets in a more primitive economy. Unlike the fragmented coastal tribes of West Africa, the mainland Asian governments, and even the major Indonesian sultanates until 1660, could guarantee the safety of English factories against Dutch or Portuguese attack.

The pattern of English settlement in Asia was not only determined by existing opportunities for free trade and the Company's antipathy to expensive fortresses; an Asian government which could ensure English immunity *vis-à-vis* other Europeans could also thwart an English attempt to acquire a local fort by force. Few Asian governments welcomed European encroachments upon their territory or sovereignty. Indeed, the reputed Indonesian

[1] K. Glamann, *Dutch-Asiatic Trade, 1620–1740* (Copenhagen–The Hague, 1958) 7–8.

insistence upon English factories being built of easily destruc-
tible timber and palm leaves was ascribed by contemporaries to
the conversion of the Dutch stone factory at Jakarta into the fort
of Batavia in 1618–19. In West Africa the choice between building
forts or factories seems to have lain with the European companies,
perhaps because the African coastal chiefs welcomed a stable
market in either form. African attacks upon the forts were usually
provoked by the occupants or instigated by rival Europeans, and
the struggle for possession of the forts was predominantly inter-
European, especially during national wars.[1] Admittedly in Asia the
Dutch conquests in Malabar, Ceylon and Malacca were wrested
in similar fashion from the declining Portuguese, but the Dutch
attitude to indigenous states was more aggressive than in Africa,
because their subjects flouted Dutch restrictions on Asian maritime trade. During the seventeenth century the Dutch imposed
unprecedented restraints upon the expansionist plans of Achin in
Sumatra and Mataram in Java. They also conquered the sultanate
of Gowa-Tallo' (Macassar) in Celebes in 1667–9 and of Bantam
in west Java in 1682. Not even the Dutch, however, could
challenge the powerful mainland governments of Persia or Mogul
India, except indirectly by naval blockade. The English company, which was much weaker than its Dutch counterpart in
capital and shipping, could hope to acquire its own political
base in Asia only by peaceful negotiation, either directly from
an Asian government, or indirectly from the hard-pressed Portuguese through Anglo-Portuguese national diplomacy. It was
the latter arrangement which finally secured Bombay for the
Company.

The Company's activities in Asia in the first thirty years of the
seventeenth century had two main aspects: the creation of an
extensive system of factories and a reluctant trial of strength with
the Dutch and Portuguese. In both respects the Company was
hampered by its weak organisation and capital. Until 1613, when
it adopted the joint-stock system, the Company sent out a series
of separate voyages, so that the opening of factories was slow and
sporadic. The Company's first factory was opened at Bantam in
west Java in 1602, but no additions were made for a decade.
Masulipatam in Golconda, on the east coast of India, was
opened in 1611 and Surat, on the western seaboard of the Mogul

[1] Davies, 263–4, 266–8, 272, 281–4, 286.

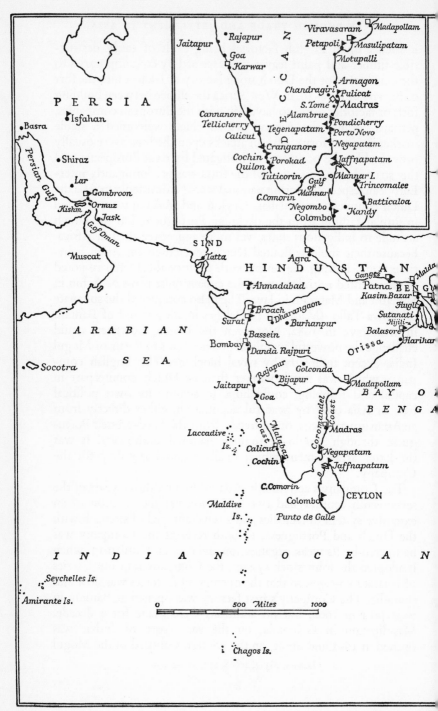

Dutch and En

English Factories ◻
Dutch "

C H I N A

Yellow Sea

Hirado ◻
Deshima ◻ Nagasaki

SHIKOKU

KYUSHU

J A P A N

E A S T
CHINA
SEA

Chusan ◻

Amoy ◻

TAIWAN
(Formosa)

Canton ●

Macao ●

Tongking ◻

S O U T H

C H I N A

S E A

Manila ●

P H I L I P P I N E S

B U R M A

S I A M

Mekong

Ayuthia ◻
Bangkok ●

Mergui

Pulo Condore ●

Patani

Achin

Kedah
M A L A C C A

Malacca ▲
Johore
Riau

B O R N E O

Macassar Str.

C e l e b e s
S e a

Menado ●

Ternate
Makian ◻
Batjan

M O L U C C A S

Spice Is.
Ceram
Buru
Amboina Is.

Banda

S U M A T R A

Barus ◻
Siak ▲
Priaman ▲
Salida
Padang ▲
Jambi ◻

Pulo Chuico
Palembang ◻

Benkulen ◻
Silebar ◻

Princes' I.

Bangka
Biliton
Sunda Str.

Sukadana

Batavia (Jakarta) ◻
Bantam ▲
Cheribon
Tegal
Japara

Banjarmasin ◻

Martapura

Macassar ●

Celebes

Buton

Banda Sea

J A V A S E A

Semarang
Mataram
Preanger

J A V A
Gresik
Surabaya
Rembang
Madura

Bima ▲

Sumba

S u n d a

Sumbawa I.s.

Timor

empire, in 1612. The first Far Eastern factories were established in Patani and Ayuthia (the capital of Siam) in 1612, and at Hirado in Japan in 1613. Macassar in Celebes and Jambi in east Sumatra were added to the Company's Indonesian factories in 1613 and 1615. The Company's trade in Persia began at Jask in 1616 and was subsequently moved to Gombroon. In broad terms, the Indian factories supplied textiles for Indonesia, calicoes and indigo for London; the Persian trade was mainly in silk for London; the Indonesian factories sent pepper and spices to England; Patani and Ayuthia marketed textiles for local products; and Japan was mistakenly treated as a promising market for English broadcloth and woollens. After the reorganisation of 1613, presidencies were created at Bantam and Surat, which supervised the factories in eastern and western Asia respectively.

A contemporary development was Anglo-Dutch rivalry in the Spice Islands, the only source of cloves, mace and nutmegs. Realising Dutch monopolistic intentions there belatedly, the English wrested a precarious foothold in the Banda Islands in 1615–16, but suffered heavy naval losses at Dutch hands in 1618–1619, when local officials resorted to war. The Company was saved from further disasters by the Treaty of Defence of July 1619, by which it joined the Dutch in an anti-Catholic naval offensive in Asia and assumed a third of the cost of the Dutch forts in the Spice Islands in return for a third of the spices.[1] In practice, mutual suspicion was too strong and the English company lacked the means to meet its political obligations without neglecting its many factories. In February 1623 Anglo-Dutch recrimination culminated in the Dutch execution of the English merchants in the Spice Island of Amboina, on a charge of conspiracy to overthrow the Dutch government. This episode, known in England as 'the Amboyna Massacre', is sometimes claimed to have caused a drastic retrenchment of the English factories in Indonesia and the Far East. In fact, the English president at Batavia had already decided to withdraw his agents in the Spice Islands as an economy measure. He had also recalled the Company's factors in Patani, Ayuthia and Japan because the trade was unprofitable. The Amboina Massacre was a dramatic epilogue, which simply confirmed the English decision to vacate the Spice Islands, ended

[1] Sir W. Foster, *England's Quest of Eastern Trade* (1933) 165–9, 198–207, 253–75; *EFI, 1618–1621*, pp. xxxviii–xliii.

Anglo-Dutch collaboration in Indonesia, and provided anti-Dutch propaganda as late as the Anglo-Dutch war of 1672–4.[1]

In western Asia, English free trade was opposed by the Portuguese, who held fortresses at Ormuz in the Persian Gulf, Muscat on the Arabian coast, and Goa on the west coast of India. Unlike the Dutch in the Spice Islands, the Portuguese could not compel the Mogul and Persian governments to exclude the English, but they could destroy English shipping and reputation. In fact, the English ships at Swally, the anchorage near Surat, defeated the Portuguese galleons in 1612 and 1615. Captain Shilling was equally triumphant off Jask in the Persian Gulf in 1620, although he was mortally wounded.[2] In 1622 the English fleet helped the Persians to capture the Portuguese fortress of Ormuz. This, incidentally, was the only aggressive action of the English company in Asia until 1686 and was undertaken by the local merchants and sea-captains under pain of Persian reprisals on their silk trade.[3] Swally was raided by the Portuguese as late as 1630, and until 1634 the English president at Surat sent ships to Madagascar or the Comoro Islands to protect merchant ships coming from London. Anglo-Dutch collaboration in western Asia survived the Amboina Massacre in consequence. The Anglo-Dutch fleet which blockaded Goa and Mozambique in 1621–3 was created by the Treaty of Defence, but the joint Anglo-Dutch voyages to Persia in 1625, 1626, 1628 and 1629 were arranged spontaneously for mutual protection against the Portuguese. The raid on Portuguese Bombay in 1626 was an Anglo-Dutch venture. Fortunately for the English, the Portuguese were principally concerned to defend their over-extended empire against the Dutch. One of their best commanders, Nuño Alvares Botelho, was killed in Sumatra in 1630.

In January 1635, the hard-pressed Portuguese viceroy, the Conde de Linhares, and Methwold, the president at Surat, thankfully signed a local truce, the Convention of Goa. The peace be-

[1] D. K. Bassett, 'The "Amboyna Massacre" of 1623', *Journal of Southeast Asian History*, I (2) (1960) 4–5, 7–19.

[2] *The Voyage of Thomas Best, 1612–1614*, ed. Sir W. Foster (Hakluyt Society, 1934) pp. xxvii–xxxi, passim; *The Voyage of Nicholas Downton, 1614–1615*, ed. Sir W. Foster (Hakluyt Society, 1939) pp. xxiii–xxv, passim; *EFI, 1618–1621*, pp. xxviii–xxix, 220–5.

[3] *EFI, 1622–1623* (1908) pp. vii–xii, 13–16, 31–8, 56, 64, 82.

came official after the Anglo-Portuguese treaty of May 1642.[1]

Anglo-Dutch and Anglo-Portuguese hostilities did not weaken the Company's preference for factory trade. The issue between the English and Dutch before 1623 was that of English access to the Spice Islands, and it was only this which was denied to them after the Amboina Massacre. Elsewhere in Indonesia the major sultanates were still independent, and the English factory system could still function. Indeed, there was no other possibility unless the Company was willing and able to conquer them, as the Dutch had conquered Jakarta. Similarly, the Anglo-Portuguese struggle had been fought at sea and the status of the English merchants ashore was involved only indirectly. In the heat of the war, the Company had considered acquiring its own base on the west coast of India. Bombay was mentioned in this connection by the Company's merchants at Surat in 1626 and 1628, but the outlay to make it defensible was too great. The other English project, also raised in 1628, was the acquisition by negotiation of Danda Rajpuri or Jaitapur on the coast of Bijapur, but the Indian refusal to cede these ports was not contested by the Company.[2] Once Anglo-Portuguese hostilities ceased, Bombay could be acquired only by negotiation. The Company's factors in Persia and Surat raised this possibility in 1640 and 1653-4,[3] and even the directors hoped that Cromwell would obtain Bombay or Bassein for them in the Anglo-Portuguese treaty of July 1654.[4] The Dutch company had resumed its attacks on Portuguese Asia in 1652, but it was not until 1661 that Charles II agreed to help, if need be, in its defence. It was this political commitment, which the Company itself would never have incurred, that induced the Portuguese to transfer Bombay.

English trade in Indonesia after 1623 was much larger than is usually realised. The factories at Jambi and Macassar were retained and the presidency was re-established at Bantam in 1628. The factories at Bantam and Jambi normally supplied all the

[1] *EFI, 1630–1633* (1910) pp. xxxv–xxxvii; *EFI, 1634–1636* (1911) pp. vii–xi, 80–1, 88–96.

[2] Khan, 423–6; *EFI, 1624–1629* (1909) pp. xxi, xxvi–xxviii, 159, 197–9, 242–3, 250–61.

[3] *EFI, 1637–1641* (1912) 228; *EFI, 1651–1654* (1915) pp. xv, 169–70, 272. British losses in the Persian Gulf in the Second Anglo-Dutch War influenced the factors on the latter occasion.

[4] Ibid., p. xxiv; Khan, 429–30.

pepper which the Company could conveniently sell, while efforts to open other factories in Borneo and Sumatra were sporadic and half-hearted. Until 1643 the Company supplemented its annual pepper investment (about one million lb.) with cloves smuggled to Macassar from Amboina, but the Dutch then subdued the Ambonese rebels. The Company still had no difficulty in obtaining Indonesian pepper, but its exports were determined by a very competitive and relatively inelastic European market. A heavy over-supply of seven million pounds in 1648–50, coupled with the loss of the Company's national privileges after the Civil War, led to a drastic cut in the Company's Indonesian trade in 1651–7. After the Company's charter was renewed by Cromwell in 1657 and Charles II in 1661, English purchases of pepper were unprecedented, averaging 3.4 million pounds annually in 1669–82. Because of heavy Dutch, French and Danish competition, Bantamese pepper became unprofitable in London by 1682 and the Company had to reduce its purchases again.[1]

Although the Company's trade in Indonesia continued, its trade in India became more important. The Surat presidency extended English trade to Sind (1635), Rajapur (1637), Basra (1640–1) and the Red Sea ports of Mocha and Suakin in the 1640s. The Anglo-Portuguese truce of 1635 permitted occasional English voyages from Surat to the Malabar pepper-ports of Cochin and Calicut in the 1640s, although the Portuguese conceded this grudgingly after their truce with the Dutch in Asia in November 1644. On the eastern side of India, English trade expanded from the original factory of Masulipatam to Armagon in 1626 and to Viravasaram, Motupalli, Golconda and Petapoli in 1630. The first factories in Orissa were opened at Hariharpur and Balasore in 1633. The Bengal factory of Hugli was added in 1651.

These developments in mainland Asia were the English response to the natural commercial opportunities of the region, not a reaction to English retrenchment in Indonesia. The Indian and Indonesian markets were complementary, not mutually exclusive. Many of the new factories in eastern India were opened in the 1630s to obtain cloth for Indonesia and for England during the great famine affecting Surat. On the other hand, some of the commodities available in the mainland factories – such as calicoes, indigo, silk, saltpetre and sugar – found an expanding market in

[1] Bassett, 'Amboyna Massacre', 8–18.

93

England,[1] which contrasted with the relatively static and precariously profitable demand for Indonesian pepper. Thus the superior attractions of the Indian markets probably ensured a preponderance of English investment there, even though the actual English investment in Indonesia was greater in the 1660s and 1670s than it had ever been.

It has already been suggested that the English company was unlikely to modify its exclusively commercial style of establishment in Asia unless it was convinced of the political instability of the indigenous governments which admitted its factories. It might also do so if it became seriously dissatisfied with the conditions under which an Asian government permitted it to trade. In the Indonesian sultanates the English factors were prepared to overlook the pre-emption of commodities by the rulers and aristocracy, give them arms and presents, and transport their subjects on the Company's ships to Mecca. They were never prepared, however, to become involved in Indonesian political rivalries. Like their countrymen in Surat during Prince Murad's attack on the town in 1657, they preferred 'to bee newtors . . . endevouring to doe our business, with a great deale of submission and not much charge'.[2] The Dutch sometimes mistakenly ascribed to the English Company territorial ambitions similar to their own. They interpreted an English mission in 1642 to the Susuhunan of Mataram, the most powerful ruler in Java, as an attempt to obtain Bangka. In fact Cartwright, the English envoy, was simply seeking minor commercial adjustments in Japara.[3] The English company was offered Bangka by the ruler of Jambi in 1643 and Billiton by the Susuhunan in 1651, but neither offer was accepted.

The English also avoided political commitments to the Indonesian sultanates against the Dutch company. The English factors at Macassar, in the sultanate of Gowa, certainly gave financial encouragement to the Malays and Javanese who smuggled cloves from Dutch Amboina and they probably influenced Sultan

---

[1] Chaudhuri, 144–5, 171–2, 173–206, esp. 190–203; Bal Krishna, *Commercial Relations between India and England, 1601 to 1757* (1924) 139–50.

[2] *EFI, 1655–1660* (1921) 124.

[3] H. J. de Graaf, 'De Regering van Sultan Agung, Vorst van Mataram, 1613–1645', *VKI*, XXIII (1958) 266–7; IOL, Original Correspondence, no. 1790, fos 6–7, Bantam presidency to Surat, 25 July 1642.

Hassan Udin of Gowa to begin his last catastrophic war with the Dutch in 1666–9 by claiming fictitious English victories in the Second Anglo-Dutch war. Yet there was never any question of official English support for Gowa, even though the defeat of the sultanate inevitably led to the expulsion of all non-Dutch Europeans.[1] The Company also ignored an appeal from Sultan Abdul Fatah to break the three-year Dutch blockade of Bantam in 1659, preferring to claim damages in Europe for the temporary interruption of its trade.[2] In 1663 the Queen of Achin in north Sumatra demanded English protection in return for commercial privileges in the west Sumatran pepper trade, which the Dutch and Achin had shared since 1641. The Dutch had already begun to oust the Achinese *panglimas* (governors) from the west coast ports, but the English president at Surat could not assist Achin and admitted subsequently that English access to the ex-Achinese dependencies could only be secured by an Anglo-Dutch agreement in Europe.[3] Experienced English factors had no illusions about Dutch naval supremacy in Asia, exemplified in all the Anglo-Dutch wars of the period.

The English trust in factories under Indonesian protection was finally shattered in the 1680s. By then they had already been expelled from Macassar. The Company's factory at Jambi was destroyed in a Malay raid in 1679. As the profit margin on Bantamese pepper in London dwindled in the 1670s, the Company made repeated appeals to Sultan Abdul Fatah to reduce his excessive export duty. He refused and also connived at the murder of the leading English merchants in Bantam in 1677. This tragedy evoked from the new English agent at Bantam the first known suggestion that the Company should conquer Bantam or seize an alternative site for a fort in Bangka Strait.[4] The directors

---

[1] D. K. Bassett, 'English Trade in Celebes, 1613–1667', *Journal of the Malayan Branch Royal Asiatic Society*, XXXI (1) (1958) 5–7, 9–10, 14–15, 35, 37. Apparently the British factors at Macassar fired cannons at the invading Dutch in 1667, but they were belligerents at the time and remained prisoners of war at Batavia until 1668; see 'Sja'ir Perang Mengkasar: the Rhymed Chronicle of the Macassar War', ed. C. Skinner, *VKI*, XL (1963) 145, 267–8.

[2] IOL, Original Correspondence, no. 2680, Sultan Abdul Fatah to EIC, 21 February 1659.

[3] *EFI, 1661–1664* (1923) 316, 322–3; *EFI, 1665–1667* (1925) 21, 34.

[4] IOL, Original Correspondence, no. 4285, 'Propositions' of Abel Payne, May(?) 1677.

preferred to press the sultan to bring the murderers to justice, but when the Dutch expelled the English from this last Indonesian factory in April 1682, after intervening in a Bantamese dynastic struggle, the Company's attitude changed. The reappraisal of policy which followed is best examined against the background of similar changes in mainland Asia.

In India and Persia, as in Indonesia, the Company relied initially upon the goodwill of the indigenous governments. Their independence from European control was never in question. If local conditions became intolerable, the only remedies open to the Company were to withdraw its factors and impose a naval blockade. In practice, the English factors at Surat were hampered, as in 1621-2, by their failure to withdraw before Indian ships were pillaged or, as in 1623-4, by the need to return ashore eventually in order to resume their trade. In every case they were forced ultimately to pay compensation for their depredations and some of them, including President Rastell in 1624, were imprisoned temporarily.[1] The Company then abandoned the idea of naval reprisals for over thirty years, even paying compensation in 1632 and 1636 for the depredations of privateers, with which it had nothing in common except nationality.[2] Thus there was no English parallel with the Dutch attack on Kishm in the Persian Gulf in April 1645, their blockade of Gombroon in 1648, or their seizure of Mogul imperial ships in 1649. The English captain, Allison, might be tempted, after some of his crew were killed at the Gombroon customs post in 1642, 'to beate theire durty brittle town & castle about theire eares', but English goods and merchants ashore were too vulnerable.[3]

The same restraint was usually observed on the eastern side of India. The English factors withdrew from Masulipatam in 1628-30 and seized a few coastal ships because of the abuses of the local Golcondan governor, but returned without gaining new privileges after a stalemate. The Dutch naval blockade of 1629 was much

[1] *EFI, 1618–1621*, pp. xxxii, xxxvi; *EFI, 1622–1623*, pp. xv–xix, xxii–xxiii, xxix–xxxiv; *EFI, 1624–1629*, pp. v–viii.

[2] *EFI, 1630–1633*, pp. xvi–xvii; *EFI, 1634–1636*, pp. xix–xxv. The privateers – Quail in 1631-2, Cobb and Ayres in 1635-6 – held commissions from Charles I. In a sense they resembled the buccaneers of Jamaica, but their actions were wholly detrimental to the Company, whereas the buccaneers helped to protect English interests in the Caribbean.

[3] *EFI, 1642–1645* (1913) 1.

EARLY ENGLISH TRADE AND SETTLEMENT IN ASIA

more effective.[1] Aaron Baker, the English factor at Viravasaram in Golconda, was imprisoned in 1637, allegedly for beating a brahmin, but the Company simply recalled and replaced him. The factors at Masulipatam contemplated blockading the port in 1638, but were restrained by the detention of their colleague at the Golcondan capital.[2] In 1656 the agent at Madras seized Mir Jumla's ship, confident that the ex-general of Golconda faced disgrace at the Mogul court. In fact Mir Jumla's subordinates closed the landward approaches to Madras in 1657–8 and stopped the Company's trade at Masulipatam.[3] When Mir Jumla became Aurangzeb's commander-in-chief in Bengal, he hampered English trade there in 1659–60 and the Company's directors, who deplored the seizure of 1656, immediately offered him compensation.[4]

The acquisition of Madras in 1639 and the subsequent building of Fort St George did not mark a new belligerent English policy or a change in the Company's subordinate standing in the Indian states. Madras was obtained as a promising *locale* for cloth manufacture from a minor Hindu *nyak* (feudatory chief), Darmala Venkatappa, by Francis Day of the Masulipatam factory.[5] The understanding, later repudiated, was that the *nyak* would bear the initial cost of building the fort and be reimbursed. The presidencies at Bantam and Surat took no part in the decision, and the latter, which feared that the *nyak* would appropriate the fort for himself, was particularly anxious to dissociate itself.[6] By 1652 Madras had prospered sufficiently to replace Bantam as the seat of the Company's eastern presidency, but the Company's status in Madras was wholly different from that of the Portuguese in Goa or the Dutch in Batavia. The Company administered Madras as the *diwan*[7] of various Indian governments, not in full sovereignty. As Hindu–Muslim warfare raged in the hinterland of Madras, the

[1] *EFI, 1624–1629*, pp. xlvi–xlvii, 278, 280–4, 315–18, 339, 341, 357–8; *EFI, 1630–1634*, pp. xi, 78.

[2] *EFI, 1637–1641*, 28–9, 52–3, 65, 67–70, 142.

[3] *EFI, 1655–1660*, 92–7, 137, 174–6, 186–7.

[4] Ibid., 263–6, 275, 280–2, 286–8, 294–7, 389–94; *EFI, 1661–1664*, 40–2, 48–9, 148–9, 157, 164, 290.

[5] *EFI, 1637–1641*, pp. xxxvi–xliii, 154–8, 166, 183–5.

[6] Ibid., 284–6.

[7] The officer to whom the collection of revenue and the administration of civil justice were delegated.

G

Company negotiated new leases of the town with Sri Ranga Rayalu, the Hindu rajah of Chandragiri, in 1645 and with Mir Jumla, the victorious general of Muslim Golconda, in 1647.[1] Initially half the revenue of Madras from native trade had been paid to Darmala Venkatappa, but this was commuted to a fixed payment to Golconda in April 1658.[2] In January 1672 the English responded to the repeated demands of Neknam Khan, the *nawab* of Golconda, that they admit his agent to Madras to collect half the revenue, by agreeing to pay arrears of 11,000 pagodas and increasing the annual payment to Golconda from 380 to 1,200 pagodas.[3] Renewed pressure to admit a Golcondan official in 1680–1 was averted by further payments.[4] The determination of Sir William Langhorn, the agent at Madras (1670–8), to maintain English neutrality at the expense of his nominal French allies during the Dutch-Golcondan siege of S. Tomé in 1673–4 reflected English unwillingness to alienate Golconda.[5]

The only occasion before 1683 when the Company contemplated war with an Asian state was in 1658–63, immediately after the Company's domestic position had been immeasurably strengthened by Cromwell's new charter of 1657. The Company feared a prolonged civil war in the Mogul empire because of Aurangzeb's deposition of the emperor, Shah Jahan, and his subsequent struggle for power with his brothers in 1658–9. Recent Dutch successes against the Portuguese in Ceylon, the Dutch threat to the Portuguese possessions in western India, and the fear that the Dutch might then blockade Surat, as they had Bantam in 1656–9, also modified the Company's pacific tradition.[6] An English base on the west coast of India seemed an immediate necessity. The directors still hoped to buy Danda Rajpuri or Portuguese Bombay and Bassein, but their anxiety to have 'some place that wee might call our owne' led them to suggest in March 1659 that an incident in 1621 with Bijapur might provide the

[1] *EFI, 1642–1645*, pp. xxxiv, 305–6; *EFI, 1645–1650* (1914) pp. xxviii, 166–7, 213–4. By the *qaul* or grant of 1645 the Company was allowed to administer justice in Madras.

[2] *EFI, 1655–1660*, 174.

[3] *EFI, 1661–1664*, 277–8, 283, 285; *EFI*, new ser., II, ed. Sir C. Fawcett (1952), 8–15, 23–6, 32–40.

[4] *EFI*, new ser., IV, ed. Sir C. Fawcett and P. Cadell (1955) 22–4, 35–7, 40–1.

[5] *EFI*, new ser., II 58–69, 73–83, 96–108.

[6] *CCM*, pp. xxiv–xxv; *EFI, 1655–1660*, 115–17, 143–4, 157, 199, 207, 208 n. 2.

casus belli to conquer Danda Rajpuri.[1] Since helping the Persians to capture Ormuz in 1622, the Company had been promised but never received a half-share of the Gombroon customs revenue. As late as August 1655 the directors refused to blockade Gombroon to obtain it,[2] but in April 1660 they changed their minds.[3] Encouraged by the restoration of Charles II, they planned to use the fleet later to seize Danda Rajpuri and blockade Surat to obtain better treatment.[4]

These aggressive proposals were welcomed in Surat by President Wyche and Matthew Andrews, who tried unsuccessfully in 1659 to obtain Muscat on the Arabian coast from the Imam of Oman.[5] The directors rejected the Muscat scheme in any case because they wanted the new base to be the depot of the Company's trade in western India.[6] Andrews, who succeeded Wyche as president in May 1659, failed to negotiate the peaceful cession of Bombay, Bassein or Danda Rajpuri, and he pressed again for naval attacks on the latter port, as well as on Gombroon and Surat.[7] Fortunately, Andrews's council at Surat rejected his suggestions in September 1660, referring specifically to the disastrous outcome of Rastell's seizure of Indian ships in 1623–4.[8] Andrews still hoped to begin the Gombroon blockade in April–May 1662, but the council again dissented, pleading insufficient ships, possible Dutch intervention to nullify the blockade, the risk of repercussions in Surat, and the lack of an alternative base to which they could withdraw beforehand.[9] Sir George Oxenden, who replaced Andrews as president in September 1662, agreed with the council. He referred the decision to blockade Gombroon back to London in January 1663 and opposed the idea firmly a year later.[10] The directors finally accepted his advice, influenced perhaps by better treatment of their employees at Surat[11] and by new developments in Europe and India.

The Anglo-Portuguese treaty of June 1661 ceded Bombay to

[1] *EFI, 1655–1660*, 151, 207–8, 208 n. 2.   [2] Ibid., 25; cf. ibid., 172–3.
[3] Ibid., 325–9, 337–40.   [4] Ibid., 335–6, 337–40.
[5] Ibid., 230–3.   [6] Ibid., 320–1.
[7] Ibid., 213–14, 299–302, 306, 310–11, 330–3.
[8] Ibid., 315–17.
[9] Ibid., 340–1; *EFI, 1661–1664*, 16–17.
[10] Ibid., 97, 100–3, 121, 192, 203–5, 213–14.
[11] Oxenden achieved this soon after his arrival at Surat simply by giving the impression of being about to close the factory: ibid., 100–3.

Charles II as part of the dowry of Catherine of Braganza and bound Charles to defend the remaining Portuguese possessions in Asia against the Dutch if he failed to arrange a peace between them.[1] In fact, the Dutch negotiated their own peace treaty in August 1661, but they had captured Portuguese Quilon, Cranganore, Cannanore and Cochin on the Malabar Coast before it became effective in Asia in March 1663.[2] Thus Charles II's military obligations to the Portuguese were never invoked in Asia, while the Company's plans to counter Dutch gains in western India by wresting concessions from the Asian states were deferred by the Surat presidency until they lost their purpose. Dutch gains from the Portuguese in western India ceased and the English company's complementary fear of civil war in the Mogul empire was stilled by the triumph of Aurangzeb.

Thus in the pepper ports of western India north of Dutch Cochin the English company once again staked its commercial position, as in Indonesia, upon the resistance of the indigenous rulers to Dutch pressure. In Porokad, where an English factory had been opened in 1662, this trust was unjustified. The Dutch claimed a monopoly of pepper in Porokad as a dependency of Cochin. The English factors ignored the demands of the intimidated ruler that they leave, but their pepper investment dwindled, and they were captured by the Dutch in July 1665 during the Second Anglo-Dutch War. The English factories at Karwar (1659), in Bijapur, and at Calicut (1664), in the lands of the Hindu Zamorin,[3] survived, despite a brief closure in 1666–8 because of adverse internal conditions. By 1669 the president at Surat assumed, apparently rightly, that the Dutch had no intention of trying to control pepper supplies north of Cochin.[4] A new factory was opened at Tellicherry in 1682, and news of the loss of Bantam led the Company to increase its demand for pepper at Karwar and Calicut from about 600 tons in 1681 and 1682 to 2,100 tons in 1683.[5] This expectation was probably disappointed, but the pre-

[1] CCM, 1660–1663 (1922), p. xxi; EFI, 1661–1664, 123.

[2] CCM, 1660–1663, p. xl; EFI, 1661–1664, 125–6; M. A. P. Roelofsz, 'De Vestiging der Nederlanders ter Kuste Malabar', VKI, IV (1943) 252–60, 262–70, 272–89, 297–340, 344–7, 374.

[3] This term is a European corruption of Samudri Raja, meaning 'King of the Seas'.

[4] EFI, 1668–1669 (1927) 260–1, 268, 271–3.

[5] EFI, new ser., III, ed. Sir C. Fawcett (1954) 402, 406. For Calicut's independent

eminent Dutch position in the pepper trade of Malabar was partially offset throughout the eighteenth century by moderate English competition to the north.

The reversion of the English to wholly commercial objectives after the aggressive impulse of 1658–63 is apparent both in the Company's policy at Karwar and Calicut and in its attitude to Bombay. The directors declined to take over the prospective colony when sounded on the subject by the Earl of Clarendon in the autumn of 1661 and did so only with reluctance in 1668.[1] The presence of a crown colony at Bombay in 1665–8 embarrassed rather than helped the Company in western India. Humphrey Cook, the royal lieutenant governor of Bombay, seized an Indian ship from Surat and hinted at forcing others to frequent Bombay. Both he and his successors, Sir Gervase Lucas and Henry Gary, claimed the exclusive right to issue English passes to Indian ships, which the Mogul governor of Surat insisted should remain the prerogative of the Company's president.[2] Oxenden actually escorted Indian ships returning from the Red Sea to Surat in August 1668, in order to safeguard the Company's commercial interests at Surat.[3] Charles II hoped to restore unprofitable Bombay to the Portuguese for a cash payment in 1664–6, but finally transferred the island to the Company in 1668 for a loan of £50,000 and an annual quit-rent of £10. Although the president at Surat then became nominally governor of Bombay, his infrequent visits to the island were made with the prior approval of the Mogul governor of Surat, and he returned to Surat when the latter pressed him to do so.[4] Surat remained the Company's trade centre; cloth production at Bombay was negligible and was actively discouraged in 1681, and the Company's revenue there was inadequate.

Bombay soon acquired many features of English rule, including a mint and civil and admiralty courts, but it was a precarious island sanctuary, not a platform for territorial expansion. The

role in the pepper trade in the later eighteenth century, see A. Das Gupta, *Malabar in Asian Trade, 1740–1800* (Cambridge, 1967) passim.

[1] *CCM, 1660–1663*, pp. xxi–xxii, 137–8; *CCM, 1664–1667* (1925) pp. xxiv–xxv, 300–2, 401, 406, 408–9; *EFI, 1661–1664*, 124.

[2] *EFI, 1665–1667* (1925) 70, 181–6, 272–4, 295; *EFI, 1668–1669* (1927) 7–11.

[3] Ibid., 11–13.

[4] Ibid., 190, 205, 207–8.

garrison, as in Madras, consisted of 150 to 200 English soldiers with an equal number of Portuguese Eurasian militia. The directors insisted on retrenchment in 1679–82 and so provoked Keigwin's rebellion in 1683–4, when the garrison defied them for eleven months, hoping to transfer Bombay again to the crown.[1] The Bombay Marine took shape in the 1670s, but was largely an anti-piratical force. The Mogul fleet under Sidi Kasim and Sidi Sambal wintered at Bombay almost every year from 1672 to 1684 in its contest with the Maratha leaders, Sivaji and Sambhaji. The English tolerated this under protest rather than jeopardise their investments at Surat. The Bombay government was also unable to prevent Sivaji's seizure of the nearby island of Kenery in August 1679 or Sidi Kasim's retaliatory occupation of Henery Island in January 1680. That Bombay was not overrun by the resentful Marathas in 1678 and 1684 was because of Anglo-Mogul naval collaboration and the defence of the overland approaches by the Portuguese, who were at war with the Marathas.[2] The subsequent Anglo-Maratha *entente* of 1684 was only possible because the rebellious Keigwin handled the Mogul fleet with unprecedented firmness, and it never came again to Bombay.

The remarkable revision of the Company's attitude to Bombay, indeed of the whole basis of its Asian trade, in 1683–90, merits closer analysis than is possible from the available published material. The new conviction that the Company's investments should be concentrated in its own fortified settlements, that these should be increased in number and yield an adequate revenue, and

---

[1] *EFI*, new ser., III, pp. xii–xxii, 139 ff.; *Dictionary of National Biography*, x 1196–7. Richard Keigwin, formerly of the Royal Navy, served in Bombay in 1676–9, firstly as captain of the local cavalry troop and later as temporary commander of the naval squadron. In the latter capacity, he fought bravely against the Maratha fleet threatening Bombay in October 1679. He left for England at the turn of the year, because no further employment was available, but returned to Bombay in August 1681 as commander of all military forces and third member of the council. Keigwin shared the garrison's resentment at the Company's military economies and weak handling of the Mogul fleets which wintered at Bombay at this time. He joined and led, rather than instigated, the rebellion which bears his name. He showed restraint during the rebellion from December 1683 to November 1684, and was instrumental in persuading his soldiers to accept Sir Thomas Grantham's offer of a general pardon. He sailed to England on Grantham's ship in January 1685, rejoined the Royal Navy, and was killed leading a naval assault on St Christopher's in the West Indies in June 1690.

[2] *EFI*, new ser., III, pp. xxiii–xxiv, 7–8.

that the Company's privileges should be maintained vigorously against English interlopers and Asian governments alike, is usually ascribed to Sir Josiah Child.[1] Child certainly dominated the court of directors in London in the 1680s: he was governor of the Company in 1681–3 and 1686–8 and deputy governor in 1684–6 and 1688–90.[2] But his role is difficult to define, and his convictions may not have been unique. During his first governorship the directors still looked askance at Bombay and only resolved definitely to develop the island as the Company's principal entrepôt in India late in 1683.[3] Sir John Banks had begun his year as governor in April 1683 and it was he, not Child, who also faced the problem of the Dutch invasion of Bantam. The Company had arranged to send the 60-gun warship *Charles II*, under Sir Thomas Grantham, to Surat and Persia in order to enforce the king's proclamation against the English interlopers who had flouted the Company's monopoly since 1680. Grantham was also instructed to attack Persian ships unless the Company's moiety of the Gombroon customs revenue was forthcoming. When he sailed in August 1683, he was sent first to Bantam to assist Sultan Abdul Fatah against his Dutch-backed son and to demand the fort and town in return. Grantham was to be followed by a large fleet under Sir John Wetwang or Captain John Nicholson,[4] but in October 1683, under pressure from Charles II to avoid war with the Dutch, this reinforcement was cancelled, and Grantham was again ordered to sail directly to Persia.[5] Before he received the amended instructions in June 1684, Grantham had occupied Princes' Island off the western point of Java, but he withdrew his men and sailed to Persia.[6] He found seven Dutch ships attacking Kishm and the Persian army fully mobilised, and so he did nothing. After

[1] Sir W. Hunter, *A History of British India*, II (1900) 279 ff.; S. A. Khan, 'The East India Company's War with Aurangzeb', *Journal of Indian History*, I (1921–2) 70–8; S. A. Khan, *The East India Trade in the 17th Century* (Oxford, 1923) 203 ff.

[2] For details of Child's standing in the directorate and domestic politics, see W. Letwin, *Sir Josiah Child, Merchant Economist* (Boston, Mass., 1959) 12–24. Letwin is concerned primarily, however, with Child's theories on interest rates. There is no study of him comparable to that of his colleague in D. C. Coleman, *Sir John Banks, Baronet and Businessman* (Oxford, 1963).

[3] *EFI*, new ser., III 155–6.

[4] IOL, Letter Book VII, fos 199–203, 206–7: EIC to Grantham, 27 July and 1 August 1683, and EIC to Sultan Abdul Fatah of same dates.

[5] Ibid., fos 223a, 223d: EIC to Grantham, 9 and 19 October 1683.

[6] BM, Harl. MS. 4753, fos 2–10: Grantham's journal, May–June 1684.

resolving Keigwin's mutiny at Bombay, he sailed for England in January 1685.

Since the recovery of Bantam was now unlikely, the Company sought an alternative site for a fort outside Dutch control in Sumatra and Malaya. Instructions to this effect were sent to Madras in October 1683, preference being given then to Achin in north Sumatra,[1] although Silebar in south-west Sumatra, Kedah in north-west Malaya, and Johore on Singapore Strait were also recommended in the next three years.[2] The objectives sought by Banks and his colleagues in Achin in 1683–4 also applied to the other places. They hoped to buy enough Indonesian pepper to deny the Dutch a monopoly, raise an adequate revenue, and promote Chinese immigration as at Batavia. Benkulen in south-west Sumatra, where the agents from Madras finally settled in 1685, was badly placed in all respects. The directors deplored the choice,[3] but the Company was to retain Benkulen, known successively as Fort York and Fort Marlborough, until 1825, rather than yield its share of Indonesian pepper.

The decisions made in London before Child became deputy governor in April 1684 and governor in April 1686 suggest that his advocacy of fort-based trade was shared by his fellow-directors. It may be significant, however, that after Grantham's dispatch to Bantam the Company's plans in South-East Asia did not involve force; even at Gombroon a peaceful settlement was preferred to war.[4] Child's mistake was to combine the general enthusiasm for self-supporting fortified entrepôts with a show of strength against Siam and the Mogul empire, which might yield additional forts incidentally. Anglo-Mogul relations at Surat had been remarkably amicable in the 1670s, but Aurangzeb's raising of the Surat customs duty from 2 to $3\frac{1}{2}$ per cent in 1680 evoked hints of force by 1684 from the president, John Child, Josiah's reputed kinsman. Sir George Oxenden was wiser in his day. In Bengal, the English factors suffered continuously after 1678 from

[1] IOL, Letter Book VII, fos 223e–223f5: EIC to Madras, 19 October 1683.

[2] Ibid., fos 254, 326–7; Letter Book VIII, fos 37, 67: EIC to Madras, 29 February and 2 July 1684, 14 January 1686.

[3] *The British in West Sumatra, 1685–1825*, ed. J. Bastin (Kuala Lumpur, 1965) pp. xi–xiii. The directors favoured Priaman, further north on the Sumatran coast, but their factors pleaded prior Dutch occupation.

[4] IOL, Letter Book VII, fo 223a: EIC to Grantham, 9 October 1683.

a bewildering succession of Mogul officials who extorted large bribes by impeding the Company's trade, imprisoning factors and threatening to impose the $3\frac{1}{2}$ per cent duty for the first time.[1] In Siam, the Company's ten-year-old factory failed in 1684, so the directors believed, because of the machinations of Phaulkon, the Greek deputy foreign minister of Siam.[2] English interlopers were welcomed in Surat and Bengal, while many former employees of the Company entered Siamese service, notably Samuel White, who became governor of Mergui, the chief Siamese port on the Indian Ocean. White and his English subordinates in the Siamese navy seized a number of ships registered in Madras, nominally as official Siamese reprisals against Golconda.[3] Child was prepared to use force to recall these adventurers to their allegiance, suppress the interlopers and claim redress for other abuses from their Asian hosts.[4]

The directors authorised naval reprisals against Siamese ships in January 1686, but urged the capture and fortification of Mergui in October, after Child had become governor.[5] In the latter month, while Captain Nicholson's troops and warships were outward bound from London to demand redress from the Mogul emperor and seize Chittagong – under the impression it lay on the Ganges, – war broke out in Bengal. Two frigates were sent from Madras to Mergui in June 1687 to recall the local English community and issue an ultimatum to Siam, but in August there followed some slender reinforcements to help capture Mergui in keeping with Child's latest instructions. The English ashore at Mergui had already been massacred in July 1687, as soon as the Siamese suspected Samuel White's intention to surrender the port, and the Company lost heavily in ships and men before

[1] *EFI*, new ser., III, p. xxix; ibid., IV, passim.

[2] D. K. Bassett, 'English Relations with Siam in the Seventeenth Century', *Journal of the Malayan Branch Royal Asiatic Society*, XXXIV (2) (1961) 98–104. For more sympathetic views of Phaulkon, see J. Anderson, *English Intercourse with Siam in the Seventeenth Century* (1890) and E. W. Hutchinson, *Adventurers in Siam in the Seventeenth Century* (1940).

[3] White's career and final predicament at Mergui are discussed most ably in M. Collis, *Siamese White* (1936). My references are to the 1965 reprint.

[4] See above, p. 103, n. 1.

[5] *Records of the Relations between Siam and Foreign Countries in the 17th Century*, IV (Bangkok, 1920) 6, 37–9. The Siamese were claimed to be 'a sheepish, cowardly people, like your Gentoos [Hindus], who will not fight'!

withdrawing.[1] The French company, with the support of Louis XIV and the connivance of Phaulkon, installed garrisons at Bangkok and Mergui in 1687-8, but they were expelled in the wave of Siamese resentment which overthrew Phaulkon in May 1688. In India, the English factories in the Surat area were destroyed, Bombay was besieged from February 1689 to June 1690, and in Bengal Job Charnock and his men found a tenuous refuge lower down the Ganges at Sutanati (Calcutta) and at Hijili. Had the Mogul government treated the affair as anything more than a minor irritant, the English would have been overwhelmed. Suitably penitent, they accepted Aurangzeb's peace terms in February 1690 and resumed trade on the old footing, except that their Bengal investment was based henceforth on Calcutta rather than Hugli. A month earlier the directors advised the Bombay government to make peace with Siam.[2]

If its political illusions were shattered, the commercial opportunities open to the Company in India and China were encouraging. English trade with China had developed almost fortuitously after the Company's failure to gain readmission to Tokugawa Japan in 1673.[3] By the end of the century, the 'old' Company and the New East India Company, which challenged its monopoly from 1698 to the amalgamation of 1708, had begun an intermittent but profitable trade with the Manchu régime at Amoy, Chusan and Canton.[4] Trade was later confined to Canton. The closing of the Old Company's extraneous factories in Siam (1684), Taiwan (1685) and Tongking (1697), all of which had been expected to supply the Japanese market, intensified English concentration in the Far East upon China. The New Company was similarly impelled by the destruction of its prospective Far Eastern entrepôt at Pulo Condore, off the mouth of the Mekong, in 1705. The united East India Company ultimately benefitted from the expanding British demand for Indian and Chinese

[1] Ibid., 151-6, 169-77; Collis, 226-38, 262-4. White escaped the massacre and was a vocal critic of the Company after his arrival in England.

[2] *Records of the Relations between Siam and Foreign Countries*, v (Bangkok, 1921) 106: 'Pha[u]lkon is killed, and the French being gone our war is at an end with those people.'

[3] D. K. Bassett, 'The Trade of the English East India Company in the Far East, 1623-1684', *Journal of the Royal Asiatic Society* (1960) 47, 150-7.

[4] H. B. Morse, *The Chronicles of the East India Company trading to China, 1635-1834*, I (Oxford, 1926) 52-65, 78-98, 109-10.

commodities, while Indonesian spices and pepper, upon which the Dutch had expended so much effort, declined in relative importance. The Company's political expansion in India, under wholly different circumstances later in the eighteenth century, and its domination of the Canton market helped to consolidate British ascendancy in Asia.

FURTHER READING

1. *Collections of Documents*

Letters received by the East India Company from its Servants in the East, ed. F. C. DANVERS and W. FOSTER, 6 vols (1896–1902), brings together the extant letters from the various Asian factories in 1602–17, drawn primarily from the Original Correspondence series at the India Office Library, London.

The Calendar of State Papers, Colonial Series, East Indies, 1513–1634, ed. W. NOEL SAINSBURY, 6 vols (1862–92), summarises the Court Minutes of the Company, the letters of the factors in Asia, and diplomatic papers relating to the Company until 1634.

A Calendar of the Court Minutes etc. of the East India Company, 1635–1679, ed. E. B. SAINSBURY, 11 vols (Oxford, 1907–38) [*CCM*], carries the publication of the Court Minutes to its present limit. They include occasional policy decisions, as well as routine sales, price lists, the dispatch of ships and goods, the raising of capital and the election of officers. Vol I of the Court Minutes has been published *verbatim* as *The Dawn of British Trade to the East Indies, 1599–1603*, ed. H. STEVENS (1886) and vol IA as *The First Letter Book of the East India Company, 1600–1619*, ed. Sir G. BIRDWOOD and W. FOSTER (1893; reprint 1965).

The English Factories in India, 1618–1669, ed. W. FOSTER, 13 vols (Oxford, 1906–27) and *The English Factories in India (New Series), 1670–1684*, ed. Sir C. FAWCETT, 4 vols (Oxford, 1936–54) [*EFI*], are a magnificent collection of almost all the documentary material originating in the Indian factories in this period. Considerable attention is also paid to Persia, although this declines after *c.* 1660. All references to Indonesia and the Far East after 1623 have been omitted unless the Indian factories are directly involved. Each volume has a masterly introduction and commentary.

Records of the Relations between Siam and Foreign Countries in the 17th Century (1607–1700), published by the Council of the Vajiranana National Library, 5 vols (Bangkok, 1915–21). These volumes have no introduction or commentary, but the documents of the second half of the century are particularly valuable. A better source for English activities in Siam in 1612–23 is *Letters Received by the East India Company* [above, p. 107] or W. H. MORELAND, *Peter Floris, his Voyage to the East Indies, 1611–1615* (1934).

The British in West Sumatra, 1685–1825, ed. J. BASTIN (Kuala Lumpur, 1965) includes documents describing early English settlement at Benkulen. There is an excellent general introduction. A more extensive collection can be found in P. WINK, 'Eenige Archiefstukken betreffende de Vestiging van de Engelsche factorij te Benkoelen in 1685', *Tijdschrift voor Indische Taal-, Land- en Volkenkunde*, LXIV (1924) 461–520.

2. *Secondary Works*

ALEXANDROWICZ, C. H.: *An Introduction to the History of the Law of Nations in the East Indies – 16th, 17th and 18th Centuries* (Oxford, 1967). A scholarly survey of the interaction of Asian and European concepts of diplomatic and political relations before the assertion of complete European dominance in Asia.

ANDERSON, J.: *English Intercourse with Siam in the Seventeenth Century* (1890). Extensive quotations from documents but inclined to misinterpret them, especially in 1660–88.

BAL KRISHNA: *Commercial Relations between India and England, 1601 to 1757* (1924). A useful pioneer analysis of English import-export trade with Asia.

CHAUDHURI, K. N.: *The English East India Company: the Study of an Early Joint-Stock Company 1600–1640* (1965). An excellent description of the Company's internal financing, imports, exports and sales, with consequent repercussions on policy.

COLLIS, M.: *Siamese White* (1936). An impartial and perceptive study of Samuel White's career in Siamese government service.

FOSTER, Sir W.: *England's Quest of Eastern Trade* (1933). Still the best account of early English travellers and merchants in Asia by the greatest historian of the East India Company. The book is devoted mainly to events before 1623.

GLAMANN, K.: *Dutch-Asiatic Trade, 1620–1740* (Copenhagen–The Hague, 1958). Some useful analogies between the Dutch and English East India Companies' difficulties in buying and selling particular commodities.

HUTCHINSON, E. W.: *Adventurers in Siam in the Seventeenth Century* (1940). Very knowledgeable about the French connection with Siam until 1688, but has misunderstood the English company's attitude to some extent.

KHAN, S. A.: 'The East India Company's War with Aurangzeb', *Journal of Indian History*, I (1921–2) 70–91. A series of extracts from the Company's letters to India in 1685–9 which casts indirect light on Sir Josiah Child's policy. Khan also discusses Child's role in *The East India Trade in the Seventeenth Century* (Oxford, 1923), but there seems to be no adequate study of the development of policy in London at this time.

MORSE, H. B.: *The Chronicles of the East India Company trading to China, 1635–1834*, 5 vols (Oxford, 1926–9). Vol. 1 has the best account of Anglo-Chinese negotiations and trade in Portuguese Macao and the Chinese ports, but is less concerned with the Company's general policy.

PRITCHARD, E. H.: *Anglo-Chinese Relations during the Seventeenth and Eighteenth Centuries* (Urbana, Ill., 1929) discusses the general circumstances which hindered the development of the Company's China trade, but some of his conclusions are debatable.

WILSON, C. R.: *The Early Annals of the English in Bengal*, I (1895) contains a detailed account of the development of the Company's trade in Bengal in the seventeenth century and of the Anglo-Mogul War there in 1686–90. Some of Wilson's value-judgements are debatable today, but he used his sources well.

5 Britain as a European Power, from her Glorious Revolution to the French Revolutionary War

ALICE C. CARTER

THE Glorious Revolution of 1688 transformed England's relations with Europe. There ascended to the English throne the francophobe William III, at a time when England's external policy was still under the direction of her sovereign and had recently been far from hostile to Louis XIV. But after William III became king England's power was aligned with the Netherlands against France, where the spearhead of the party bringing in William III wanted to see it anyway.

This is not, however, to say that William III's accession determined the long-run alignment of England's *future* power in alliance with the Dutch against France. It is only historians indulging in the doubtful benefit of hindsight who have accustomed us to thinking that at the Revolution the shift of England's future weight was preordained. In particular, the view is too simple that at the Revolution the marriage between the so-called Maritime Powers, England and the United Provinces, was fully consummated. This alliance was indeed at its most viable during the Nine Years War of 1689–97. But, in the Spanish Succession struggle which followed, the supposedly unbreakable link between the two powers was fretted and chafed by many strains. By mid-eighteenth century it was to snap; and the link was only resoldered after the defeat of Napoleon, and then without much craftsmanship. All the same, England began her career as a front-rank European power among the enemies of France, among the allies of the Dutch Republic and the Imperial Habsburgs – under the direction of a half-Stuart, a Stuart-consort, and a Netherlands stadholder who was passionately anti-French. We will return at a later stage to the working-out of this theme.

There were also more subtle changes in England's European involvement after 1688, changes more of degree than of direction.

Inevitably there followed, after the Revolution, an increasing awareness of what was going on in Europe, and of what was implied in becoming a European power. These changes, it is hardly necessary to state, were not only the result of our having sought a king from over the water to rescue us from a domestic impasse. But they were inevitably intensified by William's presence on the throne, if only because thereafter English politicians were obliged to familiarise themselves with his continental preoccupations. And where politicians led, the careerist and courtier followed. No longer were there only a round hundred politicians and merchants aware of what was happening in Europe.[1] Before 1689 there were already some ties between the 'second-wave' Exclusionists – who followed on those defeated in 1681 and who acquired many adherents after James ascended the throne – with William of Orange, francophobe Orangists and others at The Hague. The politically ambitious, as always, sought to please the King and Queen. They mixed with the internationally experienced Dutch entourage; and they acquired a better knowledge of what was happening in Europe than their predecessors had learnt from the French-orientated Catholics round Charles II or his brother, when the Court was still cut off from all but its own supporters.

It was not only courtiers and politicians who were increasing their contact with Europe after the Revolution. To begin with, more people were beginning to have personal ties with the Continent. The army, though still small by European standards, had been trebled by James II and was to be enlarged still further in the course of the Nine Years War. The navy was soon to become the greatest among all the European nations. And the armed services were increasingly employing Englishmen rather than aliens, both in the ranks and among the commissioned. This meant that as the forces moved abroad more and more relations, friends, fellow-townsfolk and contacts of all kinds began to take an interest in the fate of their menfolk 'overseas'. The failure of Parliament to renew the Licensing Act in 1695 resulted in the rapid growth of printed matter to satisfy curiosity about political questions of the day, including the fate of the armed forces. In the early eighteenth century the growth in the number of newspapers,

[1] Cf. above, pp. 40–1.

and in the habit of reading them, was phenomenal.[1] William himself, by formalising his communications to the House of Commons, so that the reply had to take the form of a written Address, subsequently printed as a Vote, added to the amount of information available to satisfy awakened public opinion. The famous Kentish Petition of 1701 was significant. It expressed 'deep concern at the dangerous Estate of this Kingdom and of all Europe', and urged that the King's desire to assist his allies – that is, to renew the war with France – should be furthered with a vote of supply.[2] It is true that William could write in 1698 to his Grand Pensionary Heinsius that 'it is as if no other country existed but this island, and that it need not concern itself with what happened elsewhere in the world';[3] yet all around him lay the evidence that so insular an outlook was fading, at least among those in England who were concerned with her politics.

Many factors were in fact moving England, after 1688, from a position which had seldom been better than 'non-isolation' to one that could become splendidly interventionist. First was the credit-worthiness of the newly constituted régime, aided by what contemporaries called 'the money'd interest'. After the Revolution, for the first time, it became possible for England to fight her foreign wars on the shoulders of the future. The Nine Years War was the last fought principally on a debt commonly regarded as repayable, and after the beginning of the eighteenth century it was found possible to pile up public debts. These provided an outlet for the increasing investible surplus of those holders who preferred semi-liquidity for their marginal funds. Once the interest payments were

[1] See G. A. Cranfield, *The Development of the Provincial Newspaper, 1700–1800* (Oxford, 1962) esp. 67–70, and E. S. de Beer, 'The English Newspapers 1697–1702' in R. Hatton and J. S. Bromley (ed.), *William III and Louis XIV: essays by and for the late Mark A. Thomson* (Liverpool, 1968) 117–29. Cf. G. C. Gibbs, 'Newspapers, Parliament, and Foreign Policy in the Age of Stanhope and Walpole', *Mélanges offerts à G. Jacquemyns* (Brussels, 1968) 293–315.

[2] *Commons Journals*, XIII 518, 8 May 1701. The Petition is printed in W. C. Costin and J. S. Watson, *The Law and Working of the Constitution*, 2 vols (1952) I 191–2.

[3] A new Parliament in this year was even more unfavourable to a standing army (declared illegal in the Bill of Rights) than its predecessors. William even let it be known that he was half-contemplating abdication. But the political situation precluded any party's daring to call his bluff. G. N. Clark, *The Later Stuarts* (Oxford, 1934) 180–1.

securely founded on specified duties, and backed by Act of Parliament, debt-stock was taken up, often quite eagerly, and European action on an effective scale became practicable.[1]

The funding of interest payments upon special duties on trade, along with war expenses generally, involved a major increase in indirect taxation. In fact between 1689 and 1713 England changed from being on the whole a free-trade country to one which put heavy duties on many imports.[2] This in itself made for changes both subtle and obvious in her European position, and increased the circle of her native traders who found their interests directly at stake in Europe. As the degree of 'protection' afforded to our home industries, for fiscal rather than for consciously protectionist purposes, increased, so did the number of petitions from industrial and trading groups, and also complaints from our foreign customers and suppliers. Foreign reactions created yet further need for information about local conditions: instructions to diplomatic representatives on trade affairs proliferated on a scale hitherto unknown in eighteenth-century correspondence, as did memoranda describing economic growth, the birth of new enterprises, the discovery of new processes.

A public debt, with the resulting change from free trade to protection, made it possible for England to go into Europe after

[1] P. G. M. Dickson, *The Financial Revolution in England* (1967) 39 ff. Table I (ibid., 10) establishes a relation between war expenditure and public borrowing. The following expresses the same idea even more dramatically:

Year	Approximate total of funded debt (£ million)
1700	4.75
1710	7
1720	50 (reflects mainly delayed funding operations following peace of 1713)
1730	47
1740	43
1750	72
1760	97
1770	127 (over £130 m. in 1767)
1780	155
1790	233
1800	402

Figures of approximate debt-total from *History of the Earlier Years of the Funded Debt, 1694–1786* (1898, C. 9010) and *Report . . . of the Proceedings of the Commissioners for the Reduction of the National Debt, 1786–1890* (1891, C. 6539).

[2] R. Davis, 'The Rise of Protection in England, 1689–1786', *Econ. Hist. Rev.*, second ser., XIX (1966) esp. 306–7.

the Revolution. The European commitments of our foreign kings made it necessary. William's concern with the Netherlands, and with the danger to be expected from France, was not only an incentive to politicians to study the European scene. The Netherlands' peril, and our own growing concern with the fate of the southern Low Countries, inevitably drew us into the Spanish Succession disputes; in spite of objections to William's high-handed partition treaties, we had to prevent French aggression around the Scheldt area. This was still strategically necessary in view of Louis XIV's ambition. Moreover, many of our merchants still believed that London could only prosper if grass grew on Antwerp's quays. That other classic merchant misconception – that direct trade with the Spanish Main was a passport to riches untold – took us further into the question of the Spanish Succession. When the Hanoverian kings arrived, with their over-prized electorate among the German states still lacking but greatly coveting access to the North Sea, and with a small but significant part to play in Habsburg politics, English ministers were landed with a European assignment even heavier than before. The ministers who aimed to stay in power under either George I or George II – that is to say, all politically ambitious statesmen of the years 1714 to 1760 – had to secure, or attempt to secure, or at least to appear to be attempting to secure, the safety of their master's 'despicable electorate'. Thus they had to pay attention to the wishes and concerns of the King of Prussia and of the Emperor, already on the verge of combat. By mid-century, when the battle for hegemony in central Germany reached the stage of a spirited rearguard action by the Habsburgs against Prussia, the situation was complicated further because either the Austrian Habsburgs or the Hohenzollerns had to assume the role of caretakers, in some sort, of Hanover.

Dutch advisers came to England with William, and many Hanoverians with George. These people, also, brought with them international expertise. They were a source of information on Baltic and central German politics. They were also very good linguists, better far than the English. The quarrels, apparently inevitable in electoral life, gave us a new political element, an opposition leader in the person of the Prince of Wales, who with his wife became a focus for London life. Caroline of Ansbach and her entourage were more mundane and accessible, thus more suited to the increasingly lay but still strongly Protestant life of London than had been the Catholic consorts of the Stuarts, and their households, in the seventeenth century.

The phenomenal growth of the British armed forces had more vital results than increasing the interest of soldiers' families in Europe. Added armed strength was another reason why in the eighteenth century England could become involved in Europe. No longer, as a hundred years earlier, did foreign governments need to supply such few and poor troops as England sent to European conflicts, 'on pillage'. Problems in logistics, much to the fore during the years 1689–97, were solved with surprising success. Marlborough's service corps arrangements in the Blenheim campaign were the wonder of Europe. By the end of Anne's reign a standing army had become an accepted fact; even though it was not large by European standards, it was sufficiently well organised to act as a cadre for expansion when needed. Moreover, army interests soon became a built-in part of the English political scene. As was perhaps inevitable, promotion was a political job, commissions were bought, and dead-pay was a perquisite. Officers, contractors, paymasters, their relations and dependents, became a recognised parliamentary group; thus military pressures could be felt in a positive parliamentary way. Naturally these people had a vested interest in extra-insular happenings.[1]

By 1714 England was possessed of a navy larger, better administered, and with better fire-power than any other in Europe. She also had abundance of merchant ships and privateers. In the Nine Years War the expansion of English shipping has been described as 'dramatic'.[2] This growth stimulated the Baltic timber trade, increased the prosperity of dockyard towns, gave business to ship-chandlers, opened up a demand for coarse linen for sails, and in general quickened Britain's economic growth as well as increasing beyond measure her European standing.

Executive skills of a high order, but above all knowledge of

---

[1] J. H. Plumb, *The Growth of Political Stability in England, 1675–1725* (1967) 120 ff.

[2] Ibid., 119; J. Ehrman, *The Navy in the War of William III, 1689–1697* (Cambridge, 1953) p. xx. But cf. R. Davis, *The Rise of the British Shipping Industry* (1962) 316–17, 68: Davis indicates considerable losses of merchantmen only partly compensated for by prizes taken from the enemy.

what is going on in the outside world, are needed to co-ordinate ship movements with those of troops awaiting passage, or of merchantmen awaiting convoy. This information was available to navy board officials because of the growth of what the eighteenth century called 'intelligence', which came very near to espionage. As the century went on, payments for intelligence increased, and so did the number of persons so employed. The presence, around the capitals of Europe, of a Stuart Pretender to the British throne was as much the cause of such growth as were the needs of admiralty officials for accurate information. Sir Robert Walpole followed with frenetic zeal the movements of the Old Pretender and his family.[1] Thus Walpole as well as his agents became more fully versed in the affairs of Europe.

Britain formalised her diplomatic service on much the same strong lines as had been laid down in seventeenth-century France, rather later than did some of the other European powers. Regular appointments in the diplomatic service were not as lucrative or desirable as commissions in the armed forces.[2] There does not seem to have developed a foreign-service element in politics in any way similar to that of the army and navy, although diplomatic appointments, like service commissions, could be held by people who were also members of parliament. This may have been because the diplomatic service was not much sought after. Such salaries as were paid were sometimes in arrears, and expense accounts were left unsettled for long periods.[3] The ambassador, envoy or minister plenipotentiary was, moreover, expected to entertain at his official residence the young men who made the Grand Tour and introduce them to the local potentates, while their fathers were not always ready to further in return the career interests of the host or his relations.[4] There is, however, little doubt that an expanding and more formalised diplomatic service – with its need for clerks, interpreters, copyists, linguists, cypher-

[1] J. H. Plumb, *Sir Robert Walpole*, II: *The King's Minister* (1960) 15. Walpole's obsession with Jacobitism is interestingly related to the background of assassination and treason inherent in European aristocracy of the early eighteenth century.

[2] D. B. Horn, *The British Diplomatic Service, 1689–1789* (Oxford, 1961) esp. ch. iii.

[3] Ibid., 61.

[4] Sir Joseph Yorke, British ambassador at The Hague, mentioned this difficulty in family letters: cf. ibid., 63, quoting a similar opinion.

breakers and intelligence officers – not only brought more British people into contact with Europe than hitherto, but also assisted the mother country to become herself a more influential member of the European family of nations. The fact that members of the less senior branches of the diplomatic service were by no means among 'the politer sort of people' (as Blackstone called them) extended the social area which in the eighteenth century became more involved personally in Europe than formerly.

Attention was directed some years ago to the effects on seventeenth-century England of the Grand Tour, undertaken by young gentlemen as an established part of their education.[1] By the eighteenth century a larger social grouping was undergoing this educational process; their parents were *ipso facto* among the moneyed, but not necessarily among the landed classes. Although these two classes were becoming less and less easy to distinguish, the influence of foreign travel on young men and on their so-called tutors, or bear-leaders, often much of their own age, was often quite dramatic. We all know how Boswell reacted to travel in the Netherlands.[2] These experiences were conducive to greater understanding, not only by the travellers but by their parents and relations, of what Europe was like. These travellers, whose numbers were increasing all the time, brought Europe and England closer together, accumulating experience and enlarging horizons.

Another influence of the same kind was that of the young merchants, or would-be merchants, who went abroad to study other countries' ways of doing business, or to promote their family concerns in foreign parts. There was the famous trading academy at Warmond, north of Leiden, from which one of the sons of the Bishop of Hereford was expelled in 1747.[3] There were international trading families like the originally Huguenot Thomases, with family members in Cork, Bordeaux and Rotterdam; or like

[1] J. W. Stoye, *English Travellers Abroad, 1604–1667* (1952); cf. J. R. Jones, *Britain and Europe in the Seventeenth Century* (1966) 5–6.

[2] *Boswell in Holland 1763–1764*, ed. F. A. Pottle (1952). Boswell alternates between idleness and devotion to learning, the ladies, the table and the cultivation of the fashionable.

[3] BM, Egerton MS. 1714, fos 31, 33, 48, 52, 65, 122. Cf. A. C. Carter, 'The Family and Business of Belesaigne, Amsterdam, 1689–1809', *Proceedings of the Huguenot Society of London*, XX no. 3 (1962 for 1961) 308 n. 3.

the Scots-Irish Peace family, with four brothers who divided their time between Glasgow, Dublin, Amsterdam and La Rochelle.[1] These people had, of course, their seventeenth-century counterparts. But by mid-eighteenth century there seem to be so many of them, doing so much, that one cannot help feeling they are now a new factor in the situation. By the 1750s a third of the names of the depositors in the Bank of Rotterdam were English, Scots or Irish. Some of them were found, on investigation in the Notarial Archives there, to be those of people who had taken, or of the sons of those who had taken, Dutch nationality. Some were growing rich by continuing in war-time to conduct the trade of Britain with French ports, flying for the purpose the flag of the most highly privileged neutral power of all time.

These more extended contacts, at a deeper level than formerly, were also promoted by the migration of skilled European craftsmen to Britain early in this period, and by the intensified search for British technologists to spread industrial skills in Europe towards the end of it. The Huguenot immigrants have been traditionally associated with ornamental crafts, such as lustrine taffetas and other advanced textile skills, silverwork, bookbinding, glassmaking and the manufacture of jewellery. Among them were sometime financial servants of the French Crown, bankers, even ordinary middle-class rentiers with skills in making money breed money, all of whom contributed significantly to the growth of business connected with the public debt, to banking and to the development of credit instruments in England. Huguenots who remained permanently domiciled here gradually became anglicised, but retained a preference for investment in stocks rather than in land. Many of them, especially those who were merchants or entrepreneurs, retained multiple contacts with other expatriate family members or former associates spread around Dutch, Mediterranean and trans-Atlantic ports. They also gradually resumed former relations with family members who had abjured their faith and remained in France. Like British merchants domiciled abroad, they are to be found conducting Anglo-French trade, via neutral ports, during mid-century Anglo-French wars.[2]

[1] Information from Notarial Archives in the Gemeente Archief, Amsterdam, supplied by Dr S. Hart.
[2] A. C. Carter, 'The Huguenot Contribution to the Early Years of the Funded Debt', *Proceedings of the Huguenot Society of London*, XIX no. 3 (1955) 21 ff. and idem,

Their visits to relations abroad, or journeys on business, must have contributed enormously to general awareness in the host-country of what was going on in Europe.

Other efforts were made at technical cross-fertilisation between Britain and Europe. Dublin linen manufacturers looked all over the Netherlands for Dutchmen to spread southwards the skills brought to the Lurgan valley by Louis Crommelin. And later in the century British technicians were sought by European entrepreneurs.[1] Even though numbers were small, study and research, the reporting back of results of industrial espionage, all contributed to increase contact between Britain and the Continent.

The Declaration of Rights settled in February 1689 England's acute domestic crisis. Thereafter sheer urgency soon drove England into the Grand Alliance. She embarked on the Nine Years War, in fact, for specifically English reasons; its old-fashioned title, the War of the English Succession, is apt. Naturally Louis XIV extracted from the English succession crisis every ounce of its nuisance value against William III. James II was sent, with good wishes, a magnificent campaign kit (and little else) to 'poison England through the Irish thorn in her side'. James, who did not want to stay in Ireland, desiring his English crown again, over-stretched his slender resources, disillusioned the Irish, and so was soon once more a pensioner in France. Nevertheless, England still saw, until Louis in 1697 recognised her Protestant Succession, that her major interests were the same as those of William's other subjects. Thereafter for a time, unlike the Dutch, the English Whigs contrived to close their eyes to the approaching Spanish crisis, and were castigated by William for attempting to cut down the army and for not renewing the Mutiny Act.[2] Meanwhile the Dutch were acutely aware of French pressure on their southern

---

'Financial Activities of the Huguenots in London and Amsterdam in the mid-eighteenth century', ibid. no. 6 (1959) 313 ff.

[1] W. O. Henderson, *Britain and Industrial Europe* (Liverpool, 1954) 6–7, 104–6.

[2] This Act, 1 W. & M. c. 5, was passed as an emergency measure in 1689 for a period of six months only. It gave effective control over the armed forces of the Crown by enabling courts martial to pronounce the death penalty, although only under carefully regulated conditions. It was renewed for a year, and thereafter annually, during the war, but was allowed to lapse temporarily after 1697. See M. A. Thomson, *A Constitutional History of England, 1642–1801* (1938) 292–7.

frontier and of the danger, in whatever form, of French influence in the Southern Netherlands. Hence there developed at an early stage the weakness in the link between the Maritime Powers which has so conspicuously escaped the attention of many non-Netherlands historians.

It was also English, rather than European, factors which dictated England's entrance into the Spanish Succession War. Louis recognised the Pretender as James III, which by itself might not have caused us to go to war. But he also opened the Spanish American trade to his own merchants. As French forces were about to enter the Southern Netherlands the grass could conceivably be worn once more from the quays of Antwerp. Louis in fact touched off no fewer than three of eighteenth-century England's most dearly cherished prejudices: that the sovereign must be a Protestant; that the Scheldt must remain closed; and that if English merchants were excluded from direct trade with Spanish America, so also must all others.

This brings us to a consideration of how, in eighteenth-century Britain, uninformed emotional reactions entered into politics. There was as yet no machinery for ensuring that members attended the House, and division lists seldom add up to more than three to four hundred out of a membership of 558. So long as no excitement was generated, the Revolution and the ensuing settlements gave the executive, in general, a *modus vivendi* with the House of Commons,[1] because within it was a caucus of 'court' members, whose interest, even whose idealism, kept them at Westminster furthering 'the king's business' by voting for government measures. Apparent immediate danger, however, to the Protestant Succession, interference with an Englishman's domestic privacy, or with his overseas trade, could let loose on the government a flood of 'independent' members who would hasten to the House, there to cast an unpredictable vote for or against government policy, according as oratory, the press or local pressures of an incalculable kind should dictate. Thus Britain's European as well as her domestic politics were 'at risk' from the eighteenth-century counterpart of today's 'floating voter', to whom later on in the century might be added the majority of

[1] J. H. Plumb, *The Growth of Political Stability in England*, 188–9. Cf. J. B. Owen, *The Pattern of Politics in Eighteenth-Century England* (Historical Association, Aids for Teachers Series, no. 10, 1962).

government stock-holders (though not, be it noted, the few who held the majority of the stock).[1]

Like its predecessor, Marlborough's war was entered into as a result of what were conceived to be urgent English interests, and was prosecuted as such whilst French forces remained in the Southern Netherlands. But, like its predecessor, as time went on, it exposed again the weakness in the link between the so-called Maritime Powers. The Dutch, expecting almost hourly in 1703 a French attack on their frontiers, extended successfully the *casus foederis* of their most recent defensive treaty with England, that of 1678.[2] Henceforth warlike preparations, as well as outright acts of aggression, could call forth armed assistance from *either* side. Now the Dutch had always traded, and advisedly, with their enemies, regarding trade as a source of wealth and wealth, however gained, as necessary to the prosecution of a war. What eroded the Anglo-Dutch alliance, turning it from what was admittedly a mere *mariage de convenance* into one on the road to divorce, were the suspicions of merchants on both sides that 'trading with the [mutual] enemy' was enriching not only the enemy, but their allies more than themselves. There was also acute Anglo-Dutch rivalry for both trade and domination in the recaptured Southern Netherlands. After these became Austrian territory, trade rivalry there continued to divide the former allies throughout the eighteenth century. Moreover, the Anglo-French settlement of 1713 and the disappointing Barrier Treaty of 1716, more or less imposed on the Dutch by the powers, including Britain, made it clear that Dutch interests were far from prominent in British foreign policy.[3]

Between the settlements terminating the War of the Spanish Succession and the renewed outbreaks of total European war in 1740, there intervened a period of mainly diplomatic British participation in continental affairs, coupled with tremendous

[1] A. C. Carter, 'Analyses of Public Indebtedness in Eighteenth Century England', *Bulletin of the Institute of Historical Research*, XXIV (1951) 173 ff.

[2] R. Hatton, *Diplomatic Relations between Great Britain and the Dutch Republic, 1714–1721* (1950) 96 n. 3, and sources there cited.

[3] The Barrier diplomacy is discussed fully in R. Geikie and I. A. Montgomery, *The Dutch Barrier 1705–1719* (Cambridge, 1930): see esp. 334 ff. For the high figures of Dutch shipping in some French ports from 1705 to 1710, see J. S. Bromley, 'Le Commerce de la France de l'ouest et la guerre maritime, 1702–1712', *Annales du Midi*, 65/21 (1953) 49–66.

advances in the field of Anglo-European trade. Britain's main concern in this period was with expansion in the East and West Indies, and with the advancing trade and frontiers of her American seaboard colonies. She was, in fact, storing up the riches, from expanding world as well as European trade, which would later enable her to take part in all-out war. Expansion outside Europe would also later make it possible to strangle at source, when advisable, France's wealth from the West Indies, and to put a stop to her ambitions in North America, Africa and the Indian continent itself. All this time the Barrier to France's expansion north-east and in Europe, with its supporting Anglo-Dutch alliance, helped to maintain stability in that area with which majority opinion in England still felt itself to be most concerned. It is curious to note how completely the navalist school of historians of the early twentieth century, like Sir Julian Corbett, clung to this majority opinion as explaining our policy then, but failed to note that the Anglo-Dutch mortar in the Barrier was crumbling to decay.

In reality it was less the strength of the Old Alliance, with the Barrier fortresses it supported, than a shift of stress in Europe, first to the Baltic and then to the Mediterranean, that preserved stability in the area of the French north-east frontiers, which had earlier proved the storm-centre. Britain played a secondary part in the settlement of a Baltic balance when the empire of Charles XII broke up. Out of this settlement there came access to the North Sea for the King-Elector George I, and thus some stability for his ministers, together with better conditions for those European powers which depended on Baltic naval stores, and continuity for Dutch services in supplying these stores to French dockyards.[1] Out of the Mediterranean settlement Britain gained some betterment of the conditions under which she conducted her trade to the Levant, undisputed possession for a time of Minorca and, as it turned out, of Gibraltar in addition. But the Mediterranean did not receive, in British strategy, the attention that might have been expected of a major maritime power.

One event significant for the future was the marriage, in 1734, of Willem Carel Hendrick Friso, son of William III's cousin and heir, to the daughter of George II. This alliance of Orange and Hanover was in a very different category from the earlier alliance

[1] P. W. Bamford, *Forests and French Sea Power* (Toronto, 1956) ch. ix.

of Orange and Stuart. For it was markedly an alliance of parties, both in Britain and in the Netherlands. The Netherlands as a whole had not given the Orange-Nassau house any of the standing accorded to William III, partly because necessity did not, after the latter's death, appear to require it. Anthonie Heinsius, grand pensionary of Holland, had long pursued the Orangist policy of hostility to France. But his regent opponents had been able more and more to develop their positive policy of neutrality under the stress of increasing friction with England and of 'live and let live' with France. The transfer of the Southern Netherlands to the Emperor Charles VI – inimical to, and later the enemy of France – suited the regents well. What we may call their 'Maginot' complex grew along with their trade in the Austrian Netherlands; both, at the beginning of the Austrian Succession War, appeared to be serving them well.

Between 1740 and 1763 Britain could be said to have reached a peak in her eighteenth-century European commitments. For a time her non-isolation can almost be described as 'splendid'. In the 1730s, and still more as the European war developed, the factors dividing her politicians notably included considerations of foreign policy, and of ways in which war, if and when it should come, ought to be conducted. Since George II was a German prince, and ministers were above all royal servants, government policy, with Hanover in mind, was still that of defensive alliance and, as far as possible, of peace. We remained neutral in the Polish Succession War – fought in Italy, not Poland. But the English opposition was turning more and more to what might be called a blue-water line of policy. England's destiny, they felt, was to be rich from conquests outside Europe, and from control of all Europe's overseas trade. Political spite against Walpole, coupled with a characteristic failure of the Duke of Newcastle's nerve, enabled these opposition leaders to project the country, by means of the 'independent' House of Commons element, into a totally unnecessary war with Spain in 1739 on the grounds that our merchants were being hindered from trading in Spanish American waters, the emotive symbol being the bottled ear of a former sea-captain of the name of Jenkins. This is dubiously to be classified as a war for strictly British interests, since it was a war that Britain did not need to fight.[1] But next year Prussian aggression against

[1] R. Pares, *War and Trade in the West Indies, 1739–1763* (Oxford, 1936) esp. 43–52.

her Austrian ally involved her in the cause of Maria Theresa, and thereafter we took for a while a major part in Europe. In return for the discontinuance of an East India company operating from Ostend, and for the general furtherance of the English king's German objectives, we had earlier agreed to guarantee the succession of all Austrian Habsburg territories to the daughter of Charles VI. We were thus enmeshed not only in our then still undeclared colonial rivalry, active in both America and India, with the French, but also in the battle for hegemony in central Europe which broke out between Hohenzollern and Habsburg. On the touchline, as it were, was the royal electorate, and opposed to Austria in Europe the colonial enemy France.

It is not easy to see how English ministers could have kept us out of this major European development. It is, however, also difficult to justify our intervention on specifically English grounds, especially since there was, as formerly, a Pretender to the throne, a threat-card ready in the hands of France. This card was played with aplomb in 1745, when the French had already won success, after an initial set-back, in the Southern Netherlands. By landing the famous 'Seven Men of Moidart' on the Scottish coast the French achieved, at no cost to themselves, a major victory in the principal western theatre of the war. The Duke of Cumberland's army was immediately withdrawn across the Channel. With it came, under the terms of our defensive alliance with the Dutch, 6,000 of their already insufficient troops. Their frontiers were left undefended; although the French did not immediately approach, Dutch alarm was intense, and in 1747 a French declaration of war brought about the return to power, on the analogy of 1672, of the House of Orange. Until 1747 the Netherlands, though fielding what they described as a strictly defensive army in the Austrian cause, were not the declared enemies of France. They were still relying on the utility to the French of their shipping, and of their other services to all belligerents. But it was continuously being borne in on them that the superior English navy, and above all English privateers, were not going to allow them to trade in naval stores, or to carry home to French ports the rich produce of the French West Indian islands. In fact, as neutrals in the Austrian Succession War, the Dutch learnt two useful lessons. One was that Britain could well defend her own Protestant Succession. The other was that she would interpret to her own advantage the terms of the long-ago commercial treaty of 1674, which like all seventeenth-century Dutch commercial treaties excluded as many articles as possible from lists of contraband of war.[1]

However, the neutral role, practised for most of the Austrian Succession War, served the Dutch Republic well, and better still in the Seven Years War. Their still ample shipping, and their much sought-after credit facilities, enabled them to serve all warring countries to their own considerable advantage.[2] French naval strength depended still on Dutch shipments of Baltic timber; and French resources in seamen, though adequate in peace-time, could not stretch to reinforce the navy without loss to the merchant marine in time of war. Britain's wars were fought on credit; and although the extent of Dutch investment in our stocks was nothing like as great as contemporaries supposed (or as some modern historians would have us believe) the steady trickle of Dutch money, especially into war-time issues of a size demoralising to the English investor, was useful and credit-promoting.[3] Our overseas trade was hungry for Dutch as well as native credit finance; and Dutch ports, especially Rotterdam, acted as entrepôts for our own considerable French trade, which could hardly continue direct. Imperial loans and Silesian mines, as well as Baltic timber and West Indian shipments to Europe, also awaited the neutral services of the Dutch during the mid-eighteenth-century wars.

One difficulty, however, facing the neutral as well as the belligerent powers of the period, was that the respective rights and duties of both had not as yet been at all clearly defined.

---

[1] P. C. Jessup and F. Deák, *Neutrality, its History, Economics and Law*, I (New York, 1935) 35 ff.

[2] By mid-eighteenth century the relative economic position of the Republic in Europe had declined considerably, especially in labour-intensive sectors. But in qualitative and quantitative terms decline was much slower, and wars in which the Republic remained neutral still acted as a stimulant. See Joh. de Vries, *De Economische Achteruitgang der Republiek in de Achttiende Eeuw* (Amsterdam, 1959) esp. 19 ff. and tables of yields of various taxes.

[3] Dickson, 320–8, discusses in masterly fashion Dutch holdings in English funds down to the 1750s. Cf. A. C. Carter, 'Dutch Foreign Investment, 1738–1800', *Economica*, new ser., xx (1953) 333, where reasons are given for supposing that Dutch investment represented 6.9 per cent of the 4 per cent loan of 1760, with (by the standards of those days) the enormous total of £8 million.

England had always adopted the position that the seas were not free. Habitual neutrals, like the Swedes, the Danes and the Dutch, took the view that a neutral-owned ship, manned by a majority of neutrals, flying neutral colours and clearing originally from a neutral port, was free to ply where she chose, and that her cargo, unless it contained actual armaments of war, was covered by her neutral status; their only concession was that her activities should not directly contribute to the war potential of the power to whose ports she plied. Effectively, all shipping services to a belligerent could be held so to contribute. By mid-eighteenth century, *force majeure*, conspicuously on the side of the English navy and still more of the English privateers, settled this question in Britain's favour, more or less without benefit of lawyers. All the same, when unrestricted interference in Dutch sea-borne trade, especially in the Seven Years War, appeared likely to result in the Dutch regents being able to consummate an alliance with France, some regulation, by way of the English admiralty courts, was brought into force. An Act of 1759 regulated privateering. Decisions in Doctors' Commons, the admiralty court of first instance for European waters, and in the High Court of Admiralty, which heard appeals from lower courts all over the world, made clear to Dutch owners and skippers the limitations which would be placed on their trade on behalf of Britain's enemies. Defiance of these limits, it was made clear, would lead to condemnation of ship, cargo or both in the courts.[1] There was, however, sufficient margin left for the Dutch to continue trading profitably; it is noticeable that the few available figures of Dutch shipping show an upward turn as soon as the series of test cases was complete early in 1760. Here the English showed as much care for Dutch neutral susceptibilities as did the French. The Diplomatic Revolution of 1756, with its unexpected – and to some eighteenth-century politicians almost immoral – alliance between Habsburg and Bourbon, made nonsense of the Barrier system. Although France was now allied to the guardian of the Southern Netherlands, French troops never approached the Dutch frontier without long and careful diplomatic preparation, and many assurances of benevolent intentions. The objective in each case was the same:

[1] I discussed 'The Dutch as Neutrals in the Seven Years' War' in *The International and Comparative Law Quarterly* for July 1963. Cf. R. Pares, *Colonial Blockade and Neutral Rights* (Oxford, 1938) esp. section iii.

neither Britain nor France wanted the Dutch to be forced by popular agitation to abandon the neutral role.

What, besides a Churchillian 'finest hour' or two, mainly in 1759, did Britain gain from her period of European power between 1740 and 1763? The Peace of Paris, negotiated as in 1713 and 1748 by a ministry very different from that which had fought the war, brought substantial colonial advantages. Canada was retained, there were Caribbean gains, French expansionist hopes of Indian trade were dashed. But, as Pitt declaimed in the House of Commons, we returned to France – with Guadeloupe, Martinique, Dakar, above all with the right to fish off Newfoundland – 'the means of recovering her prodigious losses, and of becoming once more formidable to us at sea'.[1] In Europe the British position after 1763 was arguably worse than before 1740. No longer obliged to consider German politics, for George III cared not a whit for Hanover, Britain's sights were set even more firmly than before on East and West, and no account was taken of any supporting European alliance, beyond that of ever-faithful Portugal. More and more, colonial affairs absorbed all attention, coupled with attempts to cut down the ever-mounting public debt. Britain's earlier concerns with Baltic balance, Mediterranean bases, even the safety of the Southern Netherlands, were left to look after themselves.

This turning of Britain's back on Europe might well have been to the national interest. But having been a European power, she could hardly withdraw without creating some kind of resulting vacuum. Neither Prussia, abandoned in the field, nor the northern neutrals, whose ships had been taken up, nor Spain – whilst neutral also 'at risk', and when involved in war a victim – had any particular reason to love her. The row of old Barrier fortresses was now possessed by France's ally. The French were no longer alarmed at the prospect of Dutch reaction to aggression from the south, if only because a Stuart succession to the British throne was by now unthinkable. And anyhow, the anglophile Orangist party in the Netherlands was in eclipse. The hereditary Stadholder was a minor until 1766 and after that a cypher, at least until the mid-1780s. Moreover, the Baltic was overshadowed by increasing Russian power. In time, that power could conceivably threaten

[1] Quoted and discussed by J. H. Plumb, *England in the Eighteenth Century* (Pelican History of England, VII, 1950) 114.

the vital supplies of naval stores for which Britain's need was increasing more and more. In the Mediterranean she did regain Minorca at the peace, its price the return to France of Belle Ile, captured late in the Seven Years War; but even upkeep costs, let alone re-fortification, were regarded as expenses which could well be avoided. And the acquisition of Corsica by France, in 1768, worsened to some extent our comparative position in the Mediterranean, about which at the time we did not care very much.

When it became clear that the War of American Independence was one that could not be decided quickly, our European enemies, including former allies, seized gladly on a chance to humiliate us. French military professionalism stiffened American guerrillas. British military professionalism, on the other hand, lacking contacts with more informal methods of warfare, remained inflexible; this proved to be a major cause of defeat. It has been argued that French naval strength, deployed in force in the colonists' cause, won the war for them. Would Cornwallis have been obliged to surrender at Yorktown, thus relinquishing the South, if Graves had not been hopelessly outfaced in the Chesapeake by de Grasse's much superior squadrons?

The Armed Neutrality of 1781, engineered by Russia,[1] revived the earlier French ideas of 1756 and 1758 and hampered our privateers. At the end of 1780 war broke out between ourselves and the Dutch, whose dominant States party at length exchanged their long-standing policy of friendship with France for one of active co-operation. Dutch ports, for the first time for over a century, were shut to British shipping. This meant that our merchants, already embarrassed by the near-cessation of direct American trade, were obliged to find new routes for their operations to French ports. It was lucky for them that by that time arrangements by which ships could be made to seem to have changed hands, had become so sophisticated that ships' colours and ships' papers were interchangeable almost overnight. The Fourth Anglo-Dutch War can be said to have created only temporary confusion among our merchants, thanks to the laxity of international law in respect to trade.[2] But it did detach resources

[1] See I. de Madariaga, *Britain, Russia and the Armed Neutrality* (1962).
[2] I am indebted to Dr S. Hart, of the Gemeente Archief, Amsterdam, for information about rapid changes of nationality between Dutch and Prussian ships

from the major scene of the war, and thus contributed to the loss of our American colonies.

One result of the Anglo-Dutch war was a move on Britain's part to reopen the waters of the Scheldt, and thus to make Antwerp once more easily accessible from the sea. This abortive episode (for the Emperor Joseph II would not at first co-operate) is worth some reflection, for nothing illustrates so clearly the immense changes in Britain's European policy which took place between the Glorious Revolution and the War of the French Revolution. Fears of French aggression in the Southern Netherlands, alarm for London's trade should Antwerp prosper again, conviction that if the Dutch were to prosper the Scheldt must stay closed – these motives, among others, had led both powers into the wars of the English and Spanish successions. The Barrier system, with its accompanying Austro-Dutch alliance, had been regarded as a necessary stabiliser of north-eastern Europe by English ministers, affected by the need to tranquillise policies in the interests of the King-Elector. Now Antwerp's services were required again to further Britain's continental trade. The anti-Orangist Dutch had pushed to its extreme conclusion their conviction that the French were not their active enemies. In the place of the Barrier system, dead since 1755, there had arisen a Franco-Dutch entente. By now, fortunately perhaps for Britain, the Dutch Republic was no longer able to overcome its many political weaknesses; its economic strength, like the need for its shipping and its credit facilities, was being outdistanced by other developments in these fields. Thus the impact of the Fourth Anglo-Dutch War on Britain was not anywhere near as great as was its significance as an emblem of change.

After the débâcle of losing her colonies, Britain's European image, as well as her mercantilist colonialism, was damaged. Yet within ten years she had reasserted her influence on the Continent and could be described as the linchpin of the alliance system against rampaging revolutionary France. How did this come about? Let us adopt once again the scheme of considering first Britain's

---

in the winter of 1780. Also, the late Mr C. J. B. Gaskoin, who was engaged for some years before his death on a study of neutrality, used to discuss such questions with me.

¹ S. T. Bindoff, *The Scheldt Question* (1945) 138-42.

actual ability to bring pressure to bear in Europe. The first point to note is that there were certain gains, especially in maritime effectiveness, resulting from the War of American Independence. Technical changes in signalling, first used successfully in the later stages of the West Indies campaigns, gave naval commanders greater ability to manœuvre ships of war with confidence in the course of battle; and after the war was over, contrary to earlier experience, and instead of slackening control, improvements took place in naval and dockyard administration, mainly associated with the name of Lord Barham. Periods necessary for refit were cut down, stores built up, the herculean task of tackling corruption begun. The division made in 1784 between the duties of the two secretaries of state – now no longer for 'the North' and 'the South' as previously, but for Home and for Foreign Affairs respectively – improved communications on the diplomatic front, which had always been liable to break down when the secretaries did not happen to agree.

By the 1780s, also, we had reached our 'take-off' period (Rostow-style) for economic growth; our trade, even a little later with the recently relinquished colonies, was increasing all the time; we were rapidly becoming a wealthy country even by big-power standards of the day. Our population was also increasing by leaps and bounds, and we had begun to lead, not follow, in technological advance. Measures were also under way to free trade of the restrictions which had accumulated, mainly for fiscal reasons, since the beginning of the century. Besides the free-trade treaty with France of 1786,[1] seven other commercial treaties were under serious negotiation between 1785 and 1793, and three more had been considered.[2]

This policy of attempting to enlarge the markets available to us, and to improve the terms of our trade, is associated with the initiative of William Pitt the younger, who came to lead the government late in 1783. Any form of diplomatic activity helps to reinstate in the European power-club a member who has become isolated through defeat, as Britain had been after 1783. Hence, although the results of these negotiations did not prove

[1] See W. O. Henderson, 'The Anglo-French Commercial Treaty of 1786', *Econ. Hist. Rev.*, second ser., X (1957–8) 104–12.

[2] J. Ehrman, *The British Government and Commercial Negotiations with Europe, 1783–1793* (Cambridge, 1962) I.

in the long run very rewarding, their very existence conduced to mitigate her 'non-splendid' isolation. Pitt contributed also the essential stabilisation of her central government, without which she could hardly have staged a European come-back of any proportions. The onset of the physical illness which later incapacitated George III completely, combined with the general disillusion of the country as a whole with its government after 1783, made Pitt's task less difficult. From 1783 onwards, any return to old-style monarchical government, such as had been attempted by George III and his advisers, became a clear impossibility. Thereby many central tensions relaxed, and a climate prevailed in which big changes of personnel or policy in government were less likely to occur than formerly. Thus adequate means from increasing trade, a growing population, economic advance and a stable government enabled Britain to become once more an effective European power.

The pattern of alliances into which Pitt had now to reinsert his country has been recently described as 'a single political system',[1] firmly resting on the Habsburg–Bourbon alliance operative since 1756. Excluded were Prussia and the still just viable Poland, acting as the necessary 'carve-up' area for the continental imperialism then being practised by Russia and Austria, sometimes with French connivance and usually to the alarm of England as well as of Prussia. Prussia's very isolation is supposed to have drawn her towards England, also isolated, though between these two powers until 1786 remained the aged Frederick the Great, with his hatred of 'perfidious Albion'. There were, however, already strong links between Britain and Prussia. Both powers feared Russia.

Britain still felt, also, that stability in western Europe depended upon a holding operation of some kind on the north-east frontier of France. The situation in the Dutch Republic had changed dramatically as a result of the Fourth Anglo-Dutch War, and when Pitt first came to office the revolutionary Patriots were in power. In the Southern Netherlands there still ruled Joseph II, still the ally of France, still the great enemy of the King of Prussia – who might be able to embarrass Joseph, and oppose France, if he could somehow exploit his dynastic foothold in Dutch politics. These considerations formed the basis of the Triple Alliance between

[1] D. B. Horn, *Great Britain and Europe in the Eighteenth Century* (Oxford, 1967) 163.

Britain, Prussia and the United Provinces, which in 1788 appeared to recreate England's 'ancient system' against France, with Prussia playing the earlier Austrian role.

The Triple Alliance was a remarkable achievement. To understand it means glancing at developments in the Low Countries, north and south. Joseph II had first attempted to exchange his Netherlands – so distant from the scattered central and eastern provinces he was trying to order – for territories of Bavaria. But this only served to array against him all the German princes, who feared so radical a disturbance of the balance of power in central Europe; in particular, he greatly alarmed Prussia. Joseph then set about improving the economy of the Southern Netherlands. But this required urgently that he somehow open the mouth of the Scheldt: ironically, England's desire to do this late in 1780 had come too early to chime with Joseph's plans. In 1784 and again in 1787 the alarm bell clanged in the Dutch Republic, now ruled by the so-called Patriots, among whom were successors of those very merchant oligarchs who earlier had kept the Scheldt firmly closed. This latest turn of 'the Scheldt question' delayed, and at a critical time, attempts to create a Franco-Dutch alliance at the end of the Fourth Anglo-Dutch War.[1]

To turn to the Republic itself, the most noteworthy change is the broadening of the anti-stadholderian party. To a core of old-style town aristocracy, mainly of the province of Holland, had been added middling-sort intellectuals and disgruntled careerists, mainly from provinces where the House of Orange was foremost in the distribution of patronage. Some of these people were influenced by the ideas of the Enlightenment, and some had connections with the former British colonies in North America. The late Alfred Cobban saw the struggle between Patriot and Orangist in terms of foreign policy.[2] Should the Republic line up with England or with the French? Whilst it is true that William V, hereditary Stadholder and titular leader of the Orangists, was a greater lover even than his ancestors of all things British, not all Patriots were solid for France. Among them were the sons of men who had seen the French connection as one to cultivate, but not to embrace, and who had realised the advantages of neutrality.

[1] A. Cobban, *Ambassadors and Secret Agents* (1954) 27; cf. Bindoff, 143 for a somewhat different view.
[2] Ibid., passim.

By now, the duties of the neutral power were coming to be seen more in terms of 'impartial refusal' than of 'impartial concession',[1] so that neutrality was less likely to be a profitable role in war. It is difficult to say how far such considerations weighed with the Patriots, or for that matter with France. But an all-out French alliance was not regarded favourably by all Patriots, especially whilst France's ally was showing signs of wanting to reopen the mouth of the Scheldt.

Untypically, French diplomacy was less successful than was Britain's in the ensuing struggle to achieve an alliance with the Dutch. Certainly Sir James Harris, later Lord Malmesbury, British representative at The Hague, was more successful than his French opponent La Vauguyon, and a good deal abler. Within three years, working with unpromising material – William V, though intelligent and well-informed, was ineffectual and totally inexperienced – but assisted by a good deal of luck, Harris and the King of Prussia were able to bring about a stadholderian coup. A year later the Triple Alliance of Britain, Prussia and the Republic was in being; a new 'ancient system' appeared to have emerged.

This system was not, however, a substitute for its predecessor, and indeed it did not have to be. Britain was now much stronger than formerly, so stood less in need of such security as the earlier alliance had provided. Prussia was no substitute for Austria, since Prussia's interest was to check, not to support, the guardian of the Southern Netherlands. The Republic was much weaker than heretofore. The rate of her economic decline was now accelerated, measurable in quantitative and qualitative as well as in relative terms. Moreover, though the majority of Patriots had fled when the Orangists came back to power, enough remained to threaten a régime so lacking in leadership, and to propagate ideas which made the Netherlands more receptive than they might otherwise have been to revolutionary sentiments when the French armies finally arrived.

A scant year after the framing of the Triple Alliance, the revolution broke out in France. Within four years, this was to change completely Europe's power-structure, and to promote Britain to the head of a series of new anti-French coalitions. At first, however, Britain found that she could keep out of hostilities;

[1] R. J. Valin, *Traité des Prises Maritimes*, ed. A. de Pistoye and D. C. Duverdy (1855) I 339.

her attitude was at first almost benevolent, though we need not take too seriously the ecstasies of Fox upon the fall of the Bastille. In spite of dangerous ideological disputes in Britain, bound up inextricably with national politics, Pitt and Grenville could continue neutral even after the fall of the French monarchy in August 1792. It was not until the incursion of French troops into the Southern Netherlands that a real change began to take place in British policy towards France. On 16 November 1792 came a French decree declaring that the Dutch no longer had the right to close the mouth of the Scheldt, access being needed for French warships to help reduce beleaguered Antwerp. So gross a violation of international agreement presaged real danger to the British as well as to the Dutch. In January there came a French order to equip more warships: France might soon become as powerful as England was at sea, even when lacking seafaring allies or victims. This was a more potent force impelling us to war than was the execution of Louis XVI, which followed a fortnight later. The *congé* accorded to Chauvelin, French envoy to the Court of St James, on receipt of the news of Louis's death, was followed by a French declaration of war against our allies the Dutch as well as against ourselves.

Inclusion of the Republic in this declaration against Britain showed how much less cautious was the new French government than the old. For France, as in the early eighteenth century, was now obliging the Dutch again to embrace a British alliance. British and Dutch together faced once again a French north-east aggression; Marlborough's war was about to be repeated. But by now our ally was so weak, and so divided, that more even than formerly we had to take the burden on ourselves. We had perforce to look around for other allies; Pitt's earlier hope, of adopting only the role of paymaster to such allies, fell to the ground. We had to face all-out war on every front, on land, on sea, and at diplomatic conferences. The situation facing Pitt in 1793 was, in fact, so different from any with which his predecessors had had to deal that this year forms a fitting conclusion to a survey of Britain's European relations. We acquired in the course of the eighteenth century the status of a European power. When the biggest challenge came, we could step with power into the lead.

FURTHER READING

1. *Documents*

As in the case of the previous chapter, there is no single collection to illustrate Anglo-European relations generally, apart from the extracts in *English Historical Documents*, x [1714–83] ed. D. B. HORN and M. RANSOME (1957). But a few further suggestions may be made simply to represent the mass of printed correspondence and other source materials which deal with particular areas or topics. Two accessible selections from the writings of the many English travellers who committed themselves to print are C. MAXWELL (ed.), *The English Traveller in France, 1698–1815* (1932) and R. MACAULAY, *They Went to Portugal* (1946), to which may be added *The Journal of William Beckford in Portugal and Spain, 1787–1788*, ed. B. ALEXANDER (1954). Besides *Boswell in Holland*, F. A. POTTLE has also edited *Boswell on the Grand Tour* (2 vols, 1953, 1955), covering journeys made in 1764–6. Very different in outlook but by no means confined to his central concern with agriculture is ARTHUR YOUNG's *Travels in France and Italy during the years 1787, 1788, and 1789*: the best edition by C. MAXWELL (Cambridge, 1929) omits Italy. Among the diplomatic correspondence special mention may be made of *An Honest Diplomat at the Hague: the Private Letters of Horatio Walpole, 1715–1716*, ed. J. J. MURRAY (Bloomington, Ind., 1955); *The Private Correspondence of Sir Benjamin Keene, K.B.*, ed. Sir R. LODGE (Cambridge, 1933); and *The Despatches of Earl Gower, English Ambassador at Paris from June 1790 to August 1792*, ed. O. BROWNING (Cambridge, 1885). Vol. II of the *Diaries and Correspondence of James Harris, first earl of Malmesbury* (4 vols, 1844) deals with the years 1784–8 at The Hague. Insular Toryism may best be felt perhaps in J. SWIFT's *The Conduct of the Allies* (1711), reprinted in *Political Tracts, 1711–1713*, ed. H. DAVIS (Oxford, 1951). For the diversity of British reactions to the course of the French Revolution, see A. COBBAN (ed.), *The Debate on the French Revolution* (1950).

2. *Secondary Works*

ALBION, R. G.: *Forests and Sea Power: the Timber Problem of the Royal Navy, 1652–1862* (Cambridge, Mass., 1926) shows the relation of Baltic timber to British foreign policy.

BAMFORD, P. W.: *Forests and French Sea Power, 1660–1789* (Toronto, 1956) complements Albion in respect of the French government's problems of dockyard supply at home and abroad.

BAXTER, S. B.: *William III* (1966). Up-to-date, full-length biography, with detail as to Netherlands background not easily available elsewhere.

BEMIS, S. F.: *The Diplomacy of the American Revolution* (New York, 1935). Excellent introduction to the subject.

COBBAN, A.: *Ambassadors and Secret Agents* (1954) studies the mission of James Harris to The Hague, using fresh sources.

DICKSON, P. G. M.: *The Financial Revolution in England* (1967) explains lucidly how England came to command the means to intervene in Europe in strength.

EHRMAN, J.: *The British Government and Commercial Negotiations with Europe, 1783–1793* (Cambridge, 1962) situates the Anglo-French treaty of 1786 within the context of the younger Pitt's cautious but continuous efforts to improve British markets in eastern and southern Europe.

GIPSON, L. H.: 'The American Revolution as an Aftermath of the Great War for the Empire, 1754–1763', *Political Science Quarterly*, LXV (1950) 86–104, offers a succinct statement of the major theme in the author's monumental series, *The British Empire before the American Revolution*, 13 vols (New York, 1936–67) of which vol. XIII includes a useful historiographical section.

HENDERSON, W. O.: *Britain and Industrial Europe* (Liverpool, 1954) opens a topic which is ripe for more detailed treatment now that studies of individual English industrialists with European assistants, and vice versa, are proliferating.

HORN, D. B.: *The British Diplomatic Service, 1689–1789* (Oxford, 1961). The only scholarly survey, involving much fresh work.

—— *British Opinion and the First Partition of Poland* (Edinburgh, 1945). A pioneer sketch, pointing up the influence of anti-popery.

—— 'The Diplomatic Revolution', *The New Cambridge Modern History*, VII (ed. J. O. LINDSAY, Cambridge, 1957) ch. xix. Probably the clearest short account available, but tends to undervalue the United Provinces.

—— *Great Britain and Europe is the Eighteenth Century* (Oxford, 1967). Authoritative synthesis.

LODGE, Sir R.: *Studies in Eighteenth Century Diplomacy, 1740–1748* (1930). A model of clarity by a great diplomatic historian.

—— *Great Britain and Prussia in the Eighteenth Century* (Oxford, 1923). Ford lectures of 1922, especially useful for 1740–63 and 1787–91.

MICHAEL, W.: *England under George I*, 2 vols (1936–9) deals with 'The Beginnings of the Hanoverian Dynasty' and 'The Quadruple Alliance' – all that has been translated of the author's famous *Englische Geschichte im 18. Jahrhundert*, 4 vols (Berlin, 1920–37).

PARES, R.: 'American versus Continental Warfare, 1739–63', reprinted in *The Historian's Business*, ed. R. and E. HUMPHREYS (Oxford, 1961)

130–72. A brilliant article written for *The English Historical Review*, LI (1936) while the author was working on the two books to which reference has been made in the footnotes of this chapter.

RASHED, Z. E.: *The Peace of Paris, 1763* (Liverpool, 1952) illuminates the elder Pitt's breach with the traditional style of peacemaking.

READING, D. K.: *The Anglo-Russian Commercial Treaty of 1734* (New Haven, Conn., 1934) illustrates the many difficulties which surrounded England's important trade with Riga and St Petersburg.

RICHMOND, Admiral Sir HERBERT: *Statesmen and Sea Power* (Oxford, 1946) contains chapters on all our naval wars: the mature reflections of a fundamental critic.

ROSE, J. H.: *William Pitt and the Great War* (1911). Still the best account of why Britain went to war in 1793.

VAUCHER, R.: *Robert Walpole et la politique de Fleury, 1731–1742* (Paris, 1924) is not yet superseded.

WILLIAMS, B.: *Stanhope* (Oxford, 1932). Scholarly study of British continental policy 1714–21.

—— *Carteret and Newcastle: a Contrast in Contemporaries* (Cambridge, 1943). Written late in life by a great student of eighteenth-century diplomacy and particularly useful in the absence of a solid study of Carteret.

—— *The Life of William Pitt, earl of Chatham*, 2 vols (1914). Still the standard biography.

WILSON, C.: *Anglo-Dutch Commerce and Finance in the Eighteenth Century* (Cambridge, 1941). A new approach to Anglo-Netherlands relations containing much still of interest, though now shown to exaggerate Dutch investment in England.

6 The Netherlands in the European Scene, 1813-1913

J. C. BOOGMAN

MY starting-point is the memorable year 1813, when the Dutch shook off the French yoke. If that glorious event may be called a revolution, one should immediately add that it turned out to be a rather second-rate one, decidedly not conspicuous for large-scale heroism or revolutionary fervour. For its success, conditioned of course by the allied victory over Napoleon, should be credited before all others one great man, the former regent Gijsbert Karel van Hogendorp. This man wished to prevent the allied conquest of his country because it might have resulted in the treatment of the Netherlands as an occupied territory.

The social and political élite of the country as a whole, however, did not prove to be up to the crisis. Most members of the leading classes showed themselves great masters in playing a waiting game. Irresolution and passivity were more characteristic of their attitude than revolutionary courage and élan. This lack of energy, this apathy, which was to last for a considerable time to come, can easily be understood. For several decades already the situation of the Dutch commercial commonwealth had been continuously deteriorating. Years of stagnation had been succeeded since 1795 by a period of obvious decline, and after the year 1810, when Napoleon annexed the country to his empire, this decline threatened to end in sheer disaster. No wonder, then, that the great merchants and bankers, so long the leading elements in Dutch society, felt frustrated. Their feelings of impotence were naturally an important element in the generally prevailing apathy. In addition the political fortunes of the country during a considerable space of time had increased the sense of frustration. Since the end of the previous century the Dutch had been at the mercy of the autocrat in Paris. They had seen their political fate being determined by the result of incessant wars, which they could only watch from afar.

Seen objectively – which in this case also means seen in the light of later events – there is no doubt at all that the position of the liberated Dutch state among the other European powers was not a favourable one, even if compared with that of the old Republic at the end of the Ancien Régime. In general the post-Napoleonic state was more centralised than its eighteenth-century predecessor, and it was in all respects more powerful. On the whole, however, the greater states had profited much more than the smaller ones, as the situation of the new Dutch state might alone suggest. We may think, for instance, simply of the military aspect. The institution of mercenary troops had enabled the rich Dutch commonwealth to play a role in the field which evidently did not quite correspond with the small number of its inhabitants or with their rather poor military spirit. And yet the modern army system, modelled on French and Prussian example, did diminish Dutch military strength by comparison with that of most other countries.

As to the economic prospect, it seems obvious enough to us that the old Dutch staple market was doomed in 1813. At the beginning of the eighteenth century the strength of that famous system had already been sapped by the mercantilist practices of other countries, and in the course of the century its decline had continued steadily. In the year 1813, at the very moment when Great Britain's supremacy in world trade appeared unassailable and when continental governments were more inclined than ever before to promote their own subjects' economic welfare (being now more capable of doing so), at the very moment, too, when Dutch trade had come to a deadlock, the Dutch clearly had no real chance of restoring their staple market, the achievements of which during the seventeenth century had been conditioned in fact by the backwardness and political crises of its potential rivals.

How did the Dutch themselves envisage their situation after being liberated from French domination? First and most obviously, they felt greatly relieved, freed from the oppression of a recent past which was looked upon as a bad dream. Above all, they wanted to be themselves again and hankered after peace and order, security and stability. The structure conceived by them of the serene and restful heavenly city they wished to erect on earth, on their marshy Dutch soil, is to be considered a genuine product of the Restoration period, in good classicist style. A complete restoration, however, was not wanted. The unitary state, that hard-won bequest from the Batavian period (1795–1806), had to be maintained, although it was to be placed under the sovereignty of an enlightened prince of the venerable House of Orange; the vehement party struggle of the years of the federal Republic should not, on any account, ever be allowed to return. But, for the rest, present as well as future had to be closely connected to the glorious past of the old commonwealth. The slogan 'als vanouds' ('as of old') became a magical creed. Van Hogendorp himself had prophesied in his famous proclamation of 1813: 'De oude tijden komen wederom' – 'The old times will come again'.

Not less interesting in this connection is another prophecy to be found in the same proclamation: 'De zee is open. De koophandel herleeft – 'The sea is free. Trade will revive.' These assertions certainly cannot be counted as revolutionary rhetoric. Hogendorp held very high hopes indeed of his country's future. He firmly believed that world commerce would return to the funnel of the Dutch staple market, if only free trade could be re-established in the Netherlands, even though this liberal system was not to be extended to transit trade any more than it had been in the past. Hogendorp can be regarded as the spokesman of the surviving élite of former regents, great merchants and bankers, together with the host of well-to-do rentiers in their wake. After 1813 these people retained their hold on Dutch society. They had their stronghold in the conservative city of Amsterdam. The hopes of these optimists, however, who cultivated the great commercial tradition of the province of Holland and of Amsterdam in particular, turned out to be sheer illusion.

The economic failure of the Dutch in the following years cannot be adequately explained by pointing only to the unfavour-able circumstances which immediately confronted them.[1] The same flabbiness and passivity which characterised the attitude of the upper classes in general during the revolutionary crisis of the

[1] Cf. W. J. Wieringa, 'Social Circumstances and the Development of the Dutch Economy in the Nineteenth Century' in J. S. Bromley and E. H. Kossmann (eds.), *Britain and the Netherlands*, II (Groningen, 1964) 169–80.

year 1813 is to be noticed when we look at their economic activities
in particular. The past – that is to say, the glorious seventeenth
century – was an obsession with many notable Dutchmen of this
generation. One may even say that they were enslaved by it. It
afforded them beautiful arguments to avoid adapting themselves
to changed circumstances. In the eyes of many foreigners the
starchy Dutchmen of that time, with their lack of creativeness and
imagination, with their obstinate clinging to old traditions, looked
rather curious, not to say ridiculous. The Germans, especially,
were not sparing of sharp criticism. In their opinion the Dutchman, the Chinaman of Europe (as he was called sometimes),
was the embodiment of the narrow-minded, greedy philistine.[1]

In the views of the Dutch on foreign relations and on the
position their country had now to take among the other states,
the past, of course, also figured large. I have in mind here that
rather specific tradition of the province of Holland, whose main
aspects may be summed up as neutrality with respect to foreign
policy, a utilitarian pacifism, and aversion from territorial
expansion.[2] These tendencies of the dominant province – maritime and to some extent insular and anti-continental – proved to
be still quite lively in the post-Napoleonic age, particularly among
the old élite.

The political as well as the economic ideas of the Prince of
Orange, who was cheered resoundingly by the Dutch when he
arrived from England at the end of November 1813, differed
widely from those held by the leading classes in the country. His
ideas may be described as strongly continental.[3] The Netherlands,
in William I's opinion, had to be connected much more tightly
with the European continent, and in order to be a power of real
weight on the continental scene its territory must be enlarged
considerably. This view, obviously, was at complete variance with
Holland's tradition. It bore a closer resemblance to the dynamic

[1] Cf. P. J. van Winter, *De Chinezen van Europa* (Groningen, 1965).

[2] See further on this subject J. C. Boogman, 'Die holländische Tradition in der
niederländischen Geschichte', *Westfälische Forschungen*, xv (1962). Cf. above, Ch. 1.

[3] In the time of the Dutch Republic the Orange stadholders had often also
showed continental tendencies. Cf. the striking if slightly exaggerated remark of
Jules Michelet, who noted, when visiting the Netherlands in 1837, that the House
of Orange 'rejette toujours la Hollande vers les terres, l'éloignant de la mer, son
véritable élément': *Journal*, i, ed. Paul Viallaneix (Paris, 1959) 229.

and expansionist Burgundian tradition, dynastic and supra-
national, or at any rate supra-territorial.[1]

In the domain of economics the views of the sovereign were
equally in conflict with those of the mercantile élite. In many
respects he shared the ideas of the likewise continentally-minded
radical Patriots and Batavians of the end of the eighteenth century.
Like many of them, William I tried to pursue a policy of national
welfare, fighting unemployment and pauperism by advancing
industrialisation. He was decidedly more industrial than purely
commercial in outlook. 'We should not remain mere porters', he
once told an indignant Hogendorp.[2] William, it is true, was
striving also for the restoration of the staple market. In his
opinion, however, this would not be the automatic result of
a liberal policy. It needed for its realisation a revived industry
and, more generally, a policy of vigorous and well-considered
regulation.[3]

When William disembarked at Scheveningen, he already had
a long-matured plan of uniting to the territory of the old Dutch
Republic the former Austrian Netherlands, together with the
former principality of Liège, as well as the territory on the left
bank of the Rhine as far as the Moselle and, if possible, the
territory of Berg on the right bank.[4] Even if the whole of this
scheme later proved too ambitious, a major part of it was in fact
realised. The establishment of the United Kingdom of the
Netherlands was primarily due to the allied Great Powers,
particularly to Great Britain, who wished to set up a strong
bulwark at the northern frontiers of dangerous France, to be connected with the German Confederation – that other and mightier
bulwark – by the link of the Grand Duchy of Luxemburg.[5]

[1] For this Burgundian tradition and especially its after-effects, see J. C. Boogman,
'Background and General Tendencies of the Foreign Policies of the Netherlands
and Belgium in the Middle of the 19th Century', *Acta Historiae Neerlandica*, I
(Leiden, 1966) 151, 153 n. I.

[2] *Brieven en Gedenkschriften van Gijsbert Karel van Hogendorp*, v (The Hague,
1901) 146.

[3] Cf. Th. P. M. de Jong, *De krimpende horizon van de Hollandse kooplieden:
Hollands Welvaren in het Caribisch Zeegebied, 1780–1830* (Assen, 1966) 130.

[4] It is only fair to add, however, that at that time the Rhineland could be
considered a kind of no-man's-land.

[5] The Grand Duchy of Luxemburg had been given to William as compensation
for the loss of his Nassau territories in Germany. In his capacity as Grand Duke of

The Dutch themselves were not in the main particularly pleased about the union with Belgium. According to reports from the foreign ministers, they deplored the unwillingness of their sovereign to confine himself to the old frontiers. To any territorial aggrandisement on the European continent they would much have preferred the restitution of all their overseas possessions at the peace settlement.[1] In December 1814, when international relations became very tense, the Prussian envoy wrote to Berlin that the Dutch rejoiced at the eventuality of not being united to the Belgians as a result of the crisis. For some days, indeed, an immoderate joy prevailed at Amsterdam. There was to be found only one individual in the whole country, Herr von Brockhausen concluded, not without a touch of exaggeration, who sincerely desired the union 'et cet individu c'est le Prince Souverain, qui la regarde comme un bienfait pour la Hollande et un moyen d'élever sa puissance'.[2]

Nonetheless, hardly any serious internal opposition is to be noticed to the realisation, incomplete as it was, of William's ideal of territorial aggrandisement. How is this to be explained? First, there was the mental atmosphere of apathy and uncertainty prevailing at that time among the Dutch, who may be considered as then being a nation in quest of its real national identity. By contrast, the autocratically-minded sovereign, who was held in greatest respect by his new Dutch subjects, was striving after the realisation of his favourite ambition with the utmost resolution, while a cogent argument in support of accepting territorial enlargement was furnished by the attitude of the Allied Powers, which might even be interpreted as the will of Europe. In particular Great Britain, the principal champion of the Great Netherlands state, had brought pressure to bear upon the Dutch by making the return of the major part of the former Dutch colonies conditional on the establishment of the union with Belgium. Finally, considerations of security weighed heavily with the Dutch

---

Luxemburg William was made a member of the German Confederation. In defiance of the Confederation's constitutional regulations, the King and Grand Duke simply included his Luxemburg dominion as a province in his Netherlands kingdom.

[1] H. T. Colenbrander (ed.), *Gedenkstukken der Algemeene Geschiedenis van Nederland van 1795 tot 1840*, VII (RGP, XXIII, The Hague, 1914) 291, 305.

[2] Ibid., 308.

after their sad experiences in the recent past. Did not these make it clear that their state was in urgent need of being reinforced? Territorial aggrandisement might be regarded as a continuation of the old Barrier, adapted to changed circumstances and therefore much more efficient than the old one had ever been.[1]

Van Hogendorp's views on the establishment of the new kingdom were typical of the prevailing opinion in the Northern Netherlands. That great man, the most prominent among William's ministers at that moment, had advocated the union with Belgium. The 'union intime et complète', however, to be established according to formal obligations, was not at all to his taste. In his view the Northern Netherlands ought to take the lead in all respects, whereas the southern provinces would be most graciously allowed the position of an appendage. Here are the very words of this notorious Hollander:

Il faut de toute nécessité que les Pays-Bas demeurent Puissance maritime et Puissance protestante. . . . Les Pays-Bas resteront Puissance maritime et protestante aussi longtemps que le centre du pouvoir et de l'autorité se trouvera dans les provinces de Hollande, de Zélande et de Frise [the sea-provinces], qui ont été le berceau de la République des Provinces-Unies. . . . On peut accorder aux Belges tout ce qui ne portera pas d'atteinte aux principes que nous avons établis, mais on ne doit leur rien accorder de plus, si on désire de conserver son propre ouvrage.[2]

In view of opinions like these, is it any wonder that the new kingdom was not to last for a very long time?

The foreign policy pursued by William I's United Kingdom can be summarised as a policy of the utmost independence, mainly determined by economic interests. These interests, it is true, were promoted at times in a rather selfish and devious way.[3] The king wished everyone to forget as soon as possible that his Great Netherlands state might be regarded in many respects as a creation of European diplomacy. He particularly disliked the obligations imposed on his realm as a kind of European mort-

---

[1] In an interview with Castlereagh on 27 April 1813, William himself had already made use of this argument: cf. ibid., v (RGP, xvii, 1912) 1877.

[2] *Brieven en Gedenkschriften*, v 498.

[3] Rather unpalatable, in particular, was the chicanery with which the Dutch government interpreted the Rhine Navigation Act of 1815: cf. J. C. Boogman, 'The Dutch Crisis in the Eighteen-Forties', in *Britain and the Netherlands*, I 198.

gage.[1] Great Britain was considered the Netherlands' natural ally. British pursuit of balance-of-power policy on the Continent did in fact very well harmonize with Dutch interests. For the rest, a firm stand of proud independence should be made against Great Britain too. When the King believed his country's polity to be more or less consolidated, he exhibited views on the Netherlands' international position that were marked by an obvious desire for prestige. Dutch diplomats, for instance, were expected to display more self-confidence and national pride:[2] they should remember the shining example of sturdy seventeenth-century Dutch statesmen. William I certainly did not wish to imitate the glorious past slavishly. None the less, it was always present to his mind as the inspiring example of prosperity, greatness and power which was to be equalled, if not surpassed. In a way, then, the King too was held enslaved by the past.

All this can be illustrated in detail by quoting from a most interesting document, a very elaborate and circumstantial memorandum on Dutch foreign policy written by the foreign minister Verstolk van Soelen, one of the principal characters in the Dutch political scene of the day.[3] According to Verstolk, the Kingdom of the Netherlands was to be considered an important continental power, equal at least to its famous predecessor, the Dutch Republic in its happiest days. It was to pursue an entirely independent policy and not let itself be dominated by any other state, not even by any or all of the five Great Powers, who appeared to be only too much disposed to dominate the minor states of the European continent and settle all political questions arbitrarily. In Verstolk's eyes the Netherlands state was almost a Great Power, in fact on the same level of political importance as Prussia, the weakest and at the same time the *parvenu* among the Great Five; under favourable circumstances Prussia's position in the hierarchy of European states might be taken over by the Netherlands. In this connection, too, it is worth noting that Verstolk held rather excessive views on the question of territorial extent: he thought it highly desirable to extend and, if possible, even to double his country's territory at the expense of France and

[1] The occupation of the Luxemburg fortress by Prussian troops, in particular, was an abomination to him.

[2] Cf. De Jong, 128.

[3] Colenbrander, *Gedenkstukken*, IX (RGP, XXXVII, 1917) 442–513.

Prussia. He was aiming, in particular, at annexing the Prussian Rhineland.

Verstolk's ambitious designs, which undoubtedly were cherished also by his king, were doomed to failure. The Belgian revolution and its consequences put an end to these great-power aspirations once and for all. To King William, naturally, the destruction of his life's work meant bitter disappointment. During the 1830s he succeeded for years on end in escaping a final settlement of the Belgian question by artful and sometimes rather unscrupulous manoeuvring.[1] In the controversies between the Anglo-French entente and the conservative powers he took the side of the conservative powers, which supported him on the Belgian question.[2] Prince Metternich then showed himself greatly satisfied with the demeanour of the Dutch, who had taken such a firm stand with the Holy Alliance against disorder and revolution.[3] All this, however, did not prevent the King from being forced to capitulate. The great European war he had so ardently hoped for did not break out, and in 1839 he had to ratify the separation settlement, which gave the Dutch less than could have been obtained some eight years before.

The King's subjects in the Northern Netherlands had reacted in quite a different way, and one wholly in accord with the old Holland tradition, towards the revolution in the south. On the whole, they were glad to be rid of the Belgian rebels and wanted nothing better than to be themselves again. The stout-hearted fighting they did against the Belgians was not meant to undo the de facto separation, but to obtain a more favourable separation settlement, and of course to put the vain and overbearing Belgians in their place.

After the final break-up of the United Kingdom of the Netherlands in 1839 and the abdication of the disillusioned king in favour of his son the year after that, the Dutch had great

[1] Cf. J. C. Boogman, Nederland en de Duitse Bond, 1815–1851 (Groningen, 1955) 128 ff.

[2] For instance, the reactionary pretenders in Spain and Portugal, Don Carlos and Dom Miguel, received financial support from the King of the Netherlands (ibid., 148).

[3] Metternich spoke very highly of the conduct of the Dutch to Verstolk, who was in Vienna during the winter of 1833–4. According to the Austrian chancellor, the Dutch firmly occupied the right-wing position in the front line of the Holy Alliance (ibid., 140).

difficulties in finding the right solution to the challenges of the new situation. Only in the area of foreign policy was the solution fairly easy: the small Dutch state must again pursue a policy of abstention and strict neutrality. Economically the situation was very bad during the 1840s. In many respects the Netherlands could still be regarded as an underdeveloped country, in spite of the fact that it was by no means lacking in capital. Owing to inadequate employment, pauperism had risen to a much higher level than it ever had been since 1813. Whereas some people advocated a system of radical economic liberalism as the only means of escape from the impasse, others wished to preserve the shattered remains of the old staple market system.

The uncertainty and half-heartedness to be observed in economic policy can also be noticed in other fields.[1] Bitter resentment was felt against the powers, particularly Great Britain, which had left the Dutch in the lurch during the 1830s. It was to be feared they would fail again when a much more dangerous international crisis should arise in consequence of a downright democratic revolution in Paris. At the same time many Dutchmen felt uneasy as they watched nationalist tendencies gain ground, especially in Germany, after 1840. Being himself a member of a rather old historic state-nation, the average Dutchman did not at all understand the turbulent national movements abroad, which were aiming precisely at the annihilation of historic states. On the other hand, he might wonder whether the victory of the apparently modern principle of nationality could be arrested. Did not the formation of larger political communities appear to be in the line of historical development? If so, what possibilities for development remained for a small state like the Netherlands? Add to this that the economic and political position of the Netherlands was fundamentally weakened by the separation from Belgium and by the foundation of the Zollverein, which meant for Germany a concentration of economic strength. In consequence of the Belgian revolt the bridgehead separating Germany from the sea was split in two, and the Germans very cleverly played off the two parts of the former United Kingdom against each other.

Thus a remarkably defeatist state of mind is to be discerned during these years. Since the end of the sixteenth century there

[1] Cf. Boogman, 'The Dutch Crisis in the Eighteen-Forties'.

had never existed among Dutchmen, except of course in the period of French domination, such haunting doubts about their *raison d'être*, about the sheer possibilities of survival of an independent Dutch state. In the leading liberal magazine, *De Gids*, the incorporation of the country into Germany was even openly recommended as the only way out. Highly interesting are the views on the Dutch and their problems noted in his *Journal* by the French historian Michelet, who visited the Netherlands during the summer of 1847. He appeared to be greatly shocked by the defeatist state of mind among Dutchmen. Gifted with such a brilliant imagination and sublime patriotic sentiments, Michelet of course saw an easy solution, the incorporation of the Netherlands into France: 'La parfaite ignorance où se trouve de son sort, de son idée, de sa destinée, la partie la plus sérieuse des Pays-Bas, la Hollande, doit avertir assez la France qu'il lui faudra reprendre le tout, Hollande, Belgique et Rhin'.[1] The defeatism noted by Michelet is to be considered the most serious symptom of that crisis of national identity which may be said to have prevailed, in various forms and degrees of intensity, during the whole period 1813–48.

The year 1848 is indeed a landmark of the highest importance in the history of the Netherlands. The revolutionary thunderstorm of that year was to clear the air considerably. Generally speaking, one can say that Germany's political attraction for the Dutch vanished after the failure of the German revolution. German conditions during the 'fifties, naturally, did not seem at all attractive to most of the Dutch. On the other hand, the internal situation of the Netherlands improved considerably after 1848, the year of the bloodless 'revolution'. Political and constitutional development, which had been at a deadlock, took off again thanks to the introduction of a liberal system of ministerial responsibility and cabinet homogeneity, inaugurated by Thorbecke's revision of the constitution. Thorbecke's success is to be considered a victory for the middle classes, which were to play a much more important role, politically as well as economically, than previously. In consequence a more modern spirit was gradually to be seen pervading old-fashioned and traditionalist Dutch society. In the following years many Dutch intellectuals became

[1] *Journal*, I 668 ff.

more clearly conscious of the backwardness of their country and of foreign criticism. They adopted the old sneer about 'the Chinese of Europe' as a weapon to rouse their countrymen.[1] The irresolution which had recently prevailed over Dutch enterprise also came to an end. A consistent, rather radical free-trade policy was to be pursued from now onwards, and it turned out to be successful.

The year 1848 is also a landmark as regards Dutch foreign relations and the position of the Netherlands in the European scene. From now on, generally speaking, there was no further clinging to untenable positions, no more illusions derived from the seventeenth-century past, and hence no pursuit of Great Power pretensions. The character of the Netherlands as a small state was now universally accepted by the Dutch, even by the House of Orange. But to this sealing down of unreal hopes and fantasies there was a positive counterpart: Dutchmen no longer questioned the *raison d'être* of their own independent state.

At the end of February 1848, when the international crisis came to a head, King William II had definitely abandoned his ambitions to restore the United Kingdom of the Netherlands. What is more, he had taken the decisive step of extending the hand of friendship to the King of the Belgians, his former fervently-hated rival and enemy. In this connection it needs to be emphasised that the young Belgian state had withstood a severe test during the year of revolution. It was henceforward taken much more seriously as a normal and respectable European state than it had been before 1848.[2]

Neutrality and abstention now became the catchwords of Dutch foreign policy, especially in liberal circles. A positive aversion from the idea of territorial expansion, which could even become a disposition towards territorial contraction, is to be noticed too; such an attitude, after all, was fully in harmony with the tradition of Holland. The tendency to territorial contraction, which also had something to do with the attitude assumed by the Dutch towards the Great Netherlands idea, obviously played a certain part in the so-called Limburg question. In 1848 the German

[1] Van Winter, 10.
[2] Hermann von der Dunk, *Der deutsche Vormärz und Belgien, 1830–1848* (Wiesbaden, 1966) 342.

parliament at Frankfurt laid claim to the Dutch province of Limburg, which at the same time formed part of the German Confederation. It does not look as if many Dutchmen would have been too unhappy if that remote strip of land, half-Belgian and Roman Catholic, had in fact been incorporated into the new German empire, which was to have been formed at that time.

After 1848 the Dutch were almost exclusively interested in their own internal affairs. This is especially true of the liberals, who were ardently striving after economies in public finance. National defence and diplomatic representation were the pre-eminent targets for retrenchment. Proposals were even made to suppress all legations and to replace ministers by consuls. It was generally held, but again in liberal circles in particular, that the ministry of foreign affairs should concern itself primarily with commercial matters, and that Dutch diplomats ought to become much more commercially-minded.[1] One day Finance Minister Van Bosse, one of the principal political figures of the day and a spiritual heir of the seventeenth-century polemicist Pieter de la Court, during a session of the Cabinet Council gave his honourable colleagues to understand that in his opinion the Netherlands state and nation might best be compared after all to a large grocer's shop.[2] Some years later indeed, a French newspaper rather contemptuously compared the Dutch parliament to a chamber of commerce. The young lawyer Tobias M. C. Asser, who was to make himself a great international reputation, wholly agreed with this analogy but added that it was no reason at all for disparagement: on the contrary, the description should be accepted as a name of honour, as had happened to the word 'Geuzen' [Beggars] at the outset of the sixteenth-century revolt.[3]

For diplomatic representatives from abroad, it can hardly be claimed that The Hague was any longer a very interesting post. Almost universally they commented on the obsession of the Dutch with their own affairs and well-being, with their national debt and taxation, with the harbours and railways to be constructed, and above all with their colonial problems. J. S. Pike, the American minister during the 1860s, rather drily asserted that

[1] Boogman, 'Background and General Tendencies', 147–8.
[2] Ibid., 140–1.
[3] T. M. C. Asser, *Het bestuur der buitenlandsche betrekkingen volgens het Nederlandsche Staatsrecht* (Amsterdam, 1860) 381.

'the ministers at these inferior courts have little or nothing to do, and any pretense that they have is to magnify their office, at the expense of the truth'.[1] The wife of a Prussian secretary of legation noted that the eyes of the Dutch reached no farther than their dykes. In her husband's opinion, the Dutchmen he had to deal with were on the whole rather nice people, but at the same time he felt bored to death in cosy Den Haag; Von Bunsen could not bear reading books all day long, after all.[2] An Italian envoy came to conclusions set in a higher and more positive, even a somewhat historical and philosophical, tone: the Netherlands, like all happy nations, Barone Carutti concluded in 1864, had had hardly any history since 1848.[3]

As a nation, indeed, the Dutch felt fairly happy in these years. After about 1852 the international situation turned out to be markedly favourable to small and militarily feeble states like the Netherlands. When in 1852 Napoleon III appeared to have sinister designs upon Belgium, the Dutch government pursued an active policy, especially directed at joining hands with Belgium and England against the menace of France. During the next years, however, such a menace was altogether out of the question in consequence of the Anglo-French alliance. Equally favourable to the Dutch cause was the fact that Prussia pursued a peaceful foreign policy in the 1850s.

Politically-minded Dutchmen were highly pleased by the so-called Cobden treaty, concluded by Great Britain and France in 1860. In liberal circles especially, people thought a bright future to be at hand, an era promising international peace and order, prosperity and security. Old-fashioned power politics were to be put under restraint, and the prospects for the smaller European states in particular looked extremely good.[4]

[1] Boogman, 'Background and General Tendencies', 139.

[2] Frau Carl von Bunsen, *An drei Gesandtschaften. Erinnerungen einer Diplomatenfrau* (Berlin, 1910) 306, 331.

[3] 'Come tutti i popoli felici, l'Olanda dopo il 1848 ha poca storia.' Quoted by Th. van den End, *De Italiaanse gezant Domenico Carutti over Nederland 1862–1869* (unpublished graduate student essay, 1966). In August 1865 Carutti found to his surprise that nearly all members of the government were absent from The Hague: the king as well as the ministers for foreign affairs, interior, finance, colonies and the navy: 'Questa semplice enumerazione di assenze rende immagine della felice condizione dei Paesi Bassi, meglio forse di lunghe disquisizioni.'

[4] See, e.g., Asser, 120, 368.

In this period practically nothing more can be traced of a specific Dutch sense of mission, nor even of any serious desire to take an active part in the field of international policy. We can observe this transition in the thought of Thorbecke, who for this purpose may be considered typical. Before 1840 Thorbecke thought that the Netherlands had a task to discharge in the European community of states: especially on account of its geographical situation was it a factor of significance, indeed a condition for the maintenance of the European balance of power – the 'Corner-stone of North West Europe'. After the secession of Belgium Thorbecke said nothing more about this. Apparently he considered his country to have become too small and insignificant to fulfil any special function in European politics.[1] Not that the Dutch were then lacking in self-respect, or even self-satisfaction. On the contrary, the view was widely held that the Netherlands was one of the most perfectly governed and administered countries in Europe, an example of good order and the pursuit of peace.[2] As upholders of true freedom and justice, they accounted themselves rightly deserving of an honourable place among the nations.[3]

The outlook which at the outset of the 1860s still looked so bright for the small Dutch state grew dark soon afterwards, when Bismarck's high-handed proceedings forced the German issue to a point of crisis that was to shake the whole system of international law in Europe. On the whole, Dutch opinion sided with Austria, because Prussia appeared to be the peace-breaker.[4] Besides, a lot of Dutch money had been invested in Austrian public funds.

Neither did the Schleswig–Holstein settlement promise any good to the Dutch nation, which by means of Limburg happened also to be connected to the German Confederation. In connection with the Danish disaster, Pike, the American envoy, wrote to Washington in December 1863:

[1] W. Verkade, *Overzicht der staatkundige denkbeelden van Johan Rudolph Thorbecke, 1798–1872* (Arnhem, 1935) 213.

[2] This was how Van der Maesen de Sombreff, minister for foreign affairs 1862–4, expressed himself in parliament one day: H. L. Asser, *De buitenlandsche betrekkingen van Nederland, 1860–1889* (Haarlem, 1889) 6.

[3] Cf. T. M. C. Asser, 120.

[4] In some Protestant quarters, however, an anti-Catholic and pro-Prussian tendency could be observed.

The dependent powers of Europe necessarily occupy a humiliating position. The great Powers treat them as they would not dare to treat their equals. At this moment Denmark is an example. . . . Holland is better able to defy its powerful neighbours than one of the weaker states. But even the Dutch do not want to scuttle their country to keep out the foreigner. This position of the small states breeds a public sentiment not favourable to national independence or elevation.

The minister then calls to mind the incorporation with France in 1810 in spite of the 'sturdy Dutch character'.[1]

French policy in the 1860s, which aimed at the annexation of Belgium, did not appear to offer comfort either. In an official circular letter of 16 September 1866 to all French diplomatic representatives, this ominous passage might be read: 'Une puissance irrésistible pousse les peuples à se réunir en grandes agglomérations en faisant disparaître les États secondaires. . . . Peut-être est-elle inspirée par une sorte de prévision providentielle des destinées du Monde.'[2]

It was above all during the Luxemburg crisis of 1867 that the Dutch felt seriously threatened by victorious Bismarckian Prussia. Although there was no defeatism comparable to that of the 1840s, a spirit of unease, even of pessimism about the nation's future, made itself unmistakably felt in most sections of society.

In the event, as we know, the Dutch came through the Luxemburg troubles without injury, and their neutrality remained inviolate again during the Franco-Prussian War of 1870. Afterwards from their point of view the international situation in fact improved considerably. For a long time to come direct threats to the independence of their country did not recur, and in consequence the uncertainties and fears for the future, which had prevailed during the 1860s, faded away. By the end of the century, moreover, the backward Dutch economy had been brought up to date. This economic success necessarily strengthened the self-respect of Dutchmen and so greatly influenced their sense of their country's position in the world.

The turn of the century may be seen as the heyday of Dutch neutrality. When national independence had seemed to be in jeopardy in earlier years, the Dutch had sought to entrench them-

[1] Boogman, 'Background and General Tendencies', 142.
[2] *Les origines diplomatiques dela guerre de 1870–1871*, XII (Paris, 1919–32) 301 ff.

selves behind the bulwark of international law and clung with desperate tenacity to the status of a neutral power. Since the crisis of the 1860s, which had been so happily overcome, neutrality was more and more elevated as a sacred political dogma. A policy of neutrality did indeed correspond with the real interests of a small and weak nation like the Netherlands in the nineteenth century. It has proved rather mistaken, however, to proclaim it a sacred dogma for all times.

Whereas in the seventeenth century utilitarian arguments had been advanced for the justification of national policy, the Dutch now increasingly used ethical ones, being masters in making a virtue of necessity. The practice of neutrality and isolationism brought about the accompanying phenomenon of a legalistic and moralising outlook upon international affairs, resulting especially in a rather hypocritical and condescending attitude towards the crude power politics and malpractices of the Great Powers, who were deficient (according to many Dutchmen) in that real understanding of international co-operation which the Dutch themselves possessed in good measure.

At the same time there began to emerge a clear notion of a special Dutch vocation in the world of international politics. In a pamphlet published in 1902 one may read that the Dutch state is to be considered an indispensable link in the whole system of European states, because the interests of the other powers themselves demanded, of necessity, the continued existence of an independent Netherlands state. The writer asserted that the Dutch state was of such intrinsic weight in the scales of European politics that war would break out immediately if it were ranged on the side of one of the Great Powers. Furthermore, by standing in the breach for the preservation of their independence, the Dutch were not only serving their own interests but simultaneously benefitting the whole of mankind by advancing world peace.[1]

Dutch missionary zeal of this period culminated in the writings of Cornelis van Vollenhoven, a professor at Leiden and famous expert in Indonesian and in international law. In his opinion, the country of the venerable Hugo Grotius had been predestined to play a leading role, not only in preserving the system of international law, but also in establishing a new international legal

[1] J. C. C. Den Beer Poortugael, *Nederland en Duitsland* (The Hague, 1902).

order. In a little book which appeared only one year before the
outbreak of the First World War,[1] Van Vollenhoven claimed that
the Great Powers were, as a rule, not well suited to this sublime
purpose, since egoism alone underlay their policies. Great Britain
is characterised as the nation whose egoism is the most deeply
rooted and refined; during the seventeenth century, for instance,
Dutch aims had been much more generous than English. Only
three nations might be said to have a vocation for bringing about
the new and better world order: France, the U.S.A. and the
Netherlands. Van Vollenhoven's own country is to be preferred
to France because of its healthier domestic situation – a prosperity
which clearly left its mark on Van Vollenhoven's own thought.
Finally, the Netherlands is to be preferred to the other two nations
because it surpassed both of them in its unquestionable disinterest-
edness.[2] Thus the Dutch were called upon to play the role of a
Lafayette among the nations. In a previous publication this humble
Dutchman had already vindicated his country by casting her in
the role of a heroine, even of a saint, the role of a Joan of Arc.[3]

Van Vollenhoven might be called an ethical imperialist, and his
internationalism is also to be regarded as an essential part of a
national ideology. His sometimes rather peculiar ideas did not
remain without criticism, fortunately. Yet their drift and accents
are to be considered representative of the mental atmosphere in
the Netherlands on the eve of the First World War, in that they
do reflect in such an eloquent way some of its essential elements:
optimism and national self-confidence, not to say complacency.
No wonder, then, that the centenary of the liberation of the year
1813 was celebrated with gusto and splendour.

[1] *De eendracht van het land* (The Hague, 1913; 6th impression, 1945).

[2] Van Vollenhoven may have been influenced by Thorbecke in this respect. We
know that he admired the framer of the famous liberal constitution of 1848. In
Thorbecke's pamphlet *Een woord in het belang van Europe* (Leiden, 1830) 7, we
come across the rather peculiar statement that Dutch policy, which is free from
lust of power and ambition itself, ought to be considered therefore the fairest
judge of the other powers' ambitions.

[3] 'Roeping van Holland', *De Gids* (1910).

FURTHER READING

1. *Collections of Documents*

Gedenkstukken der algemeene geschiedenis van Nederland, ed. H. T. COLENBRANDER (The Hague, 1905–22) were published in the series of the Rijks Geschiedkundige Publicatiën [RGP] as follows:

    1789–1813, RGP, vols 1–6, 11–13, 16, 17

    1813–1815, RGP, vol. 23

    1815–1825, RGP, vols 25, 27, 30

    1825–1830, RGP, vols 31, 37

    1830–1840, RGP, vols 40, 42, 44, 46, 50.

These volumes conveniently bring together many of the basic documents on home policy as well as on diplomatic relations.

Bescheiden betreffende de buitenlandse politiek van Nederland 1848–1919, 2nd period: 1871–98, ed. J. WOLTRING (The Hague, 1962–5):

    1871–1874, RGP, vol. 107

    1874–1880, RGP, vol. 118.

A useful collection of documents on Dutch foreign policy after the Franco-Prussian War, the series is still to be completed.

Bescheiden betreffende de buitenlandse politiek van Nederland 1848–1919, 3rd period: 1899–1919, ed. C. SMIT (The Hague, 1957–64):

    1899–1903, RGP, 100

    1903–1907, RGP, 102

    1907–1914, RGP, 106

    1914–1917, RGP, 109

    1917–1919, RGP, 116, 117.

This part of the series on Dutch foreign policy is already completed and yields much information on the period of the First World War and the preceding years.

Documenten betreffende de buitenlandse handelspolitiek van Nederland in de negentiende eeuw, ed. N. W. POSTHUMUS, 6 vols (The Hague, 1919–1931):

    I Documents on Anglo-Dutch commercial relations in Europe (1813–27);

    II Documents on Anglo-Dutch commercial relations in the Dutch colonies (1814–38);

    III Documents on the commercial relations of the Netherlands with Prussia and the other German States (1814–33);

    IV Documents on Dutch-Prussian negotiations on a treaty of commerce (1834–9);

    V Documents on Dutch-Prussian commercial relations (1839–66);

    VI Documents on Anglo-Dutch commercial relations and treaty negotiations (1827–70).

For students of Dutch foreign relations this series is a useful supplement because of the attention it pays to commercial aspects, so important in Dutch foreign policy.

De Tusschenwateren, 1839–1867, ed. C. GERRETSON (Haarlem, n.d.), brings together official documentary material on the influence on Dutch-Belgian relations of the semi-maritime waters in the province of Zeeland (East and West Scheldt).

SANTEN, C. W. VAN: *Het internationale recht in Nederlands buitenlands beleid. Een onderzoek in het archief van het Ministerie van Buitenlandse Zaken 1840–1850* (The Hague, 1955) shows how the Dutch government applied international law in foreign affairs. Many original documents are printed in interesting chapters on (e.g.) Dutch diplomatic institutions and relations; English introductions to each chapter and translations of all tables of contents.

2. Secondary Works

BOOGMAN, J. C.: *Nederland en de Duitse Bond, 1815–1851*, 2 vols (Groningen–Djakarta, 1955; *Historische studies uitgegeven vanwege het Instituut voor Geschiedenis der Rijksuniversiteit te Utrecht*, v). A study of the diplomatic relations between the Netherlands and the German Confederation, with attention to internal politics in Germany, the Netherlands and Belgium.

—— 'Background and general tendencies of the foreign policies of the Netherlands and Belgium in the middle of the 19th century', *Acta Historiae Neerlandica*, I (Leiden, 1966) 132 ff., analyses the social, economic, psychological and political background of the foreign policy of the Netherlands as well as of Belgium in the 1850s and 1860s.

—— 'Enkele aspecten van het Nederlandse natie-besef in historisch perspectief', *Oost-West*, v (1966) 75 ff. A study of the characteristic Dutch attitude towards foreign policy, regarded as an interesting aspect of Dutch national feeling.

CANTILLON, E.: 'Thorbecke en Europa', *De Gids*, CVIII (1944–5). An account of the uniquely active European policy of the Thorbecke government in the early 1850s.

DONGEN, F. VAN: *Tussen neutraliteit en imperialisme. De Nederlands-Chinese betrekkingen van 1863 tot 1901* (Groningen, 1966). This thorough account of Sino-Dutch political and economic relations also considers the question how far traditional Dutch neutrality in Europe was applied to China; an informative summary in English is added.

DUPARC, F. J.: *Willem II, België en Luxemburg* (The Hague, 1933). Rather superficial, but virtually the only work which deals explicitly with King William's policy towards Belgium and Luxemburg.

GOEDEMANS, A. J. M.: *Indië in de branding, een diplomatiek steekspel, 1840–1843* (Utrecht, 1953). A valuable account of Anglo-Dutch tensions over the Dutch East Indies in the 1840s.

HAAR, C. C. TER: *Nederland en Vlaanderen. Een onderzoek naar de houding der Nederlanders tegenover het Vlaamsche vraagstuk, 1830–1873* (Santpoort, 1933) illustrates the restricted character of Dutch-Flemish cultural relations in 1830–73.

HAMSTRA, J.: *De Luxemburgsche kwestie* (Groningen, 1927). Somewhat superficial, especially in its unsatisfactory interpretation of Bismarck, but indispensable.

HUISMAN, M.: 'Le problème de la sécurité de la Belgique et des Pays-Bas à l'avènement du Second Empire', *Revue de l'Université de Bruxelles*, XXXIII (April 1928) 257 ff., shows how Dutch-Belgian diplomatic co-operation resulted from the French expansionist danger at the beginning of the 1850s.

—— 'La crise révolutionnaire de 1848 et le rapprochement Hollando-Belge', *Bijdragen voor de Vaderlandsche Geschiedenis en Oudheidkunde*, seventh ser., III–IV (1935). The story of the sudden improvement in official relations between the Netherlands and Belgium because of the revolutionary situation in 1848.

JONG, T. P. M. DE: *De krimpende horizon van de Hollandse kooplieden: Hollands welvaren in het Caribisch zeegebied, 1790–1830* (Assen, 1966) shows how the defeatist mentality of Dutch merchants damaged the commercial position of the Netherlands in the Caribbean; interesting English summary.

KOSSMANN, E. H.: *In Praise of the Dutch Republic: Some Seventeenth-Century Attitudes* (1963). An Inaugural Lecture at University College, London, in which an aspect of the characteristic Dutch approach to international affairs is traced back to the seventeenth century.

LEEUW, A. S. DE: *Nederland in de wereldpolitiek van 1900 tot heden* (Zeist, 1936) covers 1895–1930, with an interesting chapter on certain Dutch pro-German sympathies shortly before the First World War.

RENIER, G. J.: *Great Britain and the Establishment of the Kingdom of the Netherlands, 1813–1815: a Study in British Foreign Policy* (The Hague, 1930) looks at some Dutch attitudes as well as at British policy.

SMIT, C.: *De handelspolitieke betrekkingen tusschen Nederland en Frankrijk, 1814–1914* (The Hague, 1923). The story of Franco-Dutch commercial relations 1814–1914.

—— *De conferentie van Londen. Het vredesverdrag tussen Nederland en België van 19 april 1839* (Leiden, 1949) surveys international relations, Dutch-Belgian tensions, and the different stages of the London negotiations, with an analysis of the ultimate Treaty of London.

—— *Diplomatieke geschiedenis van Nederland, inzonderheid sedert de vestiging van het Koninkrijk* (The Hague, 1950). A general study of Dutch diplomatic relations since 1813, using a rather old-fashioned approach to diplomatic history.

—— *Hoogtij der neutraliteitspolitiek. De buitenlandse politiek van Nederland, 1899–1919* (Leiden, 1959). An account of the foreign policy of the Netherlands as a neutral power, from the first Peace Conference at The Hague.

VANDENBOSCH, A.: *Dutch Foreign Policy since 1815: a Study in Small Power Politics* (The Hague, 1949) is mainly based on materials for the first half of the twentieth century.

VRIES A. DE: *Geschiedenis van de handelspolitieke betrekkingen tusschen Nederland en Engeland in de negentiende eeuw, 1814–1872* (The Hague, 1931). A history of commercial relations between the Netherlands and France.

VRIES, J. DE: 'De problematiek der Duits-Nederlandse economische betrekkingen in de negentiende eeuw', *Tijdschrift voor Geschiedenis*, LXXVIII (1965) 23ff. A valuable study of the many aspects of Dutch-German economic relations in the nineteenth century.

7 England and Europe, 1815-1914

ALUN DAVIES

THE bewilderment of foreign observers at the inconsistencies of Britain's relations with Europe during the nineteenth century is familiar to us all. To some extent, it is to be explained by the oft-repeated fact that although Britain counted as part of Europe, she was not primarily a European power. Her major interests lay outside the Continent. Indeed, the only possessions which she had in Europe were Gibraltar and Malta, and (after 1878) Cyprus, although Cyprus was of little importance until after the First World War, for in 1915 Britain offered to give it away to Greece in return for a Greek entry into the war – a refusal which viewed from this vantage-point in time is ironic, to say the least. Most of Britain's trade was carried on with non-European countries; most of her investments likewise were in non-European countries.

The insularity of Britain's position led, paradoxically enough, to two different attitudes towards European issues. On the one hand it led to isolationism; on the other, it led to interventionism. The isolationism is familiar enough, and there is hardly need to labour the fact that the most fundamental of Britain's interests were those which derived from her outstanding position as a maritime and commercial power. She was the first home of large-scale industrial production and trade organisation. She made no real attempt to feed her rapidly increasing population from her own resources, but on the contrary neglected her agriculture and chose the role of becoming the world's chief manufacturer, merchant, shipper and banker, drawing her supplies of food and raw materials from her Empire and from other overseas countries outside Europe.

In 1815, her world position seemed to be unchallengeable. She had a dominant industrial position; her trade was greatly expanding. Her sea power had enabled her to a considerable extent to cut off most of Europe from the rest of the world during the Revolutionary and Napoleonic wars, while she, during this period, developed new technical skills, and the industrial and financial strength which enabled her to seize and to exploit new world markets. As Professor G. S. Graham[1] has recently summed up:

In becoming the arsenal and paymaster of Napoleon's enemies, she had gained far more than victories in the field. She had become the leading, if not the only creditor nation. London had replaced Amsterdam as the central money market of the world, and British business-men and bankers, flushed with a sense of destiny, saw the universe as an oyster awaiting their prying energies, their capital and their talents. On the basis of cotton, coal, and iron, an expanding merchant marine and her ability to extend long-term credits, Britain was on the way to making the several quarters of the world her 'willing tributaries'.

Moreover, after the wars and right down to 1854, Great Britain was able to defend this vast maritime and commercial empire at the least cost, and to maintain her naval supremacy on the cheap. Britain thus had a security which no other European state enjoyed. Further, her command of the sea was a threat to others, for it denied to them the resources of other continents – a situation which was helped by the fact that at this stage the European powers attached more importance to their possessions in Europe than to possessions overseas.

But not only did her command of the sea enable Britain to maintain a balance between the European powers in order to keep the peace. The converse was also true. As the late R. W. Seton-Watson clearly showed in his great work *Britain in Europe* thirty years ago, Britain's imperial position always depended upon her relations with the continental powers, and upon the maintenance of the continental balance. This balance was shaky, and England was obliged from time to time to intervene on one side or the other in order to restore it.

Britain, then, has never been 'isolationist' in the true sense of that much abused term for very long. Her concern for her imperial and maritime interests made it impossible for her to be so. On the

[1] *The Politics of Naval Supremacy: Studies in British Maritime Ascendancy* (Cambridge, 1965) 98–9.

contrary, Britain's need for having stability on the continent, and her opposition to any violent change, of necessity made her a constant mediator in European affairs. For example, the defence of the English Channel necessitated a careful eye being kept on the ambitions of European powers regarding Belgium, and this concern for Belgium was a dominant theme in English foreign policy thoroughout the century. Similarly, control of the Mediterranean meant a curtailment of Russian ambitions in the Turkish Straits, and a concern for the future of the Ottoman Empire – a concern which, as Sir Charles Webster once remarked, 'put a heavy strain on the conscience of the British people'.[1]

Britain's influence in European affairs, as in the world at large, was at its height during the generation or so after Waterloo. Never before or since has British authority been so great either in European or for that matter in world affairs. While her trade expanded all over the world, in Europe she achieved her long-established political aim of ensuring that no power should be allowed to dominate the Continent. Moreover, differences between the European powers were great enough to make them unable to come together to take collective action against her.

This era begins with Castlereagh's dominant role in the peace settlement of 1815 and in the creation of the Congress system, which Sir Charles Webster made so well known to us. Castlereagh, in so doing, set a tradition of close co-operation with European governments for the maintenance of the peace. If he did not believe in intervention in the domestic affairs of European states, at least he was an 'interventionist' in the general affairs of the Continent. The role of his successor, George Canning, was very different. But although he was less ready for co-operation and destroyed the Congress system, Canning was still very much of an 'umpire' in international affairs, confident of British power and prestige, and a foreign secretary who carried off some considerable *coups*. Temperley's biography showed clearly, for example, how cleverly he co-operated with Russia on the question of Greece, and succeeded in preventing Russia from taking up a position at Constantinople which might have developed into a threat to British interests, and yet at the same time made certain that the Greeks would attain their national independence. As a

[1] *The Art and Practice of Diplomacy* (1961) 21.

recent writer has appropriately commented, Canning's policy was not one of foreclosing on all English interference in Europe, but only of limiting the occasions for it.[1]

From 1830 to 1851 (with only one short interruption from 1841 to 1846 when the 3rd Earl of Aberdeen was in charge) foreign affairs were conducted by Palmerston. He regarded himself as the centre of European diplomacy and energetically, sometimes impetuously and insensitively, conducted a robust foreign policy, in a highly individual style. If we care to use a more modern idiom, his was a policy of 'brinkmanship', often accompanied by much bluster and hectoring. His daring, often farsighted, and frequently provocative handling of foreign affairs was always aimed at maintaining British prestige to the utmost. He manoeuvred confidently in European affairs, taking calculated risks if he considered these necessary to the point of threatening war, as he did, for example, against France in 1831 unless she withdrew from Belgium, and again in 1840 over the question of Mehemet Ali. Yet at the same time his was a constructive foreign policy, if only for the fact that he signed the two treaties which were most important to the position of Britain in Europe throughout the nineteenth century – the one securing the neutrality of Belgium and the other the closing of the Turkish Straits.[2]

Britain's attitude to Europe right down to 1870 was conditioned to a considerable extent by her constant underlying fear of France. This is hardly surprising during the generation after Waterloo, for the threat of France had loomed so large and so long that it seemed impossible to believe that it was no longer of the same proportions. For some time, therefore, England pursued a policy of 'safety first' with France, and it was not until the foreign secretaryship of Lord Aberdeen from 1841 to 1846 that an *entente cordiale* came about between the two countries, and the success of that was short-lived enough. Thereafter, Britain's attitude fluctuated between friendship and fear, with fear predominating during most of the crises in European affairs until the Crimean War of 1853-6, when the British fear of Russia (which

[1] R. Millman, *British Foreign Policy and the Coming of the Franco-Prussian War* (Oxford, 1965) 4.
[2] Sir C. Webster, *The Foreign Policy of Palmerston*, II 780-1; also his Raleigh lecture for 1934 on 'Palmerston, Metternich and the European System, 1830-41', reprinted in *The Art and Practice of Diplomacy*.

was even greater than the British fear of France) brought the two age-old enemies together in an uneasy alliance.

Britain's attitude to Europe during this period was also conditioned by the Eastern Question – that is to say, the future of the Ottoman Empire and the repercussions of any possible changes within it upon British imperial interests, particularly in India. It was this preoccupation which led Britain to take a firm line against France and her protégé Mehemet Ali in 1839–41, and to take part in the Crimean War. Its outcome, the Treaty of Paris, left things pretty much as they were before the war, except for a fresh set of promises from the Turks, two guarantees of Turkey's frontiers, and finally, the neutralisation of the Black Sea and a veto on a Russian fleet there – a provision which Russia repudiated at the first favourable opportunity, which came in 1870 after the battle of Sedan, as the price paid by Prussia for Russia's benevolent neutrality during the crises of 1864, 1866 and 1870.

The preoccupation of the British with France and Russia helps to explain their failure really to understand the German problem. They do not seem to have comprehended the causes of the revolution of 1848, nor the significance of Bismarck in the 1860s. Richard Millman has recently shown how favourable Stanley was to Prussia, and how attracted he was to the idea of a strong Prussia between an 'aggressive' France and an 'aggressive' Russia. Even Clarendon, who was pro-French, believed that German unity was inevitable, although he disliked Bismarck's methods. Indeed, while we cannot be at all sure that a stronger line from London might have served to avoid the conflict, it is certain that there was no pressure put on Prussia in favour of France.

In fact the pattern of Britain's relations with Europe changes markedly from the 1860s. Whereas previously, as I have tried to show, Britain had acted the part of 'mediator' in European affairs with some success, from the 1860s things were changing fast. For whereas between 1815 and 1954 there had been no war involving the European great powers, between 1854 and 1870 there were five of them, in only one of which (the Crimean War) was Britain involved.

Certain disturbing personalities had appeared on the Continent like Cavour, Bismarck and Napoleon III, with large conscript armies which they were willing to use in aggressive wars. The old suspicions of France seemed to be confirmed by the annexation of Nice and Savoy in 1859. The Foreign Office papers of the 1860s again reflect traditional British nervousness about the Low Countries, and express fears about the ambitions of Napoleon III. After 1866, Napoleon's well-known obsession about compensation for what Prussia had gained in that year became a matter of considerable concern to the Foreign Office, as well as to Queen Victoria.

The tide, then, was already turning in the 1860s, and what the dramatic events of 1870 did was to turn it even more.[1] For after that date all the five great European powers came to range themselves in rival alliance groupings until by 1894 there were two of these. Great Britain was a member of neither.

On the economic front, too, the situation was changing from the 1860s. Britain's economic position was becoming less favourable, and the long period of British prosperity and of rapid economic expansion was coming to an end. While it is true that in absolute terms Britain's economic strength was increasing, in relative terms compared with other countries it was declining. Whereas, for example, in 1870 Britain's steel production exceeded that of Germany and the United States combined, by 1913 Britain was producing seven million tons of steel compared with Germany's seventeen million. Germany was also developing the lead in industrial techniques by making chemistry the basis of a new industry. For example the discovery of the Thomas–Gilchrist process made possible the utilisation of Lorraine ores which hitherto had not been used because they contained too much phosphorus. Also electricity began to be used in industry; in 1879 the electric engine was brought into use in Berlin. Again, Germany was taking the lead in forming trusts and cartels. Meanwhile Great Britain kept on exporting coal and machinery rather than making use of them herself, and in this way she equipped her rivals with the means of competition.

Further, after 1871 both Germany and France abandoned free

[1] R. W. Seton-Watson, *Britain in Europe, 1789–1914* (Cambridge, 1937) 485, pin-points the change even more precisely by saying that the events of 1866 and 1867 'were in many ways a turning point for all Europe. They represent the high-water mark of British non-intervention; for from this point of view 1870–1 was a mere sequel, as our attitude then had virtually been predetermined by our attitude in 1866. In a word, our non-intervention was most marked at the very moment when effective intervention would have had the most decisive results.'

trade and moved towards protection. It is true that London still remained the financial capital of the world, but France under the Third Republic was also playing an important role and Germany's position was improving. In Britain, both governments and business circles rather reluctantly took the view that they had more to lose than to gain by counter-measures against the protective policy and the trading practices of European powers.

Then in the 1880s there began a scramble for colonies and concessions, first in Africa and then in the 1890s in China. Tensions grew between Great Britain and France in North Africa, and even as far afield as Siam, and between Great Britain and Russia in both Central Asia and the Far East, which in the 1890s became a real storm-centre of European rivalries.

In the face of all these revolutionary developments, it is hardly surprising that British governments became less confident about their strength and influence. They remained confident enough about the ability of the Royal Navy to protect Great Britain from invasion, certainly, and to protect trade routes and overseas markets. None the less, in European affairs, politicians and civil servants showed themselves unwilling to overstep Britain's strength or interests. The consequence was an indefinite and often wavering policy.

For example, during the Polish rising of 1863, after having uttered several high-sounding phrases, and having lectured the Tsar on Russia's obligations both by treaty and as a member of the community of European states, Russell's words were not followed up by action. He told the Poles that they 'could count on our sympathies but not on our material aid'. In the same vein, Palmerston told the House of Commons that to wage war on Russia for the sake of Poland would have been 'an act of insanity' which 'we did not at any moment contemplate', that Poland was not accessible to England and France as Greece was, and that the Poles had been very short-sighted.[1]

Again, when Prussia and Austria seized Schleswig-Holstein in 1864, British public opinion was indignant, and the government expressed its disapproval. Yet again no attempt was made to provide the Danes with help, and the British protest was ignored. As Professor Mosse has shown, the events of 1863 and 1864 may

[1] Ibid., 435–77 and R. F. Leslie, *Reform and Insurrection in Russian Poland* (1963) 176–202.

be taken as marking the end of the Palmerstonian era of British policy in Europe. Not that Britain pursued a steady policy of non-intervention in European affairs, but at least Britain sought to keep clear of fresh European commitments. She did not succeed in doing so, as is shown by the Luxemburg guarantees of 1867 and the Belgian treaties of 1870. Moreover, some leading British personalities would have none of this cautious, defensive policy. A diplomat like Sir Robert Morier at Stuttgart thundered to Earl Russell against British neutrality in the Franco-Prussian War, claiming that

we were content to do chorus *off* the stage and to range ourselves amongst the wheesing, broken-kneed old grey beards, whose utmost feat consists in giving metrical expression to some miserable platitudes respecting the blessings of peace.[1]

Several looked to the towering figure of Gladstone to champion a more positive policy on Great Britain's part, to call for her increased intervention in European affairs, and to stress her moral obligation to denounce wrongdoing abroad. Gladstone's advocacy of a revived Concert of Europe and his claim that 'the high office of bringing Europe into concert, and keeping Europe in concert, is an office specially pointed out for our country to perform',[2] found full vent in the famous Midlothian campaign of 1880 during which he specifically called for a concert of the great European powers to secure the peace of Europe, and to carry out the decisions of the Congress of Berlin. His victory in the elections of that year gave a new turn to British foreign policy. On the surface his plan met with the approval of the great powers, but from the beginning Bismarck was opposed to it. He nursed a passionate hatred both of Gladstone and of his political opponents at home, and his hatred went so far as to maintain that every month of Gladstone as Prime Minister brought a republic nearer in Great Britain. Yet, in spite of Bismarck's opposition, Gladstone at first succeeded in getting the powers to agree on common action against Turkey. But the seeming unity soon disappeared, for once it came to a question of *coercing* Turkey to carry out the decisions

[1] 7 November 1870: Mrs Rosslyn Wemyss, *Memoirs and Letters of the Right Hon. Sir Robert Morier, G.C.B., 1826-1876,* 2 vols (1911) II 210.
[2] W. E. Gladstone, *Political Speeches in Scotland* (1880) II 221.

of the Congress of Berlin, the other powers would not participate. Thereafter, it is difficult to speak of a Concert of Europe. From 1886 to 1900, the Marquis of Salisbury was virtually in control of British foreign policy. As Dame Lillian Penson (who made a lifelong study of Salisbury) remarked, if he was consistent in anything it was in his reiterated assertions that British action in Europe must depend on the character of the issues and on the circumstances of the time. He never felt the need to contract formal alliances of the European type, because he was not certain that a British government at some future date would honour its commitments.[1] Faced as he was with an apparently endless series of problems which proved to be difficult but not unsurmountable, his skill in preserving British prestige and British interests, and yet retaining a free hand, put him, as Professor Medlicott has observed, very much in the Bismarck class as a diplomat.[2]

Salisbury's reluctance to assume new commitments should not, however, lead to the conclusion that his policy was one of drift. His own definition of it may have contributed much to this legend. 'English policy' he once said in a mood of exasperation, 'is to float lazily downstream, occasionally putting out a diplomatic boat-hook to avoid collisions.'[3] Yet recent work has shown quite clearly that his policy was not as negative as that. In fact he sought by means of colonial compensations, which involved mutual concessions, to reduce the tensions between the powers of Europe.

Why then did this policy of compromise fail? Firstly because European countries underestimated the malleability of Great Britain. Secondly because Britain's proposals were not taken seriously, especially by Russia. Thirdly, and perhaps most important of all, because unlike Great Britain the European powers could not pursue one single aim as Britain could. The European

---

[1] See Dame Lillian Penson, *Foreign Affairs under the Third Marquis of Salisbury* (The Creighton Lecture in History, 1960: London, 1962); 'The Foreign Policy of Lord Salisbury, 1878–1880' in A. Coville and H. Temperley (ed.), *Studies in Anglo-French History* (Cambridge, 1933); 'The Principles and Methods of Lord Salisbury's Foreign Policy', *Cambridge Hist. Journal*, v (1935) 87–106; 'The New Course in British Foreign Policy, 1892–1902', *Trans. Roy. Hist. Soc.*, 4th ser., xxv (1943) 121–38.

[2] M. Beloff *et al.* (ed.), *L'Europe du XIXe et XXe siècle (1870–1914)*, 2 vols (Milan, 1962) II 543–79.

[3] To Lord Lytton, 9 March 1877: Lady Gwendolen Cecil, *Life of Robert, Marquis of Salisbury*, 4 vols (1921) II 130.

powers sought to adapt their colonial problems to their European position. That is to say, whereas the English interpreted colonial agreements as a means of reducing rivalries on the continent of Europe, the powers of Europe saw in such agreements only a means of compelling Great Britain to take part in continental affairs. As a result, every continental power which negotiated with Britain always feared that she would parley with its enemies, an attitude which gave rise to a feeling of inferiority and explains the often open irritation which European powers felt towards Britain.

But to a British diplomat the situation seemed a very favourable one. This steady aim throughout the 1890s to be free from all dependence upon foreign powers explains the way in which Britain succeeded in resolving all potential quarrels. There was a series of patiently negotiated colonial agreements. With the exception of the special case of Japan in 1902, when the alliance had a limited objective and was concluded in order to meet a specific and obvious need, alliances were carefully avoided. The policy of Great Britain was to settle all outstanding disputes.

Thus there was the *entente cordiale* with France in 1904, the Anglo-Russian Convention of 1907 and, outside Europe, the Hay-Pauncefote Treaty of 1901, whereby Great Britain withdrew her naval forces from the West Indies and took the crucial decision to hand over the custodianship of the west Atlantic and the Caribbean to the United States – an agreement which resulted in a great improvement in Britain's relations with the United States and which has been described as 'one of the great treaties of the twentieth century'.[1]

At the same time there was a tightening of Britain's imperial bonds. Increasing account was being taken of the possibilities of empire, which was reflected not only in the increased number of subscribers to the political ideas of Milner's famous 'Kindergarten', who emphasised the overwhelming importance of British imperial interests as against her European connections: in a more practical sense it was revealed by the recognition of New Zealand as a Dominion in 1907, of the Union of South Africa in 1910, and the way in which the British government lent a closer ear

[1] J. A. S. Grenville, *Lord Salisbury and Foreign Policy: the Close of the Nineteenth Century* (1964) 388-9.

to the opinions and policies of the Dominions and to the role of the Committee of Imperial Defence.[1]

But while imperial bonds were tightening, or at least while Britain was paying more heed to imperial considerations and needs, she still resisted any form of definite commitment to European powers. The Liberal government from 1906 right down to July 1914 was constantly concerned to avoid a quarrel. In spite of constant pressure from the French, Britain continued to remain outside the alliances which prevailed upon the continent of Europe. Instead Britain sought to settle all causes of dispute with Germany – a process continuing from the cession of Heligoland in 1890 until the colonial agreement of October 1913. This readiness to come to terms with Germany, in spite of the impossibility of a naval agreement, clearly showed Britain's willingness to compromise on political issues rather than risk a naval war, which would leave her weak *vis-à-vis* a combination of the navies of France and Russia.

In sum, therefore, Britain was still uncommitted, or at least only partially committed, in European politics in 1914. It has been said that she was pledged to France or that she encouraged Russia. But the fact remains that Great Britain had no formal engagement with anyone. The British government did not want to give France and Russia a promise to intervene, yet at the same time it let Germany understand that a Franco-German war would involve Great Britain. Almost to the end of the crisis, Germany gambled on British neutrality, while Russia and France gambled on British aid. Britain does not seem to have known what she was going to do until Germany invaded Belgium. It seems quite clear that, but for the invasion of Belgium, British policy would have been much more confused and hesitant than it was, and the British people certainly less united.

From 1815 to 1914, then, Great Britain was really uncommitted in the great European issues of that period. She had frequently

---

[1] The 'Kindergarten' was the name given to the band of able and keen young men, fresh from Oxford or Toynbee Hall, whom Milner chose to help him in his schemes of reorganisation and social reform in the Orange River Colony and the Transvaal after their formal annexation to the British Empire in 1900. On the genesis of the Committee of Imperial Defence, see Norman Gibbs, *The Origins of Imperial Defence* (Inaugural Lecture, Oxford, 1955) and on its subsequent working F. A. Johnson, *Defence by Committee: The British Committee of Imperial Defence, 1885–1959* (1960).

mediated in European affairs and at times had played a leading role in the Concert of Europe, but always she had interpreted her role as that of the 'umpire' and had kept herself free from 'entangling alliances'. However, the last six years of the nineteenth century and the first four of the twentieth made it necessary to readjust foreign policy. Lansdowne and Grey embarked upon what Professor Grenville[1] has called 'a policy of partial and unforeseen commitment', which he thinks had little to commend it: possibly a whole-hearted commitment to the continent of Europe would have served Britain best.

However this may be, during the period after the First World War, Britain had to accept the role of a leading European power in a way which she had not adopted previously. For then Britain had more to bear than her share of responsibility for the Versailles settlement and for the future of Germany. There was also the prominent part played by the British delegation in drafting the Covenant of the League of Nations and the enthusiastic support given to the League by public opinion. All these factors imposed upon Britain in the inter-war years a role in Europe greater and more exacting than before.

FURTHER READING

1. *Bibliographies*

In so wide a field it is difficult to select a short list of books for further reading, but useful bibliographies may be found in A. BULLOCK and A. J. P. TAYLOR (ed.), *A Select List of Books on European History, 1815-1914* (2nd ed., Oxford, 1956); in two essays in co-operative volumes (ed. M. BELOFF, P. RENOUVIN, F. SCHNABEL and F. VALSECCHI), one by M. R. D. FOOT on 'La Grande Bretagne et l'Europe, 1815-70' in *L'Europe du XIXᵉ et XXᵉ siècles (1815-1870)*, 2 vols (Milan, 1959) II 813-38, and the other on 'La Grande Bretagne et l'Europe, 1870-1914' by W. N. MEDLICOTT in vol. II, 543-91 of the same series covering this period, 2 vols (Milan, 1962); and also in W. L. LANGER, *European Alliances and Alignments, 1871-90* (New York, 1931) and *The Diplomacy of Imperialism, 1890-1902*, 2 vols (New York, 1935).

[1] *Lord Salisbury*, 3.

2. *Documentary Sources*

Foundations of British Foreign Policy: Pitt (1792) to Salisbury (1902), ed. H. TEMPERLEY and L. M. PENSON (Cambridge, 1938) contains some basic documents, with a very good commentary. J. B. JOLL (ed.), *Britain and Europe* (1950) is on a smaller scale. H. TEMPERLEY and L. M. PENSON (ed.), *A Century of Diplomatic Blue Books* (Cambridge, 1938) is an essential guide. Sir E. HERSTLET (ed.), *The Map of Europe by Treaty*, 4 vols (1875–91) is the standard collection. G. P. GOOCH and H. TEMPERLEY (ed.), *British Documents on the Origins of the War*, 13 vols (1926–36) covers the years 1898 to 1914 in great detail.

3. *Secondary Works*

Two general works on the international history of the nineteenth and early twentieth centuries which contain stimulating analyses of British policy in Europe are P. RENOUVIN, *Histoire des relations internationales*, vols V and VI (Paris, 1954–5) and A. J. P. TAYLOR, *The Struggle for Mastery in Europe, 1848–1918* (Oxford, 1954). Wider in scope and with perceptive comments is Lord STRANG, *Britain in World Affairs* (1961).

There are some notable studies of the policies of British foreign secretaries: C. K. WEBSTER, *The Foreign Policy of Castlereagh, 1815–1822*, 2 vols (1925) and C. J. BARTLETT, *Castlereagh* (1967); H. TEMPERLEY, *The Foreign Policy of Canning, 1822–1827* (1925); C. K. WEBSTER, *The Foreign Policy of Palmerston, 1830–1841*, 2 vols (1951). *The Later Correspondence of Lord John Russell* has been edited by G. P. GOOCH, 2 vols (1930). P. KNAPLUND, *Gladstone's Foreign Policy* (1935) leaves much to be desired, but A. RAMM (ed.), *Political Correspondence of Mr. Gladstone and Lord Granville*, 2 vols (Oxford, 1961) carries further her excellent edition of *The Political Correspondence of Mr. Gladstone and Lord Granville, 1868–1876* for the Camden Series, 2 vols (1952), which throws much light on Gladstone's views on Europe. On Salisbury, besides the contributions of Dame Lillian Penson listed in note 1, p. 168 above, there is the excellent study by J. A. S. GRENVILLE, *Lord Salisbury and Foreign Policy: the Close of the Nineteenth Century* (1964). For Lansdowne and Grey see G. P. GOOCH, *Before the War: Studies in Diplomacy*, 2 vols (1936–8); Lord NEWTON, *Lord Lansdowne* (1929); Viscount GREY OF FALLODON, *Twenty-Five Years*, 2 vols (1925); and H. NICOLSON, *Lord Carnock* (1930).

On the German question see especially W. E. MOSSE, *The European Powers and the German Question, 1848–1871* (Cambridge, 1958); R. MILLMAN, *British Foreign Policy and the Coming of the Franco-Prussian War* (Oxford, 1965); and J. R. S. HOFFMANN, *Great Britain and the German Trade Rivalry, 1875–1914* (1933). The Eastern Question is well covered by M. S. ANDERSON, *The Eastern Question* (1967); C. W. CRAWLEY, *The Question of Greek Independence, 1821–1833* (Cambridge, 1930); H. TEMPERLEY, *England and the Near East: the Crimea* (1936), which covers the subject from 1808 to 1854; V. J. PURYEAR, *England, Russia and the Straits Question, 1844–1856* (Berkeley, 1931); G. B. HENDERSON, *Essays in Crimean War Diplomacy* (Glasgow, 1947); B. H. SUMNER, *Russia and the Balkans, 1870–1880* (Oxford, 1937); R. W. SETON-WATSON, *Gladstone, Disraeli and the Eastern Question* (1935); D. HARRIS, *Britain and the Bulgarian Horrors of 1876* (Chicago, 1939); W. N. MEDLICOTT, *The Congress of Berlin and After* (1938) and *Bismarck, Gladstone and the Concert of Europe* (1957).

On British policy immediately prior to the First World War, in addition to G. P. GOOCH, *Before the War* (cited above), see N. MANSERGH's short survey *The Coming of the First World War* (1949); A. F. PRIBRAM, *England and the International Policy of the European Great Powers* (1931); and especially B. E. SCHMITT, *The Coming of the War*, 2 vols (New York, 1930) and G. P. GOOCH, *Recent Revelations of European Diplomacy* (1940).

Naval aspects of the problem are discussed by G. S. GRAHAM, *The Politics of Naval Supremacy: Studies in British Maritime Ascendancy* (Cambridge, 1965); C. J. BARTLETT, *Great Britain and Sea Power, 1815–1854* (Oxford, 1964); A. J. MARDER, *The Anatomy of British Sea Power, a History of British Naval Policy, 1880–1905* (New York, 1940); and Sir E. L. WOODWARD, *Great Britain and the German Navy* (Oxford, 1935), which goes much wider than its title suggests.

8 Britain as an Imperial Power in South-East Asia in the Nineteenth Century

J. S. BASTIN

THE word 'imperialism' has had a somewhat chequered history,[1] but to many, including Asian and African nationalists, it remains indelibly associated with the concept of 'economic' imperialism popularised by the writings of J.A. Hobson and V. I. Lenin.[2] Both men focused particular attention on the period from about 1870 to 1900 when there was an enormous increase in Western territorial holdings in Africa and Asia:[3] Lenin, for example, noted that in Africa the area under European control rose from less than 11 per cent in 1876 to more than 90 per cent in 1900, and Hobson emphasised the point that one-third of the territory of the British empire in 1900 and one-quarter of its population had been acquired since 1870.[4] The acquisition by Great Britain during these years of $4\frac{3}{4}$ million square miles of territory and 88 million people was regarded as a phenomenon of especial significance,[5] and the fact

---

[1] R. Koebner and H. D. Schmidt, *Imperialism: The Story and Significance of a Political Word, 1840–1960* (Cambridge, 1964); R. Koebner, 'The Concept of Economic Imperialism', *Econ. Hist. Rev.*, second ser., II (1949–50) 1–29; A. P. Thornton, *The Imperial Idea and Its Enemies: a Study in British Power* (1959) introduction and 1 ff.

[2] References are to the following editions: J. A. Hobson, *Imperialism: a Study* (1961); V. I. Lenin, *Imperialism, The Highest Stage of Capitalism* (Moscow, 1947).

[3] Hobson (19) took the year 1870 'for convenience . . . as indicative of the beginning of a conscious policy of Imperialism . . .'; on the other hand, Lenin, who designated the beginning of the twentieth century as the turning-point from 'the domination of capital in general to the domination of finance capital' (57, 74, 76, 78) selected 1876 as 'in the main' completing 'the pre-monopolistic stage of development of West European capitalism' (97) and the year in which European colonial possessions 'increase to an enormous degree' (98). In the case of Great Britain, however, Lenin noted that 'the period of the enormous expansion of colonial conquests is that between 1860 and 1880, and it was also very considerable in the last twenty years of the nineteenth century' (95).

[4] Lenin, 93; Hobson, 18.   [5] Hobson, 18.

that during approximately the same period British capital investment overseas increased more than ten-fold[1] provided both writers
with the key for explaining imperialism, Hobson interpreting the
process as a consequence of 'under-consumption', as the pressure
of declining domestic rates of interest requiring profitable fields
of investment abroad,[2] and Lenin as the necessity of monopoly
finance capital to export to limited markets protected by the
political apparatus of the metropolitan state.[3]

If late-nineteenth-century British imperialism is to be explained
primarily as a struggle for profitable fields of investment, the
essence of the problem clearly lies in the matter of capital investment itself. This subject has attracted a good deal of critical attention in recent years. There is, if not total agreement on the actual
amounts of British capital invested overseas,[4] at least a general
consensus that during the last three decades of the century the
bulk of it went, not to the recently acquired tropical countries
of the empire in Africa and Asia, but to the United States,
Canada, Australasia, the Argentine and South Africa.[5] Nurske's
view, that British capital tended to bypass the tropical economies
and flow instead to the regions of white settlement inside and

[1] Hobson, (62) gives the figures of British overseas investment as £144 million
in 1862 and £1,698 million in 1893. Cf. D. K. Fieldhouse, ' "Imperialism": an
Historiographical Revision', *Econ. Hist. Rev.*, second ser., XIV (1960-1) 190 n. 1,
and note 6, p. 187 below.

[2] Hobson, 85: 'Imperialism is the endeavour of the great controllers of industry
to broaden the channel for the flow of their surplus wealth by seeking foreign
markets and foreign investments to take off the goods and capital they cannot sell
or use at home.'

[3] Lenin, 108: '. . . imperialism is the monopoly stage of capitalism.'

[4] For a critical evaluation of the various calculations of British overseas capital
investment see A. H. Imlah, *Economic Elements in Pax Britannica: Studies in British
Foreign Trade in the Nineteenth Century* (Cambridge, Mass., 1958) 42–81. On the
general subject of British overseas investment, see G. Paish, 'Great Britain's
Investments in Other Lands', *Journal of the Royal Statistical Society*, LXXII (1909)
465–80, and 'Great Britain's Capital Investments in Individual Colonial and Foreign
Countries', ibid., LXXIV (1911) 167–87; C. K. Hobson, *The Export of Capital* (1914;
reissued 1963); L. H. Jenks, *The Migration of British Capital to 1875* (1927; reissued
1963); H. Feis, *Europe the World's Banker 1870–1914* (New Haven, 1930); A. K.
Cairncross, *Home and Foreign Investment 1870–1913: Studies in Capital Accumulation*
(Cambridge, 1953).

[5] Cairncross, 183–5; Hobson, *Export of Capital*, 158; Feis, 19; Fieldhouse, 199;
R. Robinson and J. Gallagher, *Africa and the Victorians: the Official Mind of
Imperialism* (1961) 6–8.

outside the empire,[1] is supported by H. H. Segal and M. Simon's computer-based analysis of British 'called' capital during 1865–1894: 'Only 25 per cent of the total capital called during the thirty-year period was on issues from the tropics as against nearly 65 per cent from the regions of recent [white] settlement.'[2]

As the major part of the British empire acquired during the last thirty years of the nineteenth century was in tropical regions, and as these areas did not provide the main outlet for British overseas capital investment, recent writers like D. K. Fieldhouse, R. J. Hammond, M. Blaug and D. S. Landes have rejected the economic explanation of imperialism.[2] 'Nothing', the latter has written, 'fits the economic interpretation so poorly as the partition of Africa (South Africa and the Congo excepted) – that frantic scramble of industrial, industrialising, and pre-industrial European countries for some of the most unremunerative territory of the globe,'[4] – a view which R. Robinson and J. Gallagher have expressed in the paradox that while the 'main streams of British trade, investment and migration continued to leave tropical Africa practically untouched ... yet it was tropical Africa that was ... bundled into the empire'.[5] So, also, was a large part of South-East Asia. How well does an economic interpretation explain British territorial expansion in that part of the world?

There is certainly no question that British commitments in the region increased remarkably during the last three decades of the nineteenth century. In West Malaysia British power, hitherto confined to the Straits Settlements of Penang, Province Wellesley, Malacca and Singapore, was extended in 1874 over the Malay states of Perak, Selangor and Sungei Ujong, and in 1880–9 over the remainder of Negri Sembilan, and Pahang.[6] This power was

[1] R. Nurske, *Patterns of Trade and Development* (Stockholm, 1959) 19, cited Fieldhouse, 199.

[2] H. H. Segal and M. Simon, 'British Foreign Capital Issues, 1865–1894', *Journal of Economic History*, XXI (1961) 576.

[3] Fieldhouse, 187–209; R. J. Hammond, 'Economic Imperialism: Sidelights on a Stereotype', *Journal of Economic History*, XXI (1961) 582–98; M. Blaug, 'Economic Imperialism Revisited', *Yale Review*, L (3) (1961) 335–49; D. S. Landes, 'Some Thoughts on the Nature of Economic Imperialism', *Journal of Economic History*, XXI (1961) 496–512.

[4] Landes, 498.   [5] Robinson and Gallagher, 17.

[6] C. D. Cowan, *Nineteenth-Century Malaya: the Origins of British Political Control* (1961); C. N. Parkinson, *British Intervention in Malaya, 1867–1877* (Singa-

exercised through British Residents, appointed to the courts of the Malay rulers to advise them on all matters of administration except those touching Malay custom and religion,[1] and subsequently, after 1896, when the states were incorporated in a so-called Federation, through the Residents and their superior, the Resident-General in Kuala Lumpur.[2] During the same period North Borneo (Sabah), Sarawak and Brunei were accorded British protection (1888), and Upper Burma was annexed and joined with Lower Burma to form a province of the British Indian Empire (1886).[3] There is no doubt about the extension of British imperial power in South-East Asia during these years; the question is whether or not it was due to the operation of economic factors of the kind analysed by Hobson and Lenin.

So far as British intervention in Malaya in 1874 is concerned, the 'official' explanation is that Great Britain, as dominant power in the region, was morally bound to employ its influence to prevent further conflicts between Malays and immigrant Chinese in the tin-producing states of Perak and Selangor lest unrest should ruin trade, and that although intervention was to prove highly beneficial to British interests in the Straits, neither the Colonial Secretary, Lord Kimberley, nor the governor, Sir Andrew Clarke, nor anyone else could have foreseen its long-term economic consequences.[4] Any suggestion that British policy was determined by 'the avarice of British capitalists and their desire to exploit the riches of the Malay Pensinsula' is contradicted by the fact that 'the British Government ignored for a century the efforts of the Malay Rulers to awaken an interest in their affairs and to give them help'.[5]

---

pore, 1960); E. Thio, 'The British Forward Movement in the Malay Peninsula, 1880–1889', *Papers on Malayan History*, ed. K. G. Tregonning (Singapore, 1962) 120–34.

[1] F. Swettenham, *British Malaya: an Account of the Origin and Progress of British Influence in Malaya* (1948) 216–71; E. Sadka, 'The Colonial Office and the Protected Malay States', *Malayan and Indonesian Studies*, ed. J. Bastin and R. Roolvink (Oxford, 1964) 184–202; E. Sadka, 'The State Councils in Perak and Selangor, 1877–1895', *Papers on Malayan History*, 89–119.

[2] Swettenham, 272–305; Chai Hon-Chan, *The Development of British Malaya 1896–1909* (Kuala Lumpur, 1964) 43–83; S. W. Jones, *Public Administration in Malaya* (1953) 32–45.

[3] D. P. Singhal, *The Annexation of Upper Burma* (Singapore, 1960).

[4] Swettenham, 174.   [5] F. Swettenham, *Footprints in Malaya* (1942) 30.

Although the importance of tin to the British economy does not figure largely in the official explanation, it would appear to provide a useful economic category to account for British involvement in Malayan affairs in 1874, since the British tin-plate industry was by then the largest in the world, and was becoming increasingly dependent on foreign, especially 'Straits' tin.[1] Moreover, the fact that there was some British capital invested in the Malayan tin mines at this period is extremely suggestive so far as a Hobsonian analysis of imperialism is concerned. Unfortunately what evidence there is suggests that this investment was not large, and that it was virtually all supplied by Straits merchants, mainly Chinese.[2] Certainly the proportions from Western firms was relatively small, and in size at least can scarcely be described as significant.[3] An informed guess is that the total capital from all sources invested in the western Malay states at this period amounted to between half and one million Straits dollars,[4] and that is probably a generous estimate. Also, the investment clearly represented local surplus trading capital,[5] for it proved exceedingly difficult, even in the decade after British intervention, to raise capital on the London money market to work Malayan tin deposits.[6] Indeed, the first tin-mining company floated in London in mid-1874 to exploit a concession in Selangor was forced into voluntary liquidation fifteen months later, largely due to its failure to raise capital, and also because the Straits Government, supported by the Colonial Office, refused to recommend the concession for the approval of the Sultan of Selangor on account of its monopolistic character.[7]

It has been suggested that one of the London promoters of this company influenced Lord Kimberley's decision to adopt more positive measures in the Malay states, but whether this influence was exerted in a negative fashion, by playing on fears of possible intervention by another foreign power,[8] or more positively, by

[1] Wong Lin Ken, *The Malayan Tin Industry to 1914* (Tuscon, 1965) 6–17. A large proportion of 'Straits' tin at this period came from Thailand.

[2] Ibid., 17–40.

[3] Khoo Kay Kim, 'The Origin of British Administration in Malaya', *Journal of the Malayan Branch Royal Asiatic Society*, XXXIX (1) (1966) 57–60.

[4] Cowan, 138–9.   [5] Wong Lin Ken, 31.

[6] Ibid., 123–4.

[7] Ibid., 38–40; cf. Khoo Kay Kim, 89.

[8] Cowan, 167–8; D. McIntyre, 'Britain's Intervention in Malaya: the Origin of

enlisting Kimberley's sympathies for the aims of the company and the needs of Straits commercial interests generally,[1] is a matter for debate. The evidence adduced to support the latter interpretation cannot be ignored, and it is undoubtedly true that two of the company's promoters in the Straits were active in the governor's councils and were well informed about his intentions with respect to the Malay states;[2] but it is certainly stretching the argument to impossible limits to suggest that Kimberley's justification of a forward policy had to be expressed in broad imperial terms in order to secure the Prime Minister's support as well as to provide a device for defending the policy in the event of future criticism.[3] However favourably disposed Kimberley and the Colonial Office may have been to British mercantile interests in the Straits[4] – and the evidence on the subject is by no means unequivocal[5] – there is nothing to suggest that the Colonial Secretary's policies were determined by any but broad imperial considerations; and, in the absence of any more positive evidence, his own statements must be accepted as the best testimony for explaining the British government's decision to adopt more active measures in western Malaya. On the basis of those statements, made in July, August[6] and September 1873,[7] C. D. Cowan

Lord Kimberley's Instructions to Sir Andrew Clarke in 1873', *Journal of Southeast Asian History*, II (3) (1961) 64–6.

[1] Khoo Kay Kim, 69 ff.   [2] Ibid., 84; Wong Lin Ken, 38.
[3] Khoo Kay Kim, 91; cf. Cowan, 172.   [4] Khoo Kay Kim, passim.
[5] Cowan, passim. See also K. Sinclair, 'Hobson and Lenin in Johore: Colonial Office policy towards British concessionaires and investors, 1878–1907', *Modern Asian Studies*, I (4) (1967).
[6] On 31 August 1873 Kimberley minuted: '[W]e could not see with indifference interference of foreign Powers in the affairs of the Peninsula. . . .' (Cowan, 166; cf. a similar statement of 22 July 1873, ibid., 168).
[7] On 10 September 1873 Kimberley wrote to Gladstone: 'The condition of the Malay Peninsula is becoming very serious. It is the old story of misgovernment of Asiatic States. This might go on without any very serious consequences except the stoppage of trade, were it not that European and Chinese capitalists, stimulated by the great riches in tin mines which exist in some of the Malay States, are suggesting to the native Princes that they should seek the aid of Europeans to enable them to put down the disorders which prevail. We are the paramount power in the Peninsula up to the limit of the States, tributary to Siam; and looking to the vicinity of India and our whole position in the East I apprehend that it would be a serious matter if any other European Power were to obtain a footing in the Peninsula' (Cowan, 169).

has argued convincingly that the decision of the British government to sanction limited political intervention in the western Malay states was provoked 'not by conditions in the Peninsula, nor by any consideration of British economic interests there, but by fear of foreign intervention'.[1]

Similar factors appear to have been operative seven years later when the British government approved the grant of a royal charter to the British North Borneo Company, which had been formed to exploit 28,000 square miles of territory 'ceded' by the Sultans of Brunei and Sulu in 1877-8.[2] On advice that North Borneo would provide a useful naval base, and for fear that unless the Company were accorded some mark of official recognition another European power might occupy the country, Lord Salisbury, the Foreign Secretary, approved the grant of a charter.[3] Even after the fall of the Conservative administration, and Salisbury's replacement by Earl Granville, the decision was upheld – Granville, Gladstone and the Colonial Secretary, Lord Kimberley, all agreeing to the incorporation of the Company by royal charter in the belief that if Britain took no action Spain, Germany or the Netherlands might annex North Borneo.[4] The charter specifically stated that the Company was to remain 'British in character and domicile', and its directors were prohibited from alienating its territories and possessions without the consent of the government.[5] Although the charter gave no assurance of British government aid in the event of hostilities, this matter was resolved in 1888 when North Borneo, Brunei and Sarawak were given protectorate status.[6]

The 1888 protectorate agreements themselves reflected the political fears of the British government, being the outcome of a conference in London in October 1886 between officials of the

---

[1] Ibid.

[2] K. G. Tregonning, *Under Chartered Company Rule: North Borneo 1881–1946* (Singapore, 1959) 14–15; K. G. Tregonning, 'Steps in the Acquisition of North Borneo', *Historical Studies, Australia and New Zealand*, v (1952) 240; L. R. Wright, 'Historical Notes on the North Borneo Dispute', *Journal of Asian Studies*, xxv (1966) 475 ff.

[3] G. Irwin, 'Nineteenth-Century Borneo: a Study in Diplomatic Rivalry', *VKI*, xv (1955) 210.

[4] Ibid., 210. On Gladstone's attitude to the charter, see Tregonning, *Chartered Company*, 27–9.

[5] Irwin, 211.   [6] Ibid., 214.

Foreign and Colonial Offices to consider ways of preventing German and French intrusion into northern Borneo.[1] Whatever significance attaches to the agreements at this time, however, it is clearly only relative, for when the government agreed to appoint a consul to Kuching twenty-five years earlier, thus yielding to James Brooke's clamours for recognition, the governor-general, Lord Elgin, believed that what enhanced the importance of preserving the independence of Sarawak 'as a matter affecting British interests', was the recent acquisition of Saigon by the French and 'the persistent endeavour of the Dutch authorities to cripple British trade' in the region.[2]

A conclusion that the motivation of the British government in extending its imperial responsibilities in South-East Asia during the late nineteenth century was political rather than economic in character is also supported by a study of the annexation of Upper Burma in 1886. Although there was a clamour from mercantile interests for annexation during the 1870s, and especially during the mid-1880s,[3] the British India and Home governments maintained the view that, despite complaints by British merchants of discriminatory actions by Burmese officials, Burma had continued on the whole to honour its treaty obligations to Great Britain.[4] What altered the situation and made the government decide in favour of annexation was the treaty concluded between Burma and France in January 1885; the action of the Burmese authorities in imposing a heavy fine on the British Bombay Burmah Trading Corporation in August of that year[5] provided only the occasion for intervention. D. P. Singhal, in *The Annexation of Upper Burma*, places more emphasis on the influence exerted by British mercantile interests than on the British government's fear of French ambitions in the Indochinese peninsula;[6] but the weight of opinion is against this thesis.

[1] Ibid., 213–14.
[2] L. R. Wright, 'The Status of Sarawak under Raja James Brooke and British Recognition', *Philippine Historical Review*, I (1) (1965) 380.
[3] J. S. Furnivall, *Colonial Policy and Practice: a Comparative Study of Burma and Netherlands India* (New York, 1956) 66–8; Singhal, 71–3.
[4] Furnivall, 69.
[5] D. G. E. Hall, *A History of South-East Asia* (1966) 604–5; Singhal, 108–12; Maung Htin Aung, *The Stricken Peacock: Anglo-Burmese Relations 1752–1948* (The Hague, 1965) 79–88.
[6] Singhal, 88.

D. G. E. Hall argues political motivation,[1] and J. S. Furnivall, whom no one can accuse of ignoring economic factors, concludes that the Bombay Burmah Trading Corporation dispute served only as a 'pretext' for government action; he sees the whole issue of annexation as an episode in the rivalry between France and Britain for supremacy in South-East Asia, and considers British annexation of Burma to have removed 'at an opportune moment a potential cause of a European war'.[2]

The fact that British imperial expansion in Asia and Africa during the late nineteenth century was not determined by pressure of British capital seeking investment outlets overseas has led D. K. Fieldhouse to conclude that the race for colonies was 'the product of diplomacy rather than of any more positive force . . . as the extension into the periphery of the political struggle in Europe'. In so far as economic interests had any bearing on overseas expansion, it was that they were used by politicians as a 'diplomatic asset', as a means to justify steps already taken. The relative importance of economic pressure groups compared with the 'political criteria of the statesmen' was, therefore, 'the reverse of that assigned to them by Hobson'.[3] In emphasising the primary importance of political factors in late-Victorian imperialism, Fieldhouse draws an instructive parallel with the eighteenth century, when imperial policies were also 'largely a reflection of European politics . . . rather than of strictly economic competition'.[4] He stresses the need to view the extension of British imperial power as a whole and to avoid studying the last thirty years of the nineteenth century in isolation.[5]

The element of continuity in nineteenth-century British overseas expansion is also stressed by J. Gallagher and R. Robinson in their stimulating article, 'The Imperialism of Free Trade', which discounts the orthodoxy of contrasting a period of indifference to empire in Great Britain in the mid-century with a period of imperial expansion after 1870.[6] In terms both of formal and informal empire, the late Victorian age does not

[1] Hall, 603-6.
[2] Furnivall, 70. Cf. R. C. Crozier, 'Antecedents of the Burma Road: British Plans for a Burma-China Railway in the Nineteenth Century', *Journal of Southeast Asian History*, III (2) (1962) 10.
[3] Fieldhouse, 205-6.   [4] Ibid., 200.   [5] Ibid., 200-2.
[6] *Econ. Hist. Rev.*, second ser., VI (1953-4) 1-15. On this article, see O. MacDonagh, 'The Anti-Imperialism of Free Trade', ibid., XIV (1961-2) 489-501.

apparently introduce 'any significant novelty' in the process of British expansion.[1] If the 1870s are to be regarded in any sense as a watershed in British imperial affairs, it might be on account of greater popular notice taken of them, not the quantity of territory acquired.[2] Indeed in the three decades before 1870, quite apart from acquisitions in the Pacific and Africa, the Asian territories incorporated into the empire include the Punjab, Sind, Berar, Oudh, Lower Burma, Hong Kong, Kowloon and Labuan.[3] Well might Gallagher and Robinson ask, for all the opinion actually hostile to territorial acquisition in the middle decades of the nineteenth century, how many colonies were actually abandoned.[4]

The point is, of course, that despite all admonition to the contrary, lands of non-European settlement continued to be added to the empire throughout the whole of the nineteenth century. Hobson attaches particular importance to the 104,000 square miles of territory which were incorporated into the Indian Empire between 1871 and 1891;[5] but that area is not so large when compared with the acquisitions made at the end of the eighteenth and the beginning of the nineteenth century by Cornwallis, Wellesley and Moira, all of whom were appointed under the East India Act of 1784 which expressed repugnance to 'schemes of conquest and extension of dominion in India',[6] and in the middle years of the nineteenth century by Ellenborough and Dalhousie. The directors of the East India Company frequently reaffirmed clause XXXIV of the 1784 Act as a cardinal point of British policy in Asia, but they were unable to control from London events in India which led to territorial gains, or governors-general like Wellesley who considered it his duty to exploit every opportunity to advance British power in the sub-continent.[7] Theories of imperialism tend to obscure the influence of local factors and the activities, often unauthorised activities, of individuals in

[1] Gallagher and Robinson, 'Imperialism of Free Trade', 15.

[2] A. P. Thornton, *Doctrines of Imperialism* (New York, 1965) 45.

[3] Gallagher and Robinson, 'Imperialism of Free Trade', 2–3.

[4] Ibid., 4.

[5] Hobson, *Imperialism*, 18.

[6] *Speeches and Documents on Indian Policy, 1750–1921*, ed. A. Berriedale Keith (Oxford, 1922) I 111.

[7] J. S. Galbraith, 'The "Turbulent Frontier" as a Factor in British Expansion', *Comparative Studies in Society and History*, II (1959–60) 154.

frontier situations on the effective process of territorial expansion.

Britain's position in South-East Asia during the nineteenth century certainly owed much to the actions of the 'men on the spot'. Raffles's founding of Singapore in 1819,[1] for example, enabled Britain to establish that position of paramountcy in the region to which Lord Kimberley alluded when justifying some form of intervention in the Malay states half a century later.[2] Indeed, the whole forward movement in Malaya after 1874 owed not a little to the unauthorised action of the British governor, Sir Andrew Clarke, in concluding agreements with the Malay rulers for the stationing of British advisers in the west pensinsular states,[3] and the subsequent willingness of the Residents to exceed the limitation placed on their power by the treaties and to undertake responsibility for the direct administration of the states.[4] The important role played by individuals in extending British influence, and ultimately dominion, in South-East Asia is also well illustrated by the case of western Borneo, where in a little more than half a century James and Charles Brooke pushed the frontiers of Sarawak from the basins of the Lundu, Sarawak, Sandong and Samarahan Rivers to Kidurong Point, beyond Bintulu (1861), thence to the Baram and Trusan Rivers (1883–4), next to the Limbang (1890), and in 1905 to the Lawas River.[5] By the time a British Resident was appointed to Brunei in 1906 the once-powerful sultanate of Brunei was reduced to a tiny enclave, completely surrounded on its landward side by the territories of its former fief, Sarawak.[6]

Except for the latter phase of Sarawak's expansion, which was largely occasioned by fear of aggrandisement by the British North Borneo Company, the extension of Brooke rule from one river valley of Sarawak to another illustrates a further dynamic of Western expansion, namely the need to control elements of

---

[1] C. E. Wurtzburg, *Raffles of the Eastern Isles* (1954) 475–501; H. J. Marks, 'The First Contest for Singapore, 1819–1824', *VKI*, xxvii (1959).

[2] Cowan, 169.

[3] Ibid., 175, 203; Parkinson, 141.

[4] Swettenham, *British Malaya*, 221; Cowan, 252–3.

[5] S. Baring-Gould and C. A. Bampfylde, *A History of Sarawak under its Two White Rajahs, 1839–1908* (1909) passim; A. B. Ward and D. C. White, *Outlines of Sarawak History 1839–1946* (Kuching, 1957) 1–18.

[6] K. G. Tregonning, 'The Partition of Brunei', *The Journal of Tropical Geography*, xi (1958) 84–9.

instability on an advancing frontier of administration.[1] In wider
imperial context, J. S. Galbraith has categorised this dynamic as
'the turbulent frontier' and has demonstrated its importance as a
factor in British expansion in Africa and Asia during the nineteenth century.[2] Frontier turbulence, of course, is not a necessary
condition for explaining all acquisitions of territory, but it does
appear to have been an operative factor in a number of situations
in Asia. The case of Burma in the early years of the nineteenth
century comes easily to mind, for it was the need to protect its
Indian frontiers which led Britain to engage in hostilities with
Burma in 1824–6 in order to force the latter to forego all claim to
Assam and Manipur.[3]

In the western Malay states, also, turbulence provided the
occasion for British intervention in 1874,[4] and even before then,
despite official policy, disputes on the 'frontier' settlements of
Penang, Malacca and Singapore led to British involvement in
peninsular affairs. The war with Naning in 1831–2[5] and the
bombardment of Trengganu in 1862[6] are notable examples, but
there was also a host of incidents involving Malay pirates which
certainly constituted British interference in Malaysian affairs,
whatever the official disclaimers.[7] The unstable elements in the
peninsula necessitating British interference were often a direct
or indirect consequence of the British presence in the Straits, just
as the breakdown of African government in the nineteenth
century, which led to the Western advance in that continent, was
the culmination of 'the destructive workings of earlier exercises
of informal empire over the [African] coastal *régimes*'.[8] Robinson
and Gallagher have warned against assuming that imperial

[1] C. Hose and W. McDougall, *The Pagan Tribes of Borneo* (1912; reprinted
1966) II 257–310.

[2] Galbraith, 150–68; see also the same writer's 'Some Reflections on the
Profession of History', *Pacific Historical Review*, XXXV (1966) 1–13.

[3] Hall, 554–70.

[4] Cowan, 66 ff.; Galbraith, 'Turbulent Frontier', 156–63.

[5] L. A. Mills, 'British Malaya 1824–67', ed. C. M. Turnbull, *Journal of the
Malayan Branch Royal Asiatic Society*, XXXIII (3) (1960) 137–51; P. J. Begbie, *The
Malayan Peninsula*, ed. D. M. Banerjee (reprinted Kuala Lumpur, 1967).

[6] Mills, 200–1.

[7] N. Tarling, *Piracy and Politics in the Malay World: a Study of British Imperialism
in Nineteenth-Century South-East Asia* (Melbourne, 1963) passim.

[8] Robinson and Gallagher, *Africa and the Victorians*, 18.

expansion was necessarily the outcome of 'positive impulses' from European society or economy: 'The collapse of African governments under the strain of previous Western influences may have played a part, even a predominant part in the process.'[1]

Yet, whatever weight is attributed to factors of a local character, theorists of imperialism interpret the phenomena of expansion in largely metropolitan terms. Hobson and Lenin were not alone in this. Modern historians also tend to accept official thinking in London as the best evidence for assessing the factors leading to nineteenth-century British expansion, since it was in London that all strands of imperial policy and practice came together and where ultimately all decisions were, if not initially taken, at least finally resolved.[2] According to recent studies of nineteenth-century British imperialism those decisions were influenced more by 'political' than by other considerations, and certainly not by the secret machinations of economic pressure-groups. At the same time, decisions taken in London for political or strategic reasons do not exclude the possibility that they were taken also in full awareness of the national economic interests involved, not necessarily with respect to a specific colonial acquisition but for fear that if it were lost British interests as a whole would suffer. In Asia in the nineteenth century those interests centred on India, and it was in defence of them that much of Britain's imperial expansion in South-East Asia occurred. 'Looking to the vicinity of India and our whole position in the East' was what Kimberley considered to be the ultimate justification for British intervention in the Malay states in 1874,[3] for in India, and in India's ties with eastern and western Asia, Britain's political – and economic – stakes were high.

India, in fact, was regarded as 'the most magnificent', 'the most

[1] Ibid.

[2] Ibid., 19: 'Historically, only the government in London registered and balanced all the contingencies making for British expansion. . . . In following the occasions and motives, all roads lead ineluctably to Downing Street. The files and red boxes which passed between ministers and officials at the time contain the problem in its contemporary proportions. The collective mind of government assembled and weighed all the factors making for and against advances.' For an instructive example of how the contents of the red box containing the North Borneo Company papers escaped the attention of the principal occupant of Number 10 Downing Street, see Tregonning, *Chartered Company*, 27–9.

[3] Above, p. 179, note 7.

stupendous' part of the empire,[1] not merely because of its size or the magnitude of its military establishment,[2] but also because it offered a profitable field for trade and investment. The importance that Manchester cotton interests attached to India as a market during the middle decades of the nineteenth century is well known; but no less important, and indeed connected with a desire to make the country both an efficient cotton producer and consumer,[3] was the opportunity India afforded for capital investment, particularly in railways.[4] During the late 1850s and early 1860s the major movement of British capital was towards India, involving a total by 1870 of something like £160 million.[5] A large proportion of this was in railway development,[6] which, as it was given complete security by the government of India's guaranteed interest rate, was especially attractive to the private British investor.[7] Investment in Indian railways down to the 1880s had the additional advantage that more than one-third of the capital was actually spent in the United Kingdom on railway equipment and on transportation costs to the East.[8] By 1885 British capital investment in India amounted to £270 million, or approximately 20 per cent of the total of British overseas investment.[9] India's economic importance to Great Britain was further

[1] Phrases used in 1837 by R. M. Grindlay, a banker (D. Thorner, *Investment in Empire: British Railway and Steam Shipping Enterprise in India 1825–1849* (Philadelphia, 1950) 4) and in 1907 by Lord Morley (R. Hyam, 'British Imperial Expansion in the Late Eighteenth Century', *Historical Journal*, x (1967) 114). They, do not, of course, represent the full spectrum of nineteenth-century British opinion on India. In the middle years of the century compare the extreme view of Cobden (MacDonagh, 496) with that of *The Economist* of 6 August 1853 (Galbraith, 'Turbulent Frontier', 150). Cf. also Thornton, *Imperial Idea*, 40.

[2] Jenks, 223; Robinson and Gallagher, *Africa and the Victorians*, 12–13.

[3] A. W. Silver, *Manchester Men and Indian Cotton 1847–1872* (Manchester, 1966) passim; W. J. Macpherson, 'Investment in Indian Railways, 1845–1875', *Econ. Hist. Rev.*, second ser., VIII (1955–6) 178–9.

[4] Jenks, 210–23; Macpherson, 177–86; Thorner, passim.

[5] Cairncross, 183; Jenks, 207, 225.

[6] Macpherson, 177, estimates that between 1845 and 1875 about £95 million were invested in Indian guaranteed railways most of which came from British sources.

[7] Ibid., 180–1; Thorner, 168 ff. According to Cairncross (85), there were some 50,000-odd British investors in 1870 holding on an average nearly £1,800 in Indian Guaranteed Railway Securities.

[8] Jenks, 227. See also S. B. Saul, *Studies in British Overseas Trade 1870–1914* (Liverpool, 1960) 198.   [9] Cairncross, 183.

enhanced by virtue of the fact that, as centre of the regional system of exchange, she placed in British hands much of the trade with Asia, as well as providing the key to Britain's balance of payments.[1]

Once these economic facts are fully comprehended, deeper meaning has clearly to be assigned to such phrases as 'the defence of India' and 'protecting the sea-route to the East' which, in the words of statesmen, constituted the principal objectives of British imperial expansion in South-East Asia; for in the maintenance of the security of India lay great national economic advantage, both in terms of investment and trade. British statesmen may not have been much influenced by the specific interests of individual investors or mercantile groups in India, but they could hardly fail to be aware of the important part which India as a whole played in Britain's world trade. Official British policy may not have been manipulated by the financiers or shaped by the crude economic forces described by Hobson and Lenin,[2] nor can British territorial expansion in Asia be explained on a monogenetic basis;[3] but the recent emphasis placed on the 'political' criteria of imperialism tends to obscure the economic realities which were well understood by the statesmen of the last century in their dealings with India, and with those regions on the periphery of India.

FURTHER READING

1. Imperialism

The literature on British imperialism is too vast to attempt a bibliographical assessment of it here. An excellent guide to the subject is provided by R. W. WINKS (ed.), British Imperialism: Gold, God, Glory (New York–London, 1963) 120–2. A number of the more significant recent contributions have been cited in the references above.

2. South-East Asia

COWAN, C. D.: Nineteenth-Century Malaya (1961) discusses in an

---

[1] Saul, 188 ff.   [2] See Fieldhouse, 191.
[3] Hobson admitted the existence of non-economic factors in imperialism (Imperialism, 196–222), as did Lenin; but for various reasons the latter did not develop the subject (Thornton, Doctrines, 22).

extremely lucid fashion British policy towards the Malay states during the nineteenth century and examines the events connected with British political involvement in Perak, Selangor and Sungei Ujong in 1874–5.

GULLICK, J. M.: *Indigenous Political Systems of Western Malaya* (1958) describes and analyses the political institutions of the western Malay states immediately before British political intervention in the peninsula in 1874.

HALL, D. G. E.: *A History of South-East Asia* (1966). The standard work on the subject.

IRWIN, G.: 'Nineteenth-Century Borneo: a Study in Diplomatic Rivalry', *VKI*, xv (1955). A sound and scholarly work on British policy towards western Borneo in the nineteenth century, and on Anglo-Dutch relations during the period.

MAUNG HTIN AUNG: *The Stricken Peacock: Anglo-Burmese Relations, 1752–1948* (The Hague, 1965) presents an interesting and highly readable account of Britain's relations with Burma from a Burmese point of view.

SINGHAL, D. P.: *The Annexation of Upper Burma* (Singapore, 1960). A stimulating little book which argues that British annexation was largely the result of the pressures brought to bear on the British government by traders and chambers of commerce.

TARLING, N.: 'British Policy in the Malay Peninsula and Archipelago, 1824–1871', *Journal of the Malayan Branch Royal Asiatic Society*, xxx (3) (1957). A well documented account of the subject.

—— *Piracy and Politics in the Malay World: a Study of British Imperialism in Nineteenth-Century South-East Asia* (Melbourne, 1963). An interesting and important book which describes the part played by the 'suppression of piracy' in nineteenth-century British policy towards Malaysia.

TREGONNING, K. G.: *Under Chartered Company Rule* (*North Borneo 1881–1946*) (Singapore, 1959). A readable but unsatisfactorily documented account of the operations of the British North Borneo Company. A new edition of this book, incorporating material on post-war developments in North Borneo, has been published under the title, *A History of Sabah, 1881–1963* (Singapore, 1964).

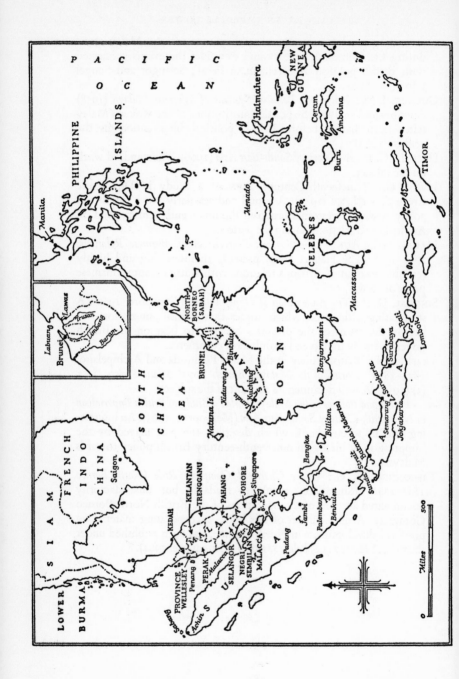

9 The Netherlands as an Imperial Power in South-East Asia in the Nineteenth Century and After

S. L. VAN DER WAL

THE British historian Richard Pares once said that 'the most important thing in the history of an empire is the history of its mother-country'.[1] We can extend his epigram by saying that the next most important thing in the history of an empire is the history of the territory towards which the expansion of the mother-country has been directed. We can also modify it in as much as the history of an empire may include a phase in which the colony, not the mother-country, assumes overriding and perhaps – for the continued existence of the empire – even decisive importance. As regards the history of the Dutch empire in Asia, we can go along with Pares until the late nineteenth century. The Dutch East Indies were ruled and exploited in accordance with the ideas and needs of the mother-country until 1870, a date which ushered in a period during which the colony's modern, post-1900 development was prepared and initiated. It is with respect to this later period, and particularly to the years after the turn of the century, that Pares's statement requires the correction I have mentioned, namely that the importance of the colony to the history of the empire may outweigh that of the mother-country, and may indeed ultimately determine the fate of that empire. We have thus indicated two periods in the history of Dutch relations with the Indonesian archipelago after the restoration of the Kingdom of the Netherlands in 1813. Although they cannot be sharply demarcated, there was a distinct transition at the beginning of the present century. It was then that the gradual but increasingly accelerated shift of influence and control from

[1] R. Pares, 'The Economic Factors in the History of the Empire', *Econ. Hist. Rev.*, first ser., VII (1937) 120; reprinted in *The Historian's Business and other Essays*, ed. R. A. and E. Humphreys (Oxford, 1961) 50.

the mother-country to the colony became clearly perceptible and irrevocable.

So vast a subject compels one to narrow the field of discussion. I shall not do so by attempting to sketch the broad outline of this stretch of colonial history, because only a longer and more comprehensive account would be really satisfying. I feel that it would be best to confine myself to a single aspect of Dutch colonialism – to one which will show how it differs from that of other European countries – and I believe I shall be drawing your attention to one of the major factors which have determined the special character of Dutch colonialism in Asia if I invite you to consider the influences that have been exerted on it from abroad: in other words, if I confine myself to suggesting the extent to which the position of the Netherlands in Europe and in the world, and that of the Indonesian archipelago in South-East Asia, have helped to shape the history of Dutch colonialism. And yet a systematic discussion of this one aspect alone would itself go far beyond the scope of a single lecture, so I must be content with a mere outline of the political and economic background, concentrating on certain palpable examples of the influence with which we are concerned. Moreover, of the two periods of Dutch colonial history already distinguished, it is on the post-1900 years that our attention will chiefly be focused. For, by then, world events and world politics had dragged the Netherlands overseas from its state of calm and isolation, and the Indonesian archipelago was proving to be part of an Asian awakening. A great deal of fresh documentary material fortunately became available a few years ago, when the official colonial archives in the Netherlands for this period were opened to scientific research. The examination of these archives, which are of inestimable value to the study of recent Dutch colonial history, and accordingly to that of the history of Indonesia, has already begun.

At the time of the establishment of the Kingdom in 1813 and for a short time after the return of the colonies by Britain, the position of the Netherlands as a colonial power among the nations was scarcely an independent one; on the contrary, it was extremely vulnerable. Nor do the later periods down to the collapse of the empire give historians any occasion whatever to pronounce as regards Dutch imperialism what Pares wrote with respect to Britain, namely that 'colonial history is made at home:

given a free hand, the mother-country will make the empire it needs.'[1] Seldom, and in very few respects, did the Netherlands have any such free hand. Certainly this was by no means the case with the young Kingdom, if only because the British interregnum gave way to a lengthy aftermath of settlement difficulties, which delayed the final determination of the new British and Dutch positions in Asia for many years. I need only recall the wrangling that went on over the Sunda and Malacca Straits – those two entrances to the Indonesian archipelago which Raffles was anxious to keep under British control – and in this connection the reluctance of the British to give up their positions in Sumatra. These difficulties led to the signing of the Treaty of London in 1824, when the British relinquished Sumatra and Billiton. But the treaty did not put an end to British influence in Sumatra. With regard to north Sumatra, the Netherlands was bound not to undertake any warlike measures against the sovereign sultanate of Achin – a restriction probably prompted by Raffles's fear of Dutch domination of the Malacca Strait. It was not until 1870 that this ban on intervention in rebellious Achin, a region that had also given the British constant trouble, was lifted: Britain then, under the provisions of the Treaty of The Hague, undertook to desist from opposing the expansion of Dutch sovereignty in Sumatra.

This treaty not only cleared the way for, but encouraged, strong-arm intervention in Achin and, indirectly, it had a considerable influence on Dutch nineteenth-century policy in the numerous native states on the islands encircling Java. Formerly, the fear of British intervention had alternately inhibited and provoked a purposeful, active policy in these regions. It was by pointing to the 'incessant complaints of the British about the expansion of our territory on the East Coast of Sumatra'[2] that the minister for the colonies, J. C. Baud,[3] in 1841 torpedoed the plans of his predecessor, J. van den Bosch,[4] to bring Bangka and Sumatra under effective Dutch control. Two years later Baud deemed it necessary to assert Dutch sovereign rights as much as possible by deed and word, because (as he wrote to the Nether-

---

[1] Ibid.   [2] J. M. Somer, *De korte verklaring* (Breda, 1934) 47.

[3] Jean Chrétien Baud (1789–1859) was governor-general *ad interim* 1833–6 and minister for the colonies 1840–8.

[4] Johannes van den Bosch (1780–1844) was governor-general 1830–3 and minister for the colonies 1834–6.

lands East Indies government) 'certain European powers were apparently bent on acquiring colonial territory'.[1] He reacted to James Brooke's settlement in Sarawak by declaring Borneo a province and appointing a governor over the island, thus clearly demonstrating that Borneo was Dutch territory and that any further settlement by the British would be regarded as a hostile act. But a few years later, when the question arose whether the same procedure should also be applied to the island of Celebes, the governor-general, J. J. Rochussen,[2] did not consider this necessary since 'so far, there has been no need to check any alien settlement on the island, as there was in Borneo'.[3]

During the first half of the nineteenth century the Netherlands was financially in no position to pursue a policy of asserting and expanding its authority in the Outer Provinces. Even if the will to develop the colonies and to establish a 'Greater Netherlands' in Asia had been more general and stronger than was in fact the case, the means of development, both financial and military, would still have been altogether inadequate. The 'cultivation system'[4] was introduced about 1830, its purpose being to provide revenue from the East Indies to alleviate the needs of the metropolitan exchequer, aggravated as these had been by the Belgian rebellion of that year; but this system did not allow of a development policy for the Outer Provinces, for that would have entailed costly expeditions and the establishment of an effective administrative system. The publication in the *Bulletin of Acts, Orders and Decrees* of a geographical inventory of traditional Dutch rights was considered sufficient, until experiences with the British revealed that *de jure* possession offered few guarantees for the future, and that paper proclamations were not worth much to the security of Dutch sovereign rights unless confirmed by *de facto* possession and administration of the territory concerned. The cultivation system, which used the revenue from the East Indies for the mother-

---

[1] Somer, 56.

[2] Jan J. Rochussen (1797–1871) was governor-general 1845–50, minister of finance 1840–3, and for the colonies 1858–61.

[3] Somer, 76.

[4] The so-called cultivation system was essentially that the Javanese population should pay little in money taxes but should put at the disposal of the Dutch government one-fifth of its soil and of its working hours for the purpose of growing mainly coffee, sugar and indigo. One of the intentions was to enrich the Dutch treasury. It led to serious abuses. From 1860 it was gradually abandoned.

country instead of for the development of the regions outside Java, indeed discouraged an active policy with respect to these Outer Provinces. It is true that Britain's attitude, towards the end of the nineteenth century, furnished a compelling reason for abandoning this restraint in favour of an active policy, but this was launched out of necessity and put into effect haphazardly.

When this policy was found to be working well and to be offering many new possibilities, it was pursued more systematically. Foreign influence, or rather fear of foreign intervention, had thus given impetus to the establishment of Dutch authority, and this was followed by Western-style administrative and economic development. In the course of this lengthy process – it was not until the beginning of the twentieth century that the entire archipelago had been brought under Dutch rule – expressions of the same fear are repeatedly encountered, even in the later years. The so-called 'Brief Declaration', which after 1900 formed the basis of the relations between the Netherlands and the self-governing territories in the Outer Provinces, provides a cogent example. This Declaration, which was in fact a uniform agreement between the Netherlands government and the native princes, embodied the recognition of Dutch supreme control, followed by the promise of the head of the indigenous principality or sultanate not to enter into any relationship whatsoever with foreign powers, for 'the enemies of the Netherlands shall likewise be my enemies and the friends of the Netherlands shall likewise be my friends'.

So far I have referred merely to one aspect, though in my opinion easily the most important aspect, of British influence on the course of Dutch colonialism in Asia in the nineteenth century. There are, of course, other examples, many of them simply the legacy of the British interregnum (1811–16), in the form of administrative, financial and economic measures. The most spectacular measure was the British introduction of a land tax, after the example of Bengal, imposed on Javanese farmers. This replaced the former compulsory supply of produce as a source of revenue for the government, and the Dutch maintained it throughout the colonial era. Other measures, particularly those resulting from Raffles's tendency to import into Java typically British institutions, such as the jury system, were revoked by the Dutch. Among the imponderables of Raffles's legacy, his impetuous desire for reform cannot have failed to impress his Dutch successors. His ideas and his urge for reform made their unmistakable mark on Herman Muntinghe (1773–1827), his highly valued adviser, who for a long time continued to fulfil an important role in various high offices.

At the beginning of the present century, in a turbulent Asia, with the Western powers bent on acquiring colonial possessions and Japan developing at a stupendous rate into a formidable power, the Dutch could scarcely feel secure in the East Indies – highly desirable territories on account of their geographical location and natural wealth. The consequences of this sense of vulnerability, and of the uncertainty whether a small power like the Netherlands would be able to assert itself in Asia, reached much farther than did the immediate after-effects of world events on the situation in the East Indies. The reaction there to the Russo-Japanese War provides a striking example. The Dutch East Indies were under an immediate and serious threat. To the threat from Japan was added the fear that Britain, Japan's ally since 1902, would support her. There were rumours that Britain intended occupying a number of strategic positions to keep the Russian fleet out of the Far East. One of these positions was reported to be Sabang, north of Sumatra, the idea being to restrain the Dutch from supplying Russian ships with coal. A Dutch squadron was sent there post-haste to prevent any violation of Dutch neutrality, which had been promulgated in the Netherlands Government Gazette of 12 February 1904 and likewise proclaimed in the colony.

The repercussions of this war were, of course, felt all over the East Indies; the rebellion in Achin, which then flared up again, was ascribed to it. The private correspondence between the then minister for the colonies and the governor-general demonstrates how far-reaching were the psychological effects of this war, and how policy decisions which ostensibly had no connection whatever with it are attributable to its influence. In the tense days of February 1904, Governor-General Rooseboom[1] included in his monthly confidential letter to the minister his reaction to Idenburg's[2] announcement that he had applied for an interest-free loan

---

[1] Willem Rooseboom (1843–1920), lieut.-general in the Netherlands Army, was governor-general 1899–1904.

[2] Alexander W. F. Idenburg (1861–1935), minister for the colonies 1902–5, 1908–9 and 1918–19, and governor-general 1909–16.

to boost East Indian economic development: 'I do not wish to discuss now the interest-free loan to which you have referred, but in view of the state of Holland's finances and the fact that these days I feel that our colonies are constantly a precarious possession, I should have preferred assistance in another form. . . .' If the Netherlands were to lose its colonies, Rooseboom argued, the financial consequences of assistance such as he envisaged would be less serious for the Netherlands.[1] We would seem justified in ascribing the governor-general's sombre view of things to the current threat of war. At least this danger had obviously made a deep impression on him.

The question whether, and if so to what extent, Rooseboom's policy was affected by other factors must be left aside in the absence of sufficient information. However, it is remarkable that it should have been this particular governor-general who hastened to build up the defences of Java and the major settlements in the Outer Provinces against a foreign foe. It was under his administration that General Van Heutsz[2] asserted Dutch authority in Achin; and Rooseboom himself contributed much towards the establishment of that rule elsewhere in the archipelago, even in New Guinea, by virtue of expeditions and other displays of power. Did the danger, the fear, of losing the colonies once again have an activating effect? If so, Rooseboom would have confirmed the truth of John De Witt's sad verdict that 'the nature of the Dutch is such that, until emergencies and danger loom large, they cannot be persuaded to attend to their own safety'.

The early twentieth century, down to the war with Japan, was a time of unprecedented development in every respect for the Dutch East Indies. It was also a time when the imperial emphasis gradually and at times haltingly shifted, or was consciously transferred, from the Netherlands to the East Indies. This ever-increasing eastwards trend had begun long ago, but not until the turn of the century did the foundations of the colony as a new state begin to take perceptible shape. Colonial policy was now geared to the principle that the mother-country should regard herself and act as the guardian of her colonies: a fundamental

[1] *De Volksraad en de staatkundige ontwikkeling van Ned. Indië*, 1: *1891–1926*, ed. S. L. van der Wal (Groningen, 1964) 66.

[2] Joannes B. van Heutsz (1851–1924), lieut.-general in the Royal Netherlands Indies Army, governor-general 1904–9.

departure from the view that the colonies were possessions to be exploited for her benefit, either by the authorities, as in the case of the cultivation system, or by private entrepreneurs, for whom the road had been opened in 1870. By accepting the role of guardian, the Netherlands had assumed the moral obligation to develop both country and people. The Speech from the Throne in 1901, which gave the new 'ethical policy' royal sanction, became famous on that account. But the principle of guardianship meant more than that. It also expressed the realisation that the colonial relationship was not permanent: rather, it would eventually give way to a situation in which the colony would be self-supporting, perhaps even independent. Although in practice the colonial administration did not adhere consistently to the new principle, it was never renounced altogether, and it provided both the Dutch advocates of independence and the Indonesian nationalist movement, which sprang up about 1910, with a legal basis for their endeavour.

Even after the most cursory enquiry into the nature and scope of the foreign influences prevalent in the East Indies in the new era, two conclusions impose themselves. First, these influences were manifest in numerous sectors of policy. Second, we can say that international factors strongly promoted the march towards independence. Consulting the archives of the former Ministry for the Colonies, we find that the impact of foreign example, whether as a model to be followed or as a warning to be apprehended, was much greater than is generally assumed. The reproach has often been heard, even among the Dutch themselves, that in the administration of the colonies the Netherlands had little comprehension of, and cared even less about, what people thought and did elsewhere in the world, particularly in Asia and in other colonial territories. This criticism need not be accepted without question. Research has shown that the reproach is unfounded as regards at least three sectors of government policy: namely, education and the political and administrative systems. On the contrary, the files relating both to the internal consultations between the various East Indian authorities and to consultations with the Netherlands government, on these subjects, reveal that the Dutch were highly receptive to foreign developments and to policies pursued in other colonies. I must confine myself to a few examples, first in the sector of education.

About 1913 plans were laid for the establishment of a College of Advanced Technology, the first institute of university education in the East Indies. The 1902 report of the Indian University Commission set up by Lord Curzon was quoted, and it was argued that the new College should be on the same level as the Colleges of Advanced Technology in Germany, Denmark and Japan; it should not become a 'mock university', as the universities in India were said to be.[1] In 1917, when secondary education was due for reform, comparative studies were made of the systems in India and Japan, which were again consulted when the decentralisation of education to provincial and municipal level came up for discussion.[2] Indian experience with private schools put the authorities on their guard as regards similar schools in the Dutch East Indies, when the inspection of this type of education was being regulated.[3]

In 1939 an educational expert was sent on a fact-finding mission to a number of countries in South-East Asia in connection with the reform plans of the head of the Education Department, a son of Idenburg. Idenburg Jr had ordered an investigation to be made in other countries in Asia. In a secret letter to the governor-general explaining the principles of educational policy in the East Indies, Idenburg advocated a reappraisal of the educational system, the most compelling reason lying according to him

in a factor which is becoming increasingly important to our colonial policy in general, namely, the position we occupy as a colonial power in this modern world. The possession by such a small power of a territory so rich, without its having the means of defending it by force of arms against foreign aggression, while large, overpopulated and well-armed nations are striving with might and main to expand their spheres of influence and their territories, has become such a conspicuous phenomenon that I feel that, if the status quo is to be maintained, we are in dire need of moral justification in the form of a colonial policy that will energetically promote the comprehensive and vigorous development of the colony. Our defensive power being weak, we must seek our strength above all in a purposeful, honest endeavour, clearly visible to all, to secure for this country and its people an honourable place in South-East Asia. We cannot afford the luxury of a colonial policy the sole criterion of which is our own discretion.[4]

[1] *Het onderwijsbeleid in Ned. Indië, 1900–1940*, ed. S. L. van der Wal (Groningen, 1963) 289.

[2] Ibid., 325. [3] Ibid., 469. [4] Ibid., 654.

Van Starkenborgh,[1] the governor-general, was in agreement, and Welter,[2] minister for the colonies, who received Idenburg's letter in London shortly after the Netherlands government had gone into exile in England, wrote in the margin against this passage: 'I fully agree.'[3]

Developments in other colonies also provided an object-lesson for the political and administrative organisation of the Dutch East Indies. Again I must limit myself to a few examples. About 1890, when the government was considering granting the people – in the first instance the European part of it – a say in the administration, the British colonies were taken as a shining example. During the preliminaries to the setting-up of a representative council, subsequently the People's Council, scrupulous attention was paid in the official correspondence to the structure of the corresponding bodies in India and in French Indo-China. Later, the Montagu–Chelmsford Report on Indian Constitutional Reforms (1918) provided useful material for comparison when constitutional reforms were under preparation in the East Indies after the First World War. Governor-General van Limburg Stirum,[4] who in 1917 had written to Pleijte[5] that 'when India is given greater freedom, the people of the Dutch East Indies will be less tolerant of interference on the part of the Netherlands',[6] remarked later that 'certain passages of the Report might well have been written with regard to the Dutch East Indies'.[7] De Graaff,[8] the conservative minister for the colonies, countered Van Limburg Stirum's pleas for a further democratisation of the East Indian administra-

[1] Jonkheer Mr Alidius W. L. Tjarda van Starkenborgh Stachouwer (born 1888), after a career as diplomat and governor of the province of Groningen in the Netherlands, was governor-general 1936–45, being interned by the Japanese 1942–5.

[2] Charles J. I. M. Welter (born 1880), vice-president of the Council of the Indies 1929–1931 and minister for the colonies 1925–6, 1937–9 and 1939–41.

[3] Van der Wal, *Het onderwijsbeleid*, 654.

[4] Mr Johan P. van Limburg Stirum (1873–1948), having served as a diplomat, was governor-general 1916–21, after which he ended his career as ambassador at Berlin.

[5] Thomas B. Pleijte (1864–1926) was minister for the colonies 1913–18.

[6] *De Volksraad en de staatkundige ontwikkeling van Ned. Indië*, I: *1891–1926*, ed. S. L. van der Wal (Groningen, 1964) 191.

[7] Ibid., 248.

[8] Simon de Graaff (1861–1948) was director of the civil service of the East Indies 1906–10, minister for the colonies 1919–25 and 1929–33.

tion by pointing to the reactions in India to the proposed reforms. True, De Graaff hoped also, 'for the sake of quiet in our Indies', that the Montagu–Chelmsford proposals would give some satisfaction in India; but he doubted whether 'any proposal from British quarters could have that effect for any length of time'.[1] Did this not apply equally to the political reforms that had been drafted for the Dutch East Indies?

The British example was quoted when the appointment of native members to the Netherlands East Indies Council was under discussion, and much later it helped to put through the indianisation of the East Indian civil service. In 1929, Welter, a member of the Netherlands East Indies Council, argued that it was necessary to revise Dutch colonial policy, which he considered far too opportunist. He referred to the consultations that Britain had initiated on the further political development of the British empire in Asia, for the purposes of which the Simon Commission in India, and in Ceylon the Donoughmore Commission, had been set up. Welter pointed out that, unlike the big colonial powers, a small country like the Netherlands, without the backing of international political power, could not afford to make mistakes: 'They can, if they wish, turn back the pages of history, but we shall undoubtedly be confronted with the consequences of our mistakes with the utmost severity.'[2] As minister for the colonies just before and during the Second World War, Welter wielded a strong influence on colonial policy, with the object of keeping the empire intact.

With regard to my other major conclusion, namely, the influence of international factors on the process of the colony's independence, I shall confine myself to one or two remarks about the effects of the First World War. Shortly after 1900 a few steps on the road to independence were taken within the framework of the 'ethical policy'. The finances of the Dutch East Indies had been separated from those of the Netherlands: the East Indies learnt to draw up its own budget and later took over from the Netherlands the responsibility for adopting it, the main idea being that if a country wanted to become independent it should learn to administer its national finances itself. A few minutes ago, I had occasion to mention the establishment, in 1916, of the People's

[1] Van der Wal, *De Volksraad*, I 455.
[2] Ibid., II: *1927–1942*, ed. S. L. van der Wal (Groningen, 1965) 79.

Council, which acted first as an advisory and later as a joint legislative body. It had been preceded by the appointment of the first local and regional councils for the autonomous districts, a process which continued down to the Second World War. The influences of the First World War ran parallel with this independence policy, but were chronologically far in advance of it.

The war of 1914 had reduced the links with the mother-country, and in consequence direct trade with the Netherlands declined steeply. Long before that, when the cultivation system, which had monopolised East Indian produce for the mother-country, had been abolished, the East Indies had sought more remunerative and less distant export markets in the Pacific area, whence they also obtained their imports in increasing quantities. This development had been much stimulated by the Great War. As a result, the economic importance of the East Indies to the Netherlands shifted. It came to hinge on income deriving from increased investment and from the trade of Dutch firms established in the East Indies, little of which, however, was directed towards the Netherlands. In 1925 only 18 per cent of imports came from the Netherlands and only 15 per cent of exports went to the Netherlands; we must not forget that Holland was much less important as a consumer market for East Indian exports than France, Britain and the United States were for the exports of their colonies and dominions. Before the First World War colonial economic policy was designed to foster a certain unity of Dutch and East Indian interests. After the war, however, doubts grew as to whether the two spheres of interest would be compatible in the long run. In practical politics signs of this doubt, and of the realisation that it was justified, clearly manifested themselves during and after the economic crisis of the 1930s. The importance was stressed of the East Indies, of Indonesia, being treated as a separate entity. Dutch interests were maintained or promoted by the granting of concessions, motivated by the East Indies' dependence on foreign goodwill for the upkeep and expansion of their export production.

The considerable *de facto* independence which the East Indies had enjoyed during the First World War, together with the influence of Indonesian nationalism, had brought the march towards political independence to the stage where views and desires in the East Indies differed greatly from those prevailing in the Netherlands. Certain events in the Dutch East Indies shocked the Netherlands. Under the pressure of the revolutionary movement in Europe in 1918, which in the Netherlands took the form of a socialist bid for power, Van Limburg Stirum had promised the East Indies far-reaching political reforms in a statement to the People's Council, without any instructions from or even prior consultation with the responsible minister. What moved the governor-general to make this statement has now become clear from his private correspondence with colonial ministers Idenburg and Pleijte. He wanted to pave the way for a temporary secession of the Dutch East Indies in the event of a revolution in the Netherlands. He intended to ignore possible telegrams from any revolutionary government in the Netherlands; pending the restoration of legal authority, the People's Council was temporarily to take over responsibility for the governor-general's policy from the minister for the colonies and the States-General.

This 'November Declaration' was a painful surprise to the Netherlands. It soon became obvious that the movement towards political emancipation was not to proceed in accordance with East Indian views and expectations, and certainly not at the pace they envisaged. Progress in realising the programme of political reforms and the 'November 1918 promises' fell so far below expectations in the 1920s and 1930s as to cause disappointment and dissatisfaction in the East Indies, particularly among the nationalists.

After 1900 specifically Asian influences also made themselves felt in the Dutch East Indies. The national revival and the revolution in China had made a deep impression on Chinese expatriates. In the East Indies the renascence of their homeland inspired the Chinese to seek to improve their legal and social status. Their attempts, and particularly their demands, resulted in measures being taken on their behalf which benefited more than the interests of their own social group. What was granted to the Chinese could not be withheld from the native population. Thus the Chinese became the pacemakers as regards Western education for Asians. Western-style schools for the Chinese were established before those for the indigenous peoples. The Chinese played an important part in gradually attenuating and finally abolishing the dualism in Dutch East Indian legislation, whereby discrimination had been practised between the Asiatic and European population groups. Many more reforms might be mentioned which were originally taken on behalf of the Chinese, but which made for social progress in general. They all stemmed from the policy of the Netherlands East Indies government towards the Chinese, which was designed throughout to forestall any interference on the part of the successive governments of China.

After 1900 Japan gave cause for other and more serious anxieties. There were not many Japanese living in the Dutch East Indies; they were never more than about 7,000, but they were extremely active and they had to be closely watched. 'There is always a military angle to every Japanese activity', as Governor-General de Jonge (who had learnt from experience) wrote. Added to this, the native population was full of admiration for the rapid rise of Japan. But, while Netherlands India opposed Japanese penetration and was not much inclined to meet Japan's demands as regards trade and shipping, it was anxious not to upset its powerful neighbour more than was absolutely necessary. It was not until it became obvious during the negotiations with Japan in 1934, and more particularly in 1940, that the Japanese principle of co-existence and common prosperity would lead to the Dutch East Indies being rigidly orientated towards Japan, both economically and politically, that the Netherlands East Indies government began to offer strong resistance to the growing threat from Japan. This threat and this resistance were the harbingers of the catastrophe that was to put an end to the Netherlands' traditional policy and was to mark the beginning of the last phase, when international influences were of decisive importance to the commitments of the Dutch in Asia.

Shipping and trade were the pillars of Dutch colonial tradition. Conquest and subjugation never constituted an end in themselves; they were only, in case of need, a means of protecting vested interests overseas, which were often surrendered again under foreign pressure after a shorter or longer period of time. History has familiarised our country with the transience of colonial possession, not only in Asia. Dutch policy in the East Indies never aimed at permanent ownership. The Dutch East Indies remained a *colonie d'exploitation* despite a growing group of Eurasians who formed, as it were, a *colonie de peuplement* within the colony. The transfer and spread of European culture, including the Dutch language, always came second to the respect for and preservation of indigenous cultural values. Wherever possible, indigenous social and political structures were kept intact. The people were left under the rule of their local heads, and the colonial laws contained frequent references to religious and social institutions and customs requiring to be respected and observed by administration and judicature alike.

Dutch colonial policy was never dominated by visions of establishing a Dutch empire in Asia. Such groups as advocated this were, like the few imperialist statesmen, always overshadowed by those who realised that colonialism was essentially a progress towards an ineluctable end. In this realisation, the Netherlands' colonial policy was designed so to influence the course of this process that a new Asian state would arise, in which there would still be scope for Dutch interests, but in a different framework. The Netherlands' awareness of its vulnerability as a colonial power and of its dependence on international factors did much to crystallise this conception, the conception that pervaded Dutch colonial policy in the twentieth century.

FURTHER READING

1. *Collections of Documents*

A commission of the Historical Society at Utrecht to promote the publication of sources covering the period 1900–42 in the history of the Netherlands Indies has brought out the following volumes, edited by S. L. VAN DER WAL:

I *Het Onderwijsbeleid in Nederlands-Indië, 1900–1940* (Groningen, 1963).

II–III *De Volksraad en de staatkundige ontwikkeling van Nederlands-Indië, Eerste stuk 1891–1926* and *Tweede Stuk 1927–1942* (Groningen, 1964–5).

IV *De opkomst van de nationalistische beweging in Nederlands-Indië* (Groningen, 1967).

The main source for these publications, with an introduction and survey of the documents in English, is the archives of the former Ministry of Colonies.

2. *Secondary Works*

COOLHAAS, W. PH.: *A Critical Survey of Studies on Dutch Colonial History* (The Hague, 1960) contains a very useful bibliographical introduction to the history of Dutch colonialism; ch. iv deals with the Netherlands East Indies between 1795 and 1950.

VLEKKE, B. H. M.: *Nusantara, a History of the East Indian Archipelago* (4th ed., The Hague, 1959). A well-written introduction to the history of Dutch imperialism in South-East Asia.

FURNIVALL, J. S.: *Netherlands India: a Study of a Plural Economy* (Cambridge, 1944; repr. 1967) deals mainly with the nineteenth century.

GONGGRIJP, G.: *Schets ener Economische Geschiedenis van Indonesië* (Haarlem, 1957). A very good outline of the economic history of the Netherlands East Indies.

BAUDET, H. and BRUGMANS, I. J. (ed.): *Balans van Beleid* (Assen, 1961). A series of essays on Dutch colonial policy in the twentieth century; a useful summary in English, 'Colonial Policy Weighed: the Last Fifty Years of the Dutch East Indies in Retrospect', was published in *Acta Historiae Neerlandica*, I (1966) 212–45.

10 The Dutch Retreat from Empire

H. BAUDET

SPEAKING of contemporary history is much as when a man tells the story of his own life. It keeps getting stranded in an excess of data and a lack of outline – even though I shall commence by admitting that the data for my subject are anything but satisfactory. First, therefore, I shall have to mark out a few main lines defining a time and a situation.

On the day of the capitulation of Japan one might say that the world awoke from the long nightmare of the war into the new period of decolonisation. In so far as it had imagined these things quite differently, it was unexpectedly overwhelmed by the new revolution, which was to prove a world movement. The first scene was played out in the Netherlands East Indies, which became Indonesia. It was substantially finished when most of the others were still to begin. Thus experience was one of the many things the Netherlands lacked when the Republic of Indonesia was proclaimed on 17 August 1945 and it was necessary to take a stand and determine a policy. Moreover, all communication had been impossible for four years, four telling years. Now a whirlpool of revolutionary developments boiled up from unsuspected depths. Experience and knowledge are no guarantee of understanding, but their presence is an essential condition of it. The most unfavourable conditions of information and knowledge prevailed when the Netherlands, only three months after their own liberation and still dazed by occupation and suffering, entered upon the scene of the new world revolution – or rather, were dragged upon that scene unprepared.

Now, twenty years later, the emancipation of Europe's former colonies has become one of the facts of the world. The Indonesian revolution, which I have called the first scene of this development, is now clearly placed in history. Whether a different government,

a different judgement, or a different policy might have enabled
the Netherlands to maintain their empire, in whatever constitutional form, are questions which hardly seem worth asking today.
One might indeed wonder whether in the given political,
psychological and ethical constitution of the world any other
solution was actually attainable, particularly in that first period,
than a rigorous anti-colonial nationalism. In the vista of the years,
macro-history and micro-history seem to separate to some extent
and to loosen their organic connection, which once seemed so
decisive. Such a separation indeed existed to a certain extent.
Politics and history are made on many different levels at once.

Thus we shall need to study this past for a long time to come,
and at different levels simultaneously, if we are to form any
adequate understanding of it. We are still far from integration and
judgement. This study, though, is no easy matter. On the one hand,
the lesson of twenty years of world history is plain, although it is
neither at an end nor confined to a single interpretation. On the
other hand, comparatively little is yet available of the material
necessary to the historian. This is not a question it would be useful
to go into now, but I must confess that during the period of my
research the Dutch records had not yet been deposited in the
Algemeen Rijksarchief, which means that they were not available
to me. However, part of them are now being transferred to that
institution and can be consulted.[1]

The bibliography of the period reflects this situation. The
Netherlands, for their part, have contributed very little. The
greater part of the publications so far deemed important have
appeared abroad and are of foreign origin.[2] A few American
universities have a special programme on the subject,[3] a few
publishers a special list. In the Netherlands, however, the sources of
fundamental research are not easily accessible. The Parliamentary
Commission of Enquiry instituted after the war to form a
judgement on the conduct of the Netherlands government-in-
exile during the years of occupation extended its examination to
17 November 1945.[4] But when it reached the real Indonesian

[1] On behalf of the government M. Boon has gathered records relating to the
period, but these are mainly official papers.

[2] See Further Reading, below, pp. 232–3.   [3] E.g., Yale and Cornell Universities.

[4] *Parlementaire Enquêtecommissie Regeringsbeleid, 1940–1945 [PEC]*, VIII (The
Hague, 1956).

question it broke off its labours for rather unsatisfactory reasons. Thus we have little more to work on in the Netherlands than what has appeared in official publications (such as the reports of proceedings in the States-General) and scanty, mostly reticent memoirs (such as those of Van Mook and Drees, or those of Schermerhorn, of which we have only a certain indirect knowledge through the publication of Dr C. Smit, and recently Stikker).[1] Then there are the articles and polemics of twenty years ago and the adroit attempts of one or two historians, such as Dr Smit, using much inside information and (if you like) journalistic methods, to strike some kind of acceptable balance. Altogether this is little, though not without value. It is significant, however, that as yet not a single doctoral dissertation has been written in the Netherlands on the subject of the relinquishing of empire.

Abroad, striking publications have appeared, attracting the notice of the world. It is books like those of Kahin, Djajadinin-grat and Alastair Taylor that have laid the foundation of the historical image that is being built up. One cannot help wondering whether the meagre output of the Netherlands, by contrast, is not the mirror of a certain national indifference: there is some truth in the view that reference to the colonial past strikes on unwilling ears in the Netherlands. It is possible that the growing number of Dutch publications on Indonesia in colonial times indicates some change in this situation, although I find it difficult to answer the question whether the Dutch formerly displayed more interest in Indonesia than they did just after they had lost it.[2] It is of course true that a limited group of specialists at and outside the universities was professionally interested in Indonesian society, thought and culture generally. But I do not think that in the consciousness of the people as a whole the Dutch East Indies ever took an essential place, beyond the fact that they 'belonged to us'. Geography lessons at the elementary school inculcated this as a matter of course, and one never paused to consider it. When I was leaving school, a boy in my class who said he was going to study Indology,

[1] H. J. van Mook, *Indonesië, Nederland en de wereld* (Amsterdam, 1945); W. Drees, *Zestig jaar levenservaring* (Amsterdam, 1962); C. Smit, *Het akkoord van Linggadjati: uit het dagboek van Prof. Ir. W. Schermerhorn* (Amsterdam, 1959); D. U. Stikker, *Memoirs* (1966).

[2] H. Baudet, 'Normative Notions in Netherlands Overseas Thinking', *Trade World and World Trade*, ed. H. Baudet (Rotterdam, 1963) 183-7.

because he wanted to go into the Administration, astonished all the others, for so eccentric an idea had not occurred to any of us.

Yet during the years of retreat from empire there is no doubt that the nation was intensely gripped by the procession of events, reacting variously to each phase and decision. There was deep and stormy division in the Netherlands, ideologically and politically, and surrounding all an ethical atmosphere in which men and actions were judged good or bad, not merely politically but also morally. A history of the state of feeling during the four years from August 1945 to November 1949 (the date of the Round Table Conference) has not yet been written, and perhaps never will be. Such a history would have to take account of an exceptional strength of emotion and contrasts of mentality. It might also afford a deeper insight into the problematics of the Dutch conservative and progressive minds and traditions. Certainly the contrasts in the Netherlands were extremely pronounced. The depth of feeling will always be hard to plumb, but its extent and durability are easily shown. Far from remaining static, the situation underwent a succession of metamorphoses. On 17 August 1945 the Republic of Indonesia was proclaimed. In the spring of 1946 Dutch-Indonesian negotiations were held at the Hoge Veluwe in the Netherlands, but failed; although several times resumed during the following months and at times apparently promising, they led to no definite results. Then the Dutch tried to break the deadlock by military action. When, however, the United Nations ordered a cease-fire, fresh negotiations were opened on board the American warship *Renville*. They too proved unsatisfactory, and the Dutch took up arms again. But soon they were forced by the Security Council to stop firing, and finally, on 2 November 1949, the Indonesians and the Dutch met at the so-called Round Table Conference in the Netherlands, where they agreed on the unconditional surrender of sovereignty. While events thus ran from one situation to another, the air was continuously filled with the heated actions and reactions of the political parties and formations which for one reason or another felt themselves concerned in the great drama: with demonstrations, mass meetings, petitions from the Right and the Left; with protests, speeches at rallies, initiatives of all kinds and threatened strikes too, whenever a crucial moment seemed to have arrived – some possible turning-point, some decisive parting of the ways.

An inclination to discern decisive moments is still rather characteristic of historical analysis and will probably long remain so. At a certain level, and from a certain point of view, it is quite justified. Much, very much, has of course always depended on personal decisions. And, as the conservative opposition was fond of saying in those days, the Indonesian revolt was not a phenomenon of nature. I believe, however, that generally speaking experience has taught – at least in French Indo-China, Algeria and the Congo – that neither a policy of armed suppression nor a complete and immediate compliance with nationalist demands will ensure that matters will pass off satsifactorily.[1] Of course I do not overlook fundamental differences between one case and another.

A few words are in place here on the comparison frequently made between Indonesia and India. More than once no less an authority than J. S. Furnivall contrasted the administration of the Netherlands East Indies with that of Burma and India, praising it as the best colonial government in the world.[2] Perhaps he was right – certainly from his point of view upon the 'plural society' and its administrative requirements. Yet circumstances, and not merely a better and more realistic policy, made the retreat of the British easier than that of the more moralistic and formalistic Dutch. Some of the most noticeable of these circumstances may be summarised. To begin with, India had an unshaken sense of self-esteem, rooted in an ancient culture which has been studied with respect by the whole world, and greatly admired by Europe in particular. It had a cultivated ruling class, in part of ancient culture and tradition, and in any case feeling itself to be such. Education had been attuned to this class, not to the masses, as in the Netherlands East Indies. There a generally better educational system had probably been built up; yet too little account had been taken of the political pay-off. Furthermore India had not been occupied by the Japanese nor Britain by the Germans. There was not that total ignorance of the psychological, political and military developments during the Japanese period which so paralysed the Netherlands. Also, Britain was not taken by surprise, as was the Netherlands, by the revolutionary proclama-

[1] Drees, 193.
[2] J. S. Furnivall, *Colonial Policy and Practice* (Cambridge, 1948) 268–79; cf. idem, *Netherlands India* (Cambridge, 1944).

tion of a republic. Britain did not have 80,000 countrymen in Japanese camps, who, so far from being liberated, remained as hostages in Republican hands and were so used.[1] Nor would I neglect the accidental factor of the difference in personality between Sukarno and Nehru. Other differences were of influence too, in part perhaps differences of a more structural kind. Britain was a great nation with a great language, of enormous importance for India. The Netherlands were a small country with a small language and little faith in it, and little inclination to inspire others with such faith. Dutch did not become a collective link throughout the heterogeneous archipelago; it was indeed the deliberate educational policy of the former Netherlands Indies administration that it should not play this role. The government never did anything to make the language function in this political sense. In the course of time many Indians, but never a single Indonesian, have spoken to me of the essential meaning for them of the common tie of the colonial *lingua franca*.

Apart from all this, one can point to the great economic differences between India and Indonesia. By Asiatic standards, India already had a considerable industrial development and a comparative plenitude of capital, while the carefully protected economy of the Netherlands East Indies rested on raw materials. There were profound differences of social and racial structure between the two countries, and particularly were there contrasts in urbanisation and urban society. One might work out the effect this would have had on revolutionary feeling, though admittedly that would be speculation. Far more potent is the fact that with respect to Britain India's trading account showed a credit, while Indonesia's showed a debit with respect to the Netherlands.[2]

Then there were differences in the political and military situations. Above all, deprived of power, the Netherlands had to face events after the Japanese capitulation in a state of complete dependence on Britain, where under the new Labour government there was less inclination than ever to interfere with a hornet's nest in favour of the totally foreign views and interests of the

---

[1] Cf. *PEC*, VIII 721.

[2] After the war the Netherlands had a claim on Indonesia of about three milliard guilders, including the claim for Netherlands property confiscated by the Republic. India, on the contrary, at that moment had a claim upon England of the order of ten milliard guilders.

Netherlands. At the same time the British did not allow their retreat from India, after the transference of sovereignty there, to be influenced by the knowledge that they would leave the country in a state of bitter civil war.

Nowhere – and this goes for India too – did decolonisation take place without tremendous difficulties and terrible side-effects. For India the number of at least half a million dead is given, compared with which the hundreds of victims in Indonesia are negligible.[1] I stress this here because it brings me back to the problem of the various planes of historical reality. As soon as one regards general decolonisation as the great world phenomenon of the century, the dead become of small account and many of the ruinous consequences of the ending of Western administration no longer seem to matter. Thus in the course of the past twenty years Europe has assimilated its greater retreat and embodied it in a new image of the world and a new general outlook upon history. The speed (by historical standards) with which this was done, and the way it was taken for granted, raise some intricate questions for future historians. The ability shown to give up an entire coherent and normative system, so to say within a few years, and replace it by something else, presents curious problems to anyone who really wants to understand what took place in people's minds on the watershed between two eras.

Colonialism, whatever that may be, and trusteeship have been replaced by the new plurality of sovereign national states, and thus a system of older terms of thought has been completely superseded by another, which will not prove permanent either, although perhaps the new system may yet stabilise itself within our lifetime in a way we do not dream of now. If so, I have every confidence that our faculty of assimilation will not fail us any more than previously; no doubt we shall once again produce an historical image to support the natural logic of something like an immanent historical principle. Today self-determination, non-intervention, international co-operation, aid to under-developed countries – these are the key phrases that have taken the place of the old system. Tomorrow they may in turn be replaced or acquire a different meaning, in keeping with a new, generally accepted, self-evident reality displayed in the main lines of history.

Are all the other stratifications of historical reality thereby

[1] Cf. Drees, 194.

discredited, or at any rate degraded into accidentals and futilities? No historian will accept that. He sees a phenomenon, in this case the Netherlands' retreat from empire, as in the first place a matter of unique factual circumstances. To him it is a particular case, distinct from all others. Only on that basis is the writing of history really possible. Anatole France summed up the whole history of the world in the single sentence that men are born, suffer and die.[1] Yet recognition of this profound truth can never be the final word in history, and indeed it was not the perspective of those participating in the drama with which we are concerned. There were certain circumstances, continually multiplying, of a short-term character in themselves and greatly dependent on apparently arbitrary decisions, which could well have been otherwise. At the same time, a development had begun in the world which in the following years was to sweep away all, or nearly all, opposing measures and decisions taken or attempted. The people themselves on either side, the people whom we historians would wish to fathom in order to know what really happened, lived and acted in more than one dimension at once, and often disharmoniously. It is therefore no explanation to say on one level that the Indonesians wished *this* and the short-sighted Hollanders *that*, and that they debated and fought for four years, after which the facts themselves had simply proved that the Netherlands were weak and in the wrong and lacked vision. Any such construction is also quite untenable in a wider European context.

History, at any rate this history which we ourselves have seen and taken part in and are trying to clarify, has not the regal simplicity of chess, where the decision lies between two clearly contrasted ideas or strategies. Yet I choose this metaphor in order to point out that in another respect the comparison is valid. There was a chess board, the historical scene; and before the Netherlands had the opportunity of putting in an appearance there, the pieces had been set up and the positions determined. This broad fact is fundamental for the whole sequel. The Netherlands had to play from an unfortunate position which was not of their own choosing.

There are many facts to recall, such as the refusal of both British and Americans to allow Prime Minister Schermerhorn to be heard in Potsdam in July 1945 – though Mountbatten was

---

[1] *Les Opinions de M. Jérôme Coignard*, ch. xvi, 'L'Histoire'.

there.[1] To confine myself to a few other main points, there was Mountbatten's communication to Van der Plas[2] (Singapore, 27 September 1945) of the immutable decision of the British government that not a single British soldier (they were mostly Indians) would be used for the restoration of the Netherlands' authority; that the Hollanders would have to restore it themselves, occupy Java themselves, and so on. But at the same time the Allied Command refused to admit Dutch troops to Java. Again, there was the (then) sensational declaration of the British general, Christison, on 29 September 1945,[3] announcing the landing of British units to disarm the Japanese (though the Japanese left their weapons and munitions in the hands of the often extremist Indonesian fighting groups): the British units, Christison declared, would come as guests of the Indonesians – he did not say 'of the Indonesian government', but the intention was perfectly clear and was indeed confirmed in word and deed afterwards. Christison requested the leaders of the republican party to assist him in the carrying out of his task, adding that the Indonesian republican authorities would remain responsible for the administration of the areas under their control.[4] This amounted to a *de facto* acknowledgement, while ignoring the views immediately laid before Christison by other Indonesian parties. After Van Kleffens, the Netherlands minister of foreign affairs, had protested to Bevin, Noel-Baker declared in Parliament on 17 October that His Majesty's Government naturally acknowledged none other than the Netherlands-Indies government over all territories under Netherlands sovereignty, though this formula was obviously ambiguous.[5] It did nothing to remove the deep impression made by Christison's declaration of 29 September. In effect, the explicit agreements that had been made, first in May 1945 with the United States and subsequently with England under the Civil Affairs Agreement, were not kept.

I spoke of our inclination to look for decisive moments, on the assumption that there were crucial points when a definite chance

[1] *PEC*, VIII 475.

[2] Dr Ch. O. van der Plas, born in 1891, was from 1936 to 1942 governor of East Java and acted in 1945 as the adviser of Dr van Mook.

[3] *PEC*, VIII 654, 664, 677, 714.

[4] Ibid., 700; cf. Van Mook, 90, 93.

[5] Djajadiningrat, *The Beginnings of the Indonesian-Dutch Negotiations* (New York, 1958) 46; cf. *PEC*, VIII 674, 706.

was missed. The Parliamentary Commission of Enquiry also adopted this line, but not without reason. The hearings reflected the general opinion that the alteration of the frontiers of the areas of command in the Pacific, agreed upon again in Potsdam, was of far-reaching and possibly decisive importance.[1] Long before the end of the war the Netherlands government had requested the government of the United States to support its authority in the Netherlands East Indies. Such support was then undertaken as a temporary commitment, and MacArthur was to bear the responsibility.[2] There were related agreements of detail with the American army for providing the necessary material when the time came. Also MacArthur had projected a direct push through Borneo to Java, a plan which included the restoration of the Netherlands-Indies government in New Guinea as well. The carrying out of this project, however, was then forbidden by the Combined Chiefs of Staff in Washington for reasons unknown to us. Moreover, American public opinion, already traditionally anti-colonial, became more and more set against the idea of the restoration of a colonial empire – a feeling much quickened after the capitulation of Japan.[3]

Though there need be no doubt as to the inclination and the plans of MacArthur with regard to the Netherlands East Indies, it is at best very doubtful whether the development at the outset in a South-West Pacific Area setting would really have been more favourable for the Netherlands than it now became in the context of the South-East Asia Command. Opinion in the Netherlands government was divided. Churchill had declared to the Dutch ambassador in London, Michiels van Verduynen: 'You will get the Indies back.'[4] This might give grounds for preferring a British South-East Asia Command. But Van Mook and Van Kleffens,[5] both members of the Dutch government in London,

---

[1] Ibid., 721; cf. C. Smit, *De liquidatie van een imperium* (Amsterdam, 1962) 15.

[2] *PEC*, VIII 507 (Helfrich), 499 and the quotation of MacArthur given there; cf. Willoughby and Chamberlain, *Life of MacArthur 1941–51* (New York, 1954).

[3] *PEC*, VIII 514 (Van Kleffens).   [4] Djajadiningrat, 12.

[5] Dr H. J. van Mook (1894–1965) was a specialist in Indonesian affairs who became minister of the colonies in 1941, residing in Indonesia, then acted as governor general of the East Indies and took refuge in Australia in 1942; later he went to London where he entered the Dutch cabinet-in-exile; he played an important though unsuccessful part in the events after 1945. Dr E. N. van Kleffens, born in 1894, was from 1939 to 1946 minister of foreign affairs.

expected more from the maintenance of the existing S.W.P.A., probably also because of a mistaken estimate of American public opinion. The final result was that the government did nothing whatever; it did not react to the plans and demarcations, but trustfully accepted things as they came. The first post-war cabinet in the Netherlands, led by Schermerhorn and Drees,[1] in the end considered the situation not without optimism.[2] Though the British had no troops or war material in the Pacific, they would undoubtedly feel the sympathy of allies for the Netherlands' interests, and all the assistance within their power might be expected from them – perhaps even more than from the tradition-ally anti-colonial Americans.

In recent historiography the great significance of the division of command of 15 August, which was so essential for British prestige in particular, is rightly insisted on. It is obvious that it greatly influenced later developments, in many different directions. Yet though it must be admitted that at this parting of the ways history took a course particularly troublous for the Netherlands at the time, it does not follow that the alternative would have proved so much more satisfactory. Van Mook admitted as much afterwards in a rather convincing manner, contrary to his original views.[3] There were more of such apparently crucial moments in the succeeding years. There had been some before 1942 also. We shall return to this. However, the evaluation of alternatives and the distribution of blame, dear to the historian, is a precarious matter, as in the example given here. Equally precarious is it to estimate the motives behind the choices – in so far as there were choices to be made – especially on the basis of the exiguous information we have to make do with at present.

And what can we say of those Dutchmen who, comparatively close to the events and yet in a position of some detachment, were able to observe some matters and wanted to form an opinion? My difficulty is that in many contrary views there is some truth or reasonableness, or at least plausibility. I think I may say that

---

[1] W. Schermerhorn, born 1894, professor at the Technical University of Delft, was prime minister of the first post-war cabinet. W. Drees, born 1886, member of the Socialist party, led the cabinet of 1945 with Schermerhorn and had, in contrast with his collaborator, a long political career afterwards.

[2] PEC, VIII 519 (Schermerhorn); cf. Djajadiningrat, 13–15.

[3] Personally stated to me by Van Mook.

the idea of a new relationship to be given form at a General Conference of State, such as Queen Wilhemina had announced in her broadcast of 7 December 1942, was generally accepted in the Netherlands from the beginning. The principle of self-government for the Netherlands East Indies was not disputed: but was self-government to be the same as independence? And who were to be the leaders of that self-governing Indonesia of the future? Here the answer depended on the angle from which the participant looked out at an imagined world future, on his principles and on his stand as between principles and expediency. The great contrast was between two views, one of which envisaged a society in Indonesia mixed as it 'always' had been and unavoidably embracing various social and racial groups on different social and economic levels. The other view accepted a nationalistic society as inevitable, an Indonesian Indonesia, indeed with various groups upon different social levels, but based on other principles and above all without Europeans, at least in their traditional function.

What the new republic really was, or was intended to be, could hardly be made out from the faulty information of the time, even by the best-informed. What was the strength of the rebel movement? How far did the Indonesians in general regard it as a Japanese manoeuvre and therefore something to be rejected? Would the great mass of the population, or the moderates, approve the restoration of the Netherlands authority for a period of transition? Would the Republic collapse through inner dissension – widespread, as we now know? All this was uncertain.[1] Mountbatten's prompt assertion that Sukarno's republican government was most firmly founded, and that it disposed of a well-armed military force of 100,000 men, may have rested upon data supplied by the British agent Van der Post (who deserves the attention of historians), and it made an impression in London. All the same, it was a flight of imagination: as to the real effectives of the Republic, general ignorance still prevailed for a long time. Owing to poor communications – the radio did not penetrate, while telegrams went through British channels which restricted the Netherlands to a few hours a day and a word-limit – this state of ignorance was prolonged far more than it need have been.[2]

Nevertheless, all possible measures were at once inaugurated in

[1] *PEC*, VIII 704 (Logemann).   [2] Ibid.

the Netherlands to build up an expeditionary force: not for restoring former conditions nor for weakening the plan for a General Conference of State, but to make such a Conference possible and fruitful. All responsible persons were agreed upon this. Yet when, in the first week of October 1945, a few companies – formed of prisoners-of-war liberated in Borneo and under an Indonesian commander – landed in Tandjong Priok, the British High Command forbade their access to Batavia (now Jakarta) on the ground that it would constitute a provocation.[1] I mention this because, here again, there seemed to be a decisive moment. These are the facts we have. Nasution, who had been a resistance leader against the Japanese occupation, then offered to supply the vacancy in authority with 10,000 youngsters furnished with Japanese arms. But General Van Straten and Colonel Abdulkadir[2] found they could do nothing. In those same days, be it said in passing, Indonesian intellectuals presented to the British Admiral Patterson the draft of an agreement embodying a trusteeship, with the Netherlands as the mandatory country. Its ultimate aim was collaboration with the Netherlands, though not as part of a single state.[3] However, Admiral Patterson (who afterwards told General Spoor[4] that he was disgusted at what he had to do)[5] was merely instructed to refuse the draft as lying outside his instructions.[6] Far more important was the controversy between Sjahrir[7] and Sukarno which became acute at that time.

Sjahrir's cabinet did not take office till 14 November 1945. For a considerable time Sjahrir and his supporters, who had led the resistance against Japan, remained aloof from Sukarno, expecting the arrival of allied forces.[8] We are fairly well informed about this

---

[1] *PEC*, VIII 606 ff. (Schilling), 874 (Van Straten). Personally stated to me by Raden Sardjono Suria Santoso (born 1898, officer in the Dutch army in the East Indies and then in the Indonesian army).

[2] Th. L. W. van Straten, born 1897, acted from October 1945 as chief commanding officer in Java, Madura, Bali and Lombok. Raden Abdulkadir Widjojoatmodjo, born 1904, was a colonel in the Dutch Indonesian Army.

[3] Personally stated to me by Suria Santoso.

[4] General S. H. Spoor, born 1902.

[5] Personally stated to me by Spoor.

[6] Personally stated to me by Suria Santoso; cf. *PEC*, VIII 874 (Van Straten).

[7] Sutan Sjahrir (1909–66) studied in the Netherlands and became in the 'thirties a leading nationalist. After 1945 he tried unsuccessfully to steer a middle course between Sukarno's radicalism and the Dutch conceptions.

[8] Personally stated to me by Suria Santoso.

by Sjahrir himself, who wrote a pamphlet on the situation and his ideas about it:

At the moment when the free Indonesian state was founded, its leadership was almost entirely in the hands of former helpers and officials of Japan. This prevented the purging of our society of the Japanese sickness, which was a mortal danger to our youth. Most of those who held the reins of the Indonesian Republic were not strong men . . . they had bowed too often and run too fast in the service of Japan; finally, they thought they had got into power for the very reason that they had collaborated with Japan.[1]

Obviously this referred directly to Sukarno, and it was justified; I might well go on quoting. Yet if one were to regard these words and ideas as elements of another crucial situation in which the way was missed to a speedy peace, I think one would be over-estimating the authority of what I may call Sjahrir's conception, and underestimating the fanatical passion in the violent revolutionary stir. Also it would mean neglecting the direct link that undoubtedly existed between developments in the latter part of September and those aspects of the division of command in August to which we have already referred. Mountbatten set the condition for increased British shipment of troops to Java: namely, that 'the Netherlands-Indies government should be willing to begin discussions with Sukarno and his adherents immediately'. Later on, this was reduced to beginning 'discussions with the nationalists, Sukarno expressly not excepted'.[2] There are no serious grounds for supposing that an American command would have taken up a different attitude towards Sukarno and backed up the Netherlands' fundamental objection to him because of his collaboration with the Japanese.

There were plenty of incidents in the following months that might have been turning-points in history and were so looked on in passing. Thus the death of Brigadier Mallaby in the disturbances in Surabaya in November 1945 aroused British sentiment against the Republic. Christison himself in those days spoke of this as 'a turning-point', but this affair had no public consequences.[3] At the Singapore conference of 6 December, Mountbatten

[1] Sutan Sjahrir, *Onze Strijd* (Amsterdam, 1945) 13, 15; cf. Djajadiningrat, 35 ff.
[2] *PEC*, VIII 655 (Van der Plas); cf. Djajadiningrat, 23 ff.
[3] Djajadiningrat, 39–40; Van Mook, 100.

informed the Dutch representatives of his decision to continue
a policy of barring entrance into Java and Sumatra of any additional Netherlands forces. Despite the strongest protest of the
Dutch military commanders, Mountbatten remained adamant on
this point, according to Djajadiningrat.[1]

Now that I have the opportunity to speak of this period in
Britain, I should like to set forth these matters plainly – not in
order to conclude that a malicious anti-Netherlands policy on
Britain's part was at the root of the main difficulties, but to show
that the world situation had brought the Netherlands into an
impasse. To this impasse British policy, constrained by its own
problems and cares, contributed.

These first months decided the positions from which in the
ensuing years the negotiations were conducted and the battle was
joined. While the Netherlands government formulated the main
lines of its standpoint and intentions in a series of declarations,[2]
always trying to follow the situation and develop a political
initiative, the revolution in Indonesia went on. The Republic –
most cleverly and with a keen political sense – continually created
a situation just a little ahead of the latest feat of adaptation the
Netherlands had arrived at.[3] One might put it the other way
round and say that for four years the Netherlands vainly tried to
keep up with events. A world revolution had indeed set in, to which
the Netherlands could in the end only yield, hard though the
country might find it to do so. Yet this development was
accompanied by a Republican policy of what one might call
continually shaking off the enemy and forcing him to further
exhausting manoeuvres against continual short, quick, tactical
attacks. This was true even in the literal sense, for the Republic
never for a moment kept to the later truces, but with a bewildering
insincerity conducted and financed guerrilla warfare, murder,
sabotage and destruction.[4]

It was this phenomenon – the fact that Sukarno's republic,
which internationally was soon beyond attack, always managed
to stay some way in front – which made Schermerhorn speak of
the permanent disparity of phase between Jakarta and The Hague –

[1] PEC, vIII 623–5 (Helfrich), 626 (Van Mook); cf. Djajadiningrat, 47.

[2] For instance, the declarations of 6 November 1945 (printed in Van Mook, 247)
and 10 February 1946.

[3] Cf. Drees, 200, 238.   [4] Ibid., 238–9.

a disparity which continually blocked agreements that seemed to be on the verge of conclusion.[1] Schermerhorn was alluding in the first place to the contact between government and governor-general. This disparity of phase, however, was undoubtedly a consequence of Republican policy. It played its part in the abortive conference of Hoge Veluwe, in spring 1946. It wrecked the agreement of Linggadjati, in spring 1947, which culminated in a full-blown military conflict entirely without political perspective. At last, in 1949, the Dutch had to agree, and in majority did so eagerly, to the complete and unconditional transference of sovereignty and the ceding of all influence.

It is neither necessary nor possible to discuss all this in full at present. Might one say that the conflicts, the conferences, the armed conflict in the micro-sphere of practical politics, had yet, seen in a wider historical context, merely an instrumental function with regard to the macro-process of decolonisation that was in progress? Such a formulation would see the eventual solution as the only one fitting the historical logic of this development. The nationalism of the Republic in August 1945, however, was not the only nationalism in Indonesia. There were national movements everywhere in the heterogeneous archipelago, and ever since the conference of Malino the Netherlands had been in negotiation with them. It was to the Federal United States of Indonesia, combining all these units, that the Netherlands transferred sovereignty in 1949. Within the shortest time imaginable the Republic of Jokja had liquidated all the partners and founded the unified state.

In the first and decisive stage the international positions were, I think, indeed laid down. In another way the same might be said of the conflict of opinion in the Netherlands at home. Politically the conflict was between the left-wing government of 1945–6 and the opposition from the Right – that of 'the old colonials [wrote Van Mook] whose voice at first drowned out that of the others, and who were politically a generation behind'.[2] I think his description misjudges two things. On the one hand (and this was to have important political consequences), the opposition ran through a far wider scale, was divided in itself and also divided the parties in the government, particularly the Roman Catholic Party, which took part in the government from the beginning.

[1] Smit, *Linggadjati*, e.g. 13.   [2] Van Mook, 108, 113.

Thus there was no question of a single split as, for example, between Indonesian self-government and independence. On the other hand (and this is partly the same phenomenon), the contrast between Left and Right was at any rate not that between backward conservatism, trying to set back the clock and preserve the old system, and enlightened progressiveness blessed with a monopoly of seeing the world in true perspective. With respect to the loud voice of the old colonials that Van Mook wrote of, their standpoint may be said to have been that the former society of the Indies had indeed collapsed owing to the Japanese occupation, but that the foundations of a society which had been in vigorous development still existed.[1]

Evidence for this view included the enthusiastic reception accorded to the Dutch in other parts than Java. Perhaps this view was mistaken. Information was defective, for all parties; and perhaps certain pre-war criteria and ideas as to the future were active here, since knowledge of actual conditions only came in bit by bit and judgement was perforce based on piecemeal information. The curious thing is that these ideas were not conservative, but rather, by a pre-war standard, ideas of a slightly anti-Netherlands and progressive character.[2] They had been formed in the years of the great crisis, when the colonies bore the brunt of the Netherlands policy of maintaining the gold standard, being economically vulnerable producers of raw materials. This vision of the Right saw a society composed of different peoples living together in Indonesia, the general masses led by an intermixed upper class – a kind of South America, but without its drawbacks. There the initial Netherlands element would gradually transfer its ascendancy to the components of the indigenous upper class. This process of development would gradually continue downwards. The Right disputed that the extremists, whose only practical work before the war had been demolition, violent opposition to the Netherlands, should now be looked on as the very leaders needed in Indonesia. They wished rather for the speedy construction of a new Indonesia, with far more place assigned to Indonesians and to rapid evolution, but without the total destruction of all the old foundations of the mixed society.

[1] J. W. Meyer Ranneft, *De weg voorr Indië* (Amsterdam, 1945) 59 ff.
[2] E.g. idem, 'Nederland's fout in Indië', *De Gids* (1937). In 1937 W. K. H. Feuilleteau de Bruyn supported the petition of Sutardjo.

For, as Meyer Ranneft said, addressing the University of Groningen, 'the question for Indonesia is not whether it will become independent but how it will fit into one of the two great spheres of influence', which, as we know, had already begun to appear before the capitulation of Japan.[1]

It may be argued that the pre-war mixed society of the Netherlands-Indies had not been so peaceful as it was represented here, and that after all the vicissitudes of the war it no longer offered a starting-point for a new construction. The prediction that the struggle between the two great spheres of influence was to be of capital importance for Indonesia, however, was well judged. That, for the rest, the tremendous world problem of the near future would be the relations between 'haves' and 'have-nots', and that the revolution in Indonesia stood in just this context, this was recognised on both sides, Left and Right. One side, however, saw this only as a further argument in favour of a nationalist solution, while the other regarded it as an extra confirmation of their view that the quick restoration of order, as a condition for rehabilitating the economy and effectively combating hunger, should take priority above all else – and that this restoration necessitated the curbing of the revolution.

The opposition, however, did not have the task of actually carrying out a policy. The little I was able to see, but which on several points was more than others saw, gave me the conviction that the Netherlands governments of those first stages certainly made mistakes, but that in the main no Netherlands government would have been able to obtain much better results, considering the powers then at work. If I seem to have lingered too long over the first six months of the conflict – exactly the reverse of what most authors have done – this is to emphasise as much as possible the position from which the Netherlands had to play. Others had set the pieces on the board, the duty of the Netherlands was to make good moves from an impossible position. In such a situation one makes mistakes, unnecessary no doubt, but hardly avoidable. For instance, it was mistaken timing to negotiate at the Hoge Veluwe in the spring of 1946, immediately before the elections,

---

[1] Dr J. W. Meyer Ranneft (1887–1968) was a civil servant in the Dutch East Indies and after 1945 a conservative opponent of Dutch policy towards the colony. For what follows see Sutan Sjahrir, *Indonesische Overpeinzingen* (Amsterdam, 1966) 118–19, 144–5, 189–90.

which should and could have been held much earlier but had been put off so long on inadequate grounds. Again, it was a mistake to take no part in the politics of Indonesia, particularly in the dissension between Sjahrir and Sukarno: that we 'had no right' to do so was nonsense, of course, for every country joins in the internal affairs of other countries. Then there was the great lack of understanding of the value of publicity on the part of the government, at any rate during the first stages. They neither made an adequate political use of publicity themselves nor ever properly understood the real power of the active anti-Netherlands publicity in the world. They never got a grip upon it. Far too late, in 1949, an initiative of the Netherlands press attaché in New York, Dr Friedericy, led to the journey of the fifteen American journalists to Indonesia which came to such a tragic end: Burton Heath, Charles Gratke, Barrows, Newton, Knickerbocker, Moorad and seven others perished in an air disaster at Bombay. In the booklet *Last Testimony* their articles about the journey were brought together too late to have any effect.[1]

Generally speaking, the Netherlands encountered their opponent in the full armour of Dutch national peculiarity: paternalism, faith in discussion, constitutionalism, perfectionism, a juridical way of thinking probably characteristic of a nation of traders.[2] The Indonesians countered this with ease. Moreover, as time went on, it became clearer and clearer that the failure of negotiations was more to their advantage than success. In May 1951 Sjahrir stated to Mr Mitchener of the *New York Herald Tribune*:

I would have accomplished little if the Dutch had not sent some of the most stupid, aloof and arrogant men I have ever known. We kept our mouths shut and let the Dutch talk. They argued themselves to death. No one could hear their stupidities without knowing they had no moral right to govern any colony.

I cannot resist continuing the quotation, though it is not in context here. 'But', said Sjahrir, 'I am afraid that if China captures all of Asia we are doomed. That is why I never mention New Guinea or Malaya. What Indonesia needs is not more land in New Guinea

---

[1] Published by Knickerbocker, New York, 1949.
[2] Cf. Drees, 194–5, 235–6; Smit, *Liquidatie*, 227.

but a better land here at home. Right now we need men with low voices and high ideals. . . .'[1]

I do not believe that if all the Dutch mistakes could have been avoided – and could they? – the results would have been so much better for both countries. I will illustrate this with a single example. The crucial moment of the Hoge Veluwe conference was certainly not chosen by the government. One might say that Van Mook pushed it through, consciously or unconsciously disregarding parliamentary conditions in the Netherlands.[2] The Netherlands delegation now had to negotiate without the backing of a parliamentary mandate. For the existing emergency parliament mainly reflected the political situation of 1937[3] – new elections were set only for 17 May 1946. Naturally it was not possible or desirable to rush through elections in the two weeks between the drafting of Van Mook's agreement with Sjahrir and the beginning of discussions in the Netherlands. But of course elections should and could have been held far earlier, as was repeatedly insisted on.[4] Schermerhorn, however, who rather lacked political flair, was taken with the idea of the so-called break-through – that is, breaking through the pre-war parliamentary party system, which was regarded as fossilised – and hoped for a new political union, and so thought the time and the country far from ripe for elections. The Partij van de Arbeid (the new Labour Party) was moreover founded only in February 1946. Thus the elections were not held until it was impossible to put them off any longer. Yet Schermerhorn's views may be held to confirm the idea that earlier elections would certainly not have made for a chamber of representatives more suitable to a government that had to negotiate on the basis of the minimum Indonesian demand, which was *de facto* recognition of the Republic's authority in Java and Sumatra. The facts at least have shown that even cabinets starting out with the intention of altering policy continually found themselves in an

[1] *New York Herald Tribune*, 4 May 1951, 1 and 5 (col. 2): 'And let the Dutch talk.' In the minutes available to me of the various Netherlands-Indonesian negotiations, taken by the joint secretariat, I had the curiosity to count the number of lines on either side: the Dutch did four or five times as much talking as the Indonesians.

[2] As against Djajadiningrat see Smit, *Liquidatie*, 35–6.

[3] Cf. Drees, 145–6.

[4] Cf. W. J. van Welderen Rengers, *Schets eener Parlementaire Geschiedenis*, 4 (The Hague, 1956) 261.

impasse, both on the international and on the parliamentary plane.

Here are plenty of problems for the historian free to begin the examination of the Netherlands sources. Even the bare facts are still largely uncertain. The mere comparison of the few memoirs now available is a revelation in this respect. It will be necessary to gain far greater knowledge of the political possibilities effectively open to successive Netherlands administrations, internationally but also nationally. What relationship was there between the men and the party trends in the teams that succeeded one another in office? What was their relationship with the intelligent and self-willed governor-general, who for his part regarded the Netherlands administrations as a set of nincompoops, yet for a complex of reasons was maintained in office almost until 1948? For another thing, the internal deliberations of the government must be enquired into as well as their international consultations – particularly with the British government. The quality of the information available for these discussions must also be examined. The reports of the embassies should certainly form some of the most important material.

In this way I might go on enumerating matters in need of an exact account, where as yet we depend too much on incomplete and private information. Thus we shall not know until much later whether it was really necessary that matters should have gone quite so badly as they did, or whether it might have been possible to make a better move from an apparently hopeless position on the chessboard.

Developments that took place at various levels, at differing speeds, harmonising or not, working upon one another or not, will always confront the historian with the problem of their integration in the human mind. There is something else, however: economic data and economic movements have a force of their own with a certain measure of autonomy. The Netherlands' retreat from empire might have taken place without many of the accompanying economic phenomena and without very noticeable economic consequences, as has been known to occur in other such instances. Economic life and transactions may go their own way without being much affected by political or even psychological vicissitudes. Liquidation of the Netherlands empire might have taken place without great alterations in the structure of economic relations – at any rate in the sector of enterprise.

As is well known, the question of the remunerativeness of colonies has always been a matter of concern. 'The Indies gone, prosperity done' was an old Dutch saying – in spite of the experience, for instance, of England after 1783, when liberal economists even discovered that colonies were nothing but a drag upon prosperity. There were other sayings and favourite quotations of similar tenor. They were mainly coined in the previous century, and our century had accepted them as self-evident truths, without troubling much to enquire after more exact quantitative data. According to this view, the Indies were one of the two or three economic rafts the Netherlands floated upon; the major part of the national prosperity was due to the colonies. Was this true? We have only a single fairly exact calculation, made after the war, for not more than one pre-war year. Tinbergen and Derksen estimated in 1945 that, in the year 1938, of the total national income of 4.9 milliard guilders, 13.7 per cent came from the Indies.[1] That is a considerable proportion. One would like to see similar calculations over long periods. One vainly wishes one could make an estimate for the whole nineteenth century; at least one would wish to know the fluctuations of the share taken by the Indies in the economic development of the twentieth century, which saw the Indies become more and more part of the world economy as supplier of raw materials. In particular, one could wish for a sketch of the years of crisis before 1938.

In any case, the pre-war state was replaced by something quite different after 1945. The upward trend of the economy of the Netherlands-Indies, which had been overcoming the worst consequences of the Great Depression, was completely broken by the Japanese occupation. Theoretically everyone could see the great future reserved to the Indonesian production area; in practice that future was not so easy to realise. The companies operating in Indonesia were confronted with the destruction or neglect of their capital investment overseas in circumstances which hardly favoured their restoration and a new start. Political uncertainty, organised robbery, theft and insecurity in general were added to unwilling workers, increased cost of labour and decline in its

---

[1] J. Tinbergen and J. B. D. Derksen, 'Berekeningen over de economische betekenis van Nederlandsch-Indië voor Nederland', *Maandblad Centraal Bureau voor Statistiek*, 10/12 (1945) 10. Cf. W. Gorter, 'Enkele gedachten over de economische betekenis van het verlies van Indonesië', *De Economist*, CVIII (10) (1960).

productivity, impediments to the immigration of European experts and many other restrictive measures, while in the background the Netherlands were laboriously rising out of the morass: such were the facts and factors burdening great and small companies. The annual report of the Netherlands Bank for 1945 stated that 'the Netherlands-Indies, instead of being able again to contribute considerably to our national economy as supplier of raw materials and market for our products, have on the contrary occasioned the withdrawal of considerable assets from our national economy, partly as a result of the military effort we were obliged to make'.

There are not yet many annual reports of companies from these first years. Those which appeared were very brief and even more sketchy than usual. Were they as gloomy as they were scarce? Some of them were – necessarily so, especially in reporting factual circumstances which necessitated a plain statement. On the other hand, industry was notable in soon displaying considerable self-confidence. It may be objected that this is a matter of course in a report to shareholders. Keeping to the main lines, I will only instance Amsterdam-Rubber. In 1946 this company stated their conviction that the complete recovery of trade and industry in the Indies was only a matter of time, and said they faced the future with confidence. Other annual reports expressed their faith in their own and in the general recovery. A good deal of the optimism displayed in these vague generalities was of course mere façade, but behind that optimism a feverish activity was attacking the problems of rehabilitation and possible reorientation.

The various companies, so different in kind and placed in such varying circumstances, could not follow parallel courses ahead. And yet these courses began to be plotted, as already clearly appears in accounts of 1947. The report of the Netherlands Bank irrefutably showed the quickening of trade with Indonesia. The increasing exchange of goods reflected the gradual improvement of economic conditions in Indonesia – and in the Netherlands also. The impression might even be given, because many companies resumed the paying of dividends, that the traditional structure was reasserting itself in a remarkable way. This was also important for the Netherlands because in the pre-war system trade between the Netherlands, the Netherlands East Indies and the United States had formed one of the foundations of the national economy.

Certainly, the amounts now involved were still very far from the pre-war figures. For many plantations and mining concerns, especially small ones, the situation remained difficult owing to their location and local circumstances, often through lack of money, and because of the drastic damage done to sites and installations, particularly by incompetent handling during the Japanese occupation. Here rehabilitation could only proceed bit by bit. On the other hand, a number of other undertakings soon managed to make substantial profits. The total picture for 1947 and 1948 was already that of a general activity to put things in order, of manifest confidence and a certain optimism in spite of the way political developments kept deteriorating. Conditions had changed, but there was no reason to react with a loss of confidence. It was indeed a difficult matter to judge of the political situation in its economical aspect, especially if a change in the policy of a concern was at issue. In general terms, the question was whether Western industry would be able to continue its business whatever developments might occur.

In detail, the political, economic and social possibilities of carrying on determined the choice between remaining or switching over to other fields of enterprise, either by settling outside Indonesia and so exporting acquired experience to another part of the world, or by entire reorientation of the undertaking. Long before the transfer of sovereignty this problem had an important place in domestic discussions. One may say that in the main trade and industry adopted a positive attitude towards the new political conformation, in spite of the reserve shown by investors and the many difficulties hampering business activity. Outwardly at least, the majority remained confident to the last. Then the great blow fell in 1957–8, when as a result of the New Guinea crisis Indonesia broke off all contacts – and did far more.

In the last period before the transference of 1949 the exchange of goods with Indonesia recovered to a great extent. Nevertheless there was a considerable withdrawal of capital from Indonesia, which it was hard to offset by investment of profits, more or less enforced as this was by currency restrictions. Hence, in part, the reason why in the post-war years Indonesia repeatedly had to appeal for credit to the Netherlands state – in 1949 to an amount of over 500 million guilders. This was a heavy burden on the Netherlands economy, hardly lightened by the fact that without this credit Indonesia would probably have been unable to continue the payment of interest, pensions and other obligations. Even so, a credit of two milliard guilders, accumulated since 1945, was altogether forgiven in the financial settlement which took place at the transference of sovereignty.

Meanwhile, a considerable economic recovery was going on in the Netherlands, and thanks to Marshall Aid the dropping out of Indonesia as supplier of third-party currency was of diminishing importance. The divorce of 1949 could not but relieve the Netherlands of a heavy responsibility. If the economic links with Indonesia were broken, Van Mook was already saying in 1947, the recovery of the Netherlands economy would be much quicker. These words proved prophetic, though spoken at a moment when nobody yet foresaw that relations between the Netherlands and Indonesia would be almost completely cut.[1]

It has been said that the Netherlands would have had to forget industrialisation – which has become the sensational fact of the whole post-war economy – if they had had to finance the reconstruction of Indonesia. I prefer to say that the Netherlands might have forgotten industrialisation if they had had to carry the financial burden of Indonesia's economic recovery. All the same, awareness that the profits would never flow as before was always a stimulus after 1945 to a vigorous policy of industrialisation at home. This policy, in fact, was never in debate. Only increased exports, obviously, could in the long run pay for the unavoidable increase in the importation of food and raw materials for a fast-growing population.

The general picture that appears from the annual reports and the commentaries must evidently leave many blank spaces. We see results and decisions. We do not see, or can only glimpse, the attendant reasoning. As long as the archives of the companies have not been opened, it must remain a precarious matter to fit the judgements and conduct of commercial undertakings into the general national reaction to historical events. It is doubtful indeed whether we might one day find what we seek in the open archives: the motivation of decisions and some account of the relationship between these motivations and the relevant circumstances. Important material has even been deliberately destroyed.

[1] W. Brand, 'How the entrepreneurs from the Netherlands tried to effect reorientation', in *Trade World and World Trade*, 139 ff.

Permit me, in conclusion, to return to the image I began with: the image of a man recounting the experience of his own life. It has been a long story, as he feared, and he feels he has hardly related anything yet of the events in which he took part, even at a distance, and which he has tried to evaluate. More interesting than the facts, however, were the problems they raised. Of these I have attempted to say something. And even more interesting than the problems were the people who had to solve them or who experienced them. In those years I came to the conviction that one must fathom what went on in their minds if one is truly to understand the events themselves. How did they, and how did the Netherlands in general, see themselves? How did they see others – on what level, and in the context of what philosophy of the future? History, which comprehends everything, is also a discipline of motivations. Perhaps its primary concern is 'with the problem how men actually think – not in the sense of the thinking that appears in textbooks on logic, but in the sense of how it really functions in public life and in politics as an instrument of collective action – and thus in past and present'.[1]

The colonial era has come to an end, naturally, because of, or at least accompanied by, all those political complications of which we have discussed a few examples. Yet the fundamental point seems to me that the will for independence of the formerly dependent world coincided with a general disclination in the West after the war to retain dominion over the colonies as before. Europe no longer had that moral conviction of a right to rule, that firm will and belief in itself and its vocation to open up the world and govern it. Doubt regarding all these things had not only sapped the foundations of the power of the West to act as leader of half the world, but also of the faith of the West in its right and duty to do so. Its concept of that world and of the people in it had altered.

FURTHER READING

WOLF, C.: *The Indonesian Story* (New York, 1948) studies the birth, development and structure of the Indonesian Republic from

[1] Karl Mannheim, *Ideology and Utopia: an Introduction to the Sociology of Knowledge* (1946) 1.

February 1946 to June 1947. The author served as vice-consul of the U.S.A. at Batavia; in his view economic interests must prevail over political prestige.

WEHL, DAVID: *The Birth of Indonesia* (1948). An analysis of the diplomatic conflict, leading after two years to the recognition of the Republic by the U.N. as a party for negotiations; the book contains documents.

KAHIN, G. McT.: *Nationalism and Revolution in Indonesia* (Ithaca, N.Y., 1952) may be considered the classic account of the Indonesian Revolution. It starts with an analysis of the social background of Indonesian nationalism before 1940 and studies the whole development to the day when the independent and united republic was established.

WINT, GUY: *Spotlight on Asia* (1955) describes the transformation of Asia between 1947 and 1955. The author contrasts the peaceful development in India with the violent revolution in China.

TAYLOR, ALASTAIR M.: *Indonesian Independence and the United Nations* (1960) is a description of the debates in the U.N. from 1946 to 1948, with documents.

DJAJADININGRAT, I. H.: *The Beginnings of the Indonesian-Dutch Negotiations and the Hoge Veluwe Talks* (New York, 1958) is a factual account based on the minutes.

LYPHART, AREND: *The Trauma of Decolonization: the Dutch and West New Guinea* (New Haven, Conn., 1966). The author analyses what he considers to be the Dutch attachment to colonies which was, in his view, the cause of the New Guinea problem.

PALMER, LESLIE H.: *Indonesia and the Dutch* (1962) starts in 1900, considers the growth of Indonesian nationalism, analyses the relations of the nationalists with the Dutch authorities during the 1930s and the influence of the Japanese during the war, and finally describes the events after 1945, with a detailed survey of the dispute about New Guinea; bibliography.

TINBERGEN, J. and DERKSEN, J. B. D.: 'Berekeningen over de economische betekenis van Nederlandsch-Indië voor Nederland', in the periodical *Centraal Bureau voor de Statistiek, 10/12* (The Hague, 1945); and 'Nederlandsch-Indië in cijfers' in W. H. van Helsdingen (ed.), *Daar werd wat groots verricht* (Amsterdam, 1941). In both articles the authors analyse the economic importance of Indonesia for the Netherlands.

11 The British Retreat from Empire

A. J. HANNA

WHEN I was asked to speak on this subject, I was struck by the significance of the choice of words used in the title. I remembered how, only three or four years ago, Mr Dean Acheson had aroused a storm of patriotic indignation by his candid remark that Britain had lost her empire and had not yet found a role in the world to compensate for it. We had not lost our empire, came the indignant reply: we had transformed it into a free association of sovereign peoples, the Commonwealth. Even the Prime Minister, Mr Macmillan, thought fit to add his voice to these protestations, although Mr Acheson had spoken merely as a private citizen. It was as if men who had for many years cherished their belief in the Commonwealth suddenly found it necessary to shout down their own dawning awareness that the fine new clothes in which the British Empire had arrayed itself existed only in our own imagination, to conceal from our own eyes the reality of our nakedness.

There are still, I think, very few people in Britain who are totally disillusioned with the Commonwealth. Mrs Elspeth Huxley was probably expressing the view of a very small minority when she wrote to The Times to say how much she welcomed President Kaunda's suggestion that Britain should be expelled from it.[1] Nevertheless it does seem to command a steadily diminishing amount of confidence and enthusiasm. Too many of its states are unwilling or unable to uphold the democratic standards of government which we used to regard as its distinguishing characteristic; too many of them weary us with their persistent demands while offering nothing, not even goodwill, in return; it has not even been able to prevent an outbreak of war between two of its own members, and has had the humiliation of seeing

[1] The Times, 25 May 1966.

that war ended by the mediation of a government which professes no respect whatever for its ideals.[1] And at the same time as we have been disillusioned by the behaviour of a number of our fellow-members of the Commonwealth, we have had to recognise the still more painful fact of our own decline as a world power. Less than a quarter of a century ago we were the equal partners of the United States and the Soviet Union. Even fifteen years ago we could have had the unquestioned leadership of western Europe if we had been willing to accept it. Our decline from those heights to our present embarrassments has occurred simultaneously with the ending of our imperial role in one territory after another, and it is natural to suppose that there is a causal connection between the two series of developments. We have lost our position in the world at the same time as we have relinquished our empire. We therefore tend to assume that our former greatness was based upon the possession of that empire. In these circumstances we find it difficult to deny that our withdrawal was, in fact, a forced retreat.

Now, of course, it is true that we withdrew under pressure – pressure from world opinion as well as from impatient nationalists in our various dependencies – and that the final stages of our withdrawal were much more rapid than we originally intended. It is probably also true that our withdrawal at some date was inevitable. But, at least in the case of the African territories, we could undoubtedly have held on much longer than we did without unduly straining our economic or military resources, if we had had the political will to do so. If it is within Portugal's capacity, it would surely have been within Britain's. But Britain is not simply a greater Portugal: it is a different kind of country, with a different kind of public opinion and a different system of government. If, then, Britain withdrew from empire in response to anti-imperial pressure – as she undoubtedly did – she did so, not because the pressure was irresistible, but because she had so little inclination to resist it. This lack of inclination has sometimes been attributed to liberal-mindedness and magnanimity, and some-

[1] I have no wish to imply any feeling of resentment against Mr Kosygin's statesmanlike action in mediating between India and Pakistan to end their recent war. On the contrary, there is every reason to welcome any Russian willingness to act constructively to promote peace. What is revealing and deplorable, however, is that within the Commonwealth a situation should have arisen in which such a diplomatic initiative was found necessary.

times it has been attributed to weakness of purpose and 'the craven fear of being great'. There is probably some truth in both these attributions, but it is necessary also to take account of a third: a tolerably competent assessment of our national interest.

For, in fact, it was quite untrue that Britain's prosperity or her status as a Great Power was based upon the possession of her empire. This illusion was partly an optical one, a feeling of importance derived from seeing a large part of the map of the world coloured in deep pink; and it was partly the result of the ceaseless repetition of Leninist mythology.[1] It is true that the older members of the Commonwealth made an immensely valuable contribution in both world wars, but they made it entirely of their own free will, and it could not be counted upon as a factor in diplomacy in time of peace.[2] It is also true that the possession of strategic points like Gibraltar and Malta and Singapore was essential to the maintenance of communications. But when one thinks of the British Empire one does not think primarily of strategic points such as these. On the whole, with only minor qualifications, it is true to say that Britain's wealth and power rested on her own industry, commerce and armed forces. And in recent years our comparatively slow rate of economic growth, as compared with that of our neighbours in western Europe, has been due, partly indeed to purely domestic factors, but also to the fact that we, unlike them, still have world-wide commitments and defence burdens, because although our former colonies have become independent we still have to be prepared to prop up their independence. We are not suffering from their attainment of independence, but from the fact that their independence is still not sufficiently self-supporting.[3]

[1] Cf. above, pp. 174–5.

[2] Sir Wilfrid Laurier, the Canadian Prime Minister, was at pains to point out in 1900 that Canada's contribution to the Boer War was entirely voluntary, and arose from her own assessment of the merits of the case. South Africa, when united under Boer leadership, was no more imperially-minded than Canada. Perhaps, in the case of Australia, automatic support could still be counted upon as late as 1914, though the fact that Australia had already insisted on creating her own navy had ominous implications for the long-term unity of the empire, and contemporaries fully understood that this was so. New Zealand was, of course, the most imperially-minded of the Dominions.

[3] 'This country [Malawi] does not pay for its own keep. In blunt and simple language, if Britain stopped helping us with our recurrent budget and our

Nearly two hundred years ago, the loss of the American colonies did not involve a loss of trade as had been feared; instead, trade with America increased as the new nation expanded, and at the same time Britain was relieved of the burden of defending the American frontiersmen from the Indian tribes of the west. The lesson of American independence was not learnt immediately, and for another generation or so Britain continued to adhere to the mercantilist idea that the possession of empire was essential to the nation's commerce and therefore to its strength. But before the middle of the nineteenth century, the whole apparatus of control over imperial commerce had been abandoned, and in 1859 Britain actually acquiesced in a Canadian demand that Canada should be at liberty to impose whatever duties she thought fit, including protective duties, on imports from any source, including the mother country. This claim was expressed in the classic memorandum drawn up by the finance minister, Alexander Galt, a document which might well be described as the Canadian declaration of economic independence.[1] Once this had been accepted, the Canadians were content; they neither sought nor desired complete political independence, with its attendant burdens and responsibilities, and acquired it only gradually, by imperceptible stages, over the next hundred years.

In the mid-nineteenth century the prevailing British attitude towards the colonies was to regard them as a source of expense rather than of profit, and to welcome the prospect of an amicable transition to independence in the same way as a parent might look

---

development budget tomorrow, we would not stand and function a single day as a state. I want this truth to sink into everyone's head.' President Banda, addressing the annual convention of the Malawi Congress Party on 12 October 1966, as quoted in *The Times* on 13 October.

Fortunately no other former dependency continues to be dependent economically on Britain to the same degree as Malawi; but there is a general need for development assistance, and the need exists on a far greater scale than any British government dare ask its electorate to contemplate. It is also in this connection of continuing *de facto* dependence that the burdensome defence commitment which Britain still carries 'east of Suez' has its *raison d'être*. On the side of the former colonies, an uncomfortable awareness of this fact that political independence is not enough to terminate all *de facto* dependence gives rise to suspicions and allegations of 'neo-colonialism'.

[1] The text of the memorandum is conveniently accessible in A. B. Keith, *Speeches and Documents on British Colonial Policy, 1763–1917*, II 58–83.

forward to the day when his children would be able to support themselves in their own households. A hundred years ago the Treasury was no more enthusiastic about protecting colonists from the Basuto or the Maoris than it has been recently about protecting Malaysia from the Indonesians. It had to be done, but the sooner the trouble could be ended and our forces extricated, the better.[1] That is why Britain recognised the independence of the Orange River Colony (or Orange Free State) in 1854, and thus lost forever the opportunity to act constructively to shape the destinies of South Africa.[2] Half a century later, after the Boer War had been fought and won, it was already too late. The struggle had been so bitter and costly that the paramount necessity when it was over appeared to be the reconciliation of the defeated Afrikaners with the victorious British. The result was that the Union of South Africa was set up on Afrikaner terms, and was destined to become the instrument of uncompromising Afrikaner nationalism.

In the mid-nineteenth century what Britain wanted from the rest of the world was the greatest possible opportunities for secure, peaceful commerce. Thanks to her temporary industrial supremacy at a time when her naval supremacy was still unchallenged, it seemed that the best way to achieve this aim was to minimise commitments and remove obstacles to freedom of trade. She was prepared to act forcefully, perhaps even aggressively, to open up closed markets; the terms 'informal empire' and 'the imperialism of free trade' have become common currency of academic discussion with reference to such policies. But she was exceedingly reluctant to incur the continuing burdens of colonial administration and defence.

In the 1870s and 1880s she gradually overcame this reluctance. There was a great increase in imperial pride and a vast extension of the Empire's boundaries. It was in the last two decades of the nineteenth century that British rule was extended over most of the

[1] Both the Boers and the New Zealanders had themselves to blame for their predicament; but the home government, however little it liked such situations, did not feel able to leave the Queen's white subjects to suffer the natural consequences of their own aggressive land-hunger.

[2] See C. W. de Kiewiet, *British Colonial Policy and the South African Republics* (1929). De Kiewiet describes the decision to abandon the Free State (and also the Transvaal) as 'the eclipse of humanitarian policy' (ibid., 5).

African territories which have recently emerged from that rule as independent states. Superficially it looks as if this was a time when the tide of empire was flowing more strongly than ever before, only to ebb half a century later. And the superficial view does, of course, contain a good deal of truth. But the whole truth is much less simple, and we cannot properly understand how the British Empire was brought to an end if we suppose that the process was simply a reversal of the process by which it was built up. British imperialism in the late nineteenth century was not the result of a heightening of British national self-assertiveness. Indeed, if we compare Lord Salisbury's manner of conducting foreign policy with Palmerston's, it is apparent that the contrary was the case. Britain was being rapidly overtaken by her competitors in industrial production, and could no longer assume that all or most of the world market could be kept open to her exports by a policy of free trade supported by vigorous diplomacy. The so-called 'Little England' outlook of the mid-Victorian period was based upon a confident cosmopolitanism, and the growth of imperialism was due to the fact that this confidence was being undermined. Amid the growing economic and political dangers which Britain had to face, it seemed that Britain's future as a Great Power might depend on preserving, perpetuating and even extending her Empire, with its vast resources and potentialities. If we could not count on having the world at our feet, let us at least try to make sure of the Empire. The imperialist phase does not mark the zenith of British power, but the beginning of the long decline from that zenith.

There is another and even more important respect in which there was more continuity than is usually realised between the imperialist phase and the periods both before and after. The well-established tradition of colonial self-government survived, unchallenged and indeed unchallengeable, throughout the period of attempted consolidation and of territorial expansion. When men used the term 'the British Empire' in the late nineteenth century, they were not referring primarily to a group of tropical dependencies populated by Asians and Africans. The British Empire was, first and foremost, the great self-governing colonies of Canada, Australia, New Zealand and the Cape, which in due course came to be called Dominions in recognition of their importance. Their powers of self-government had been more and more firmly consolidated since the introduction of cabinet responsibility as recommended by Lord Durham in his famous report on Canada. Nevertheless they were not aiming at independence. They believed that they were as free within the Empire as they could be out of it, and at the same time they enjoyed the advantage of being defended against the possibility of external aggression at little cost to themselves, and the satisfaction of being associated with one of the Great Powers instead of being insignificant little states on the periphery of world affairs. When the term 'Commonwealth' began to be used, during the First World War, it was intended as an up-to-date substitute for the term 'Empire'; it was not the name for a new invention nor for a future aspiration, but for an existing fact. Throughout the inter-war period the two names 'Empire' and 'Commonwealth' existed side by side. They were more or less synonymous terms; you could use whichever you preferred. Many people in the Dominions, if they were of British origin or descent, continued to cherish the name 'Empire' and to regard 'Commonwealth' as a weak and watery substitute. But those who were of French or Dutch descent did not share this sentiment, and, of course, neither did the Irish of the Free State, who had accepted Dominion status as no more than a poor substitute for independence. It was mainly to conciliate these non-British elements among the white population that the term 'Commonwealth' was introduced. The classic Balfour Report of 1926 described the Commonwealth as *part of* the Empire: the part consisting of the fully self-governing communities, i.e. the Dominions and also Britain herself. These communities, it declared, were 'within the British Empire, . . . and freely associated as members of the British Commonwealth of Nations'.

This gradual transition from Empire to Commonwealth was not regarded as a defeat for Britain, but as a triumph, on the assumption that the unity of the whole empire would continue unimpaired, with freedom and decentralisation giving it a strength and vitality which it could never have had from bureaucratic control. There were, indeed, some people, not only in Britain but also in the Dominions, who believed that the unity of the empire could not be permanent unless it were deliberately preserved by the creation of central institutions, both legislative and administrative; but even these champions of imperial federation wished to respect the autonomy of the Dominions as much as that of the mother country herself. When Joseph Chamberlain gave the whole weight of his authority and resourcefulness to the advocacy of this cause, the champions of imperial decentralisation were, for a time, thrown on the defensive. But one has only to study the record of the two Colonial Conferences over which Chamberlain presided, in 1897 and 1902, to see how great were the obstacles in his path. However much the statesmen of the Empire might cherish common loyalties and common interests, there were also divergent interests and attitudes which were too important to be ignored. The most that was ever achieved in the direction of imperial consolidation was the decision in 1907 that, instead of occasional Colonial Conferences, there should be an Imperial Conference which would be deemed to be a permanent institution, even though it only met at intervals of about four years. Throughout the imperialist phase the self-governing colonies had, in fact, been quietly consolidating their own autonomy, as was recognised at this same conference in 1907, when it was agreed that in future they should be called 'Dominions'. A few years later, although their eager participation in the First World War was motivated by imperial loyalty, it had the unforeseen effect of fostering their own emergent national consciousness. The imperial federation movement became practically defunct in the immediate post-war years, when Lloyd George failed to preserve his imperial war cabinet as an imperial peace cabinet. The views of Smuts and Mackenzie King now definitely prevailed, and it became accepted orthodoxy in Britain as well as in the Dominions that consultation and co-operation were the only acceptable means by which to pursue common objectives. The Balfour Report gave expression to this orthodoxy. It assumed with serene confidence that the unity of the Empire (or Commonwealth) was securely based on a common loyalty to the Crown and to the principles of parliamentary democracy. 'And', it declared, 'though every Dominion is now, and must always remain, the sole judge of the nature and extent of its co-operation, no common cause will, in our opinion, be thereby imperilled.'

Pride in the Empire, then, was not necessarily an illiberal sentiment. Of course, in the late nineteenth century, it tended to be tainted by nationalistic arrogance, which was part of the spirit of the age. But, if you had asked an Englishman or indeed an

Australian at that time, 'Why are you proud of the Empire?' he would probably have replied, 'Because it is based on free institutions.'

You might well have refused to accept such an answer, on the ground that it appeared to ignore the populations of the non-self-governing territories; after all, the population of India alone was twenty or thirty times as large as the combined white populations of all the Dominions. But British opinion certainly did not ignore India in the late nineteenth century. India was Britain's best market, and her defence was one of the main preoccupations of British foreign policy. In these circumstances, any attempt at justifying British rule necessarily comes under the suspicion of being a mere rationalisation of Britain's own self-interest. Yet it can scarcely be denied that Britain gave to India an impartial rule of law and a standard of honesty and justice which she had not possessed before, and without which freedom and self-government are empty words. The late-nineteenth-century imperialist had this achievement in mind when he boasted of the Empire. The British people, he thought, not only had the qualities of mind and character to operate free institutions among themselves; those same qualities made them uniquely worthy to govern other races.[1] If such a claim now appears absurdly presumptuous, and if 'the white man's burden' has come to be despised as a hypocritical cant phrase, it is partly because a less confident and purposeful generation has arisen which is too estranged from the age of Kipling to understand its outlook, and incredulously shuns the historical fact that British officials in India and the colonies usually had a strong sense of duty to the people whom they governed, and in many cases found the greatest satisfaction of their careers in availing themselves of their wide opportunities for giving unstinted service.

Of course, the very success of British rule in India combined with its shortcomings to produce an increasingly discontented

[1] This view was held in a particularly simple and extreme form by Cecil Rhodes. But although Rhodes was a passionately convinced empire-builder, who believed that British rule was unquestionably good for any and every man who was privileged to come under it, he had not the slightest desire to extend the administrative control of the Colonial Office. His political activities were directed to the aggrandisement of the self-governing Cape Colony, and he founded Rhodesia as, in effect, a dependency of the Cape.

and vociferous middle-class intelligentsia. The unpopularity of Lord Curzon's viceroyalty at the beginning of the present century showed that the time had come when efficiency and justice were no longer enough, and from then on Britain began gradually and cautiously to build up self-governing institutions. The Morley–Minto reforms of 1909 were a first tentative step; they were intended to enable British rule to enjoy the consent of the governed by giving the governed a more influential voice in the Legislative Councils, but without any real powers or any broadly-based electoral support. At the time of their introduction these reforms seemed imaginative and enterprising, but within a few years they proved totally inadequate, because the First World War brought stresses which gave a new intensity to Indian discontent. So, in 1917, the secretary of state for India, E. S. Montagu, made the supremely important announcement that the British government's policy was 'the gradual development of self-governing institutions with a view to the progressive realisation of responsible government in India as an integral part of the British Empire'. Another thirty years were to pass before responsible government was fully attained, but I think it is fair to say that the length of the transitional period was due to the formidable difficulties which Britain encountered rather than to continuing hesitations and misgivings on the part of her own statesmen. Montagu's statement meant that in 1917 Britain had embarked upon a journey which could have no other destination than Indian independence. It is true that he did not use the word 'independence'; on the contrary, he spoke of 'responsible government in India as an integral part of the British Empire'. That might seem to make a great difference, especially as, in 1917, it was still hoped that the Empire might achieve some effective unity of action in the post-war period. But, as Lord Irwin, the viceroy, made clear in 1929, the 1917 declaration implied that the objective of British policy for India's constitutional development was the attainment of Dominion status. And in the inter-war period the Dominions had full control of their external as well as their internal affairs. If the use of the word 'independence' was still carefully avoided, this was because it seemed to imply total separation from the British Commonwealth. But in practice a Dominion was as independent as it wished to be, and the avoidance of the word was a matter of accepted good taste rather than of political substance. The

Indians for their part, however, would be satisfied with nothing less than the explicit recognition of their independence; they were not content to be called a Dominion; they would not even be prepared to remain within the British Commonwealth unless it ceased to call itself British and permitted a republic to be included within its membership. Even though the terms used by Montagu had not envisaged such an outcome, it was inevitable that when India or any other major part of the Empire attained full responsible government, it would not remain within the Empire (or the Commonwealth) except on terms acceptable to itself, however learnedly the constitutional lawyers might discuss the legal niceties of the matter.

Let us consider these events from the point of view of British national interests. Lord Alanbrooke, who was Chief of the Imperial General Staff at the time of the final decision to transfer power, commented bitterly on it in his autobiographical notes written ten years afterwards. 'With the loss of India and Burma', he wrote, 'the keystone of the arch of our Commonwealth Defence was lost, and our Imperial Defence crashed. Without the central strategic reserve of Indian troops ready to operate either east or west we were left impotent and even the smallest of nations were at liberty to twist the lion's tail.'

'And yet,' he added, 'I do not see how we could have remained in India, and I think we were right in withdrawing when we did; but few realised what the strategic loss would amount to.'[1]

In other words, the best that could be said for the transfer of power was that we were cutting our losses. And in his blunt reference to 'the loss of India and Burma' he did not make any distinction at all between Burma, which had left the Commonwealth, and India, which had remained within it. From the aspect of military strategy such a distinction was irrelevant. What he seems to have had chiefly in mind was that the triumph of Indian nationalism had given both the signal and the opportunity to Arab nationalism to put an end to the British domination of the Middle East, which had played such an important part in British strategy during the Second World War. And this was indeed true.

But let us look more closely at this matter. What, after all, was

[1] Arthur Bryant, *Triumph in the West, 1943–1946* (1959) 533. The significance of this passage in connection with the Middle East was pointed out by Elizabeth Monroe in *Britain's Moment in the Middle East, 1914–1956* (1963) 12.

the purpose of British domination in the Middle East? It was not, assuredly, for the sake of its own hot and sandy wastes. We established our control over the Middle East for the sake of the defence of India; we did not acquire India so that we could proceed to control the Middle East. If, for a time, we tried to retain that control, it was partly from force of habit, partly because we feared that our withdrawal would leave a vacuum which the Russians would be prompt to fill, partly because we were anxious about the future of our oil supplies, and partly because the Suez Canal was as important as ever to our ordinary peaceful commerce.

We are now in a position to see, thanks to the advantage of hindsight, how much less cogent these reasons were than they appeared to be. The withdrawal of British power has made it more difficult, not less, for the Russians to penetrate the Middle East, since it has removed a grievance which enabled them to make common cause with Arab nationalism. It is true that Russia has thought it worth while to invest heavily in the area, especially in Egypt, and that her prestige and influence among the Arabs have risen greatly in consequence. But influence gained through investment and technical assistance is a contribution to stability, not to subversion, and, provided she does not encourage those whom she supports to act recklessly against Israel, there is no reason why our own legitimate interests need suffer as a result of any genuinely constructive activity in which she may engage. Indeed, it may even be to our advantage, and to the advantage of the West as a whole, if, by building up her own prestige, Russia minimises the influence of Peking.

We still get our oil, and our ships still go through Suez, for the very adequate reason that the Arabs need to do business with us at least as much as we need to do business with them.[1] It is true

[1] The Israeli–Arab war of 1967 was fought several months after this paper was written. By showing the extent to which the Arab states looked to Russia as their patron, and by causing a blockage of the canal and an interruption of our oil supplies, it might be thought to have invalidated much of what has been said in these paragraphs on the Middle East. A less superficial consideration, however, reveals that Britain's discomfiture was not the result of her withdrawal, but of its incompleteness. The war broke out while we were still tied down to our base in Aden, and while we still possessed aircraft carriers which could irritate the Arabs by their ostentatious presence, even though their presence was presumably never intended for anything more serious than an incompetent policy of bluff. When, by attempting to close the Gulf of Aqaba, Egypt tried to snatch back the fruits of

that they have become masters of the art of extracting from the oil companies the highest possible royalties that the companies can afford to pay, but in making their demands they do not threaten to curtail supplies, but insist that production (and consequently royalties) be increased. And even if we had continued to exercise military control over the Middle East, we could not have used that control for the purpose of keeping down the level of oil payments without exposing ourselves to the charge of being imperialist exploiters, and appearing to write a corroborative footnote to Lenin's *Imperialism*.

I doubt, therefore, if we have lost anything at all as a result of our withdrawal from the Middle East, except some of our commitments and anxieties. If that withdrawal was the worst consequence of the transfer of power in India, we must conclude that Lord Alanbrooke's summing up was mistaken, not because his strategic judgement was in any way at fault, but because he was looking at the matter in a false political perspective.

And, after all, it was only to a relatively small extent that Indian troops had ever been required except in the defence of India itself and the approaches to India. In so far as Britain still required them for service elsewhere, they were still, in fact, sufficiently available. The valiant but impecunious Gurkhas of Nepal were and still are more than willing to enlist in Britain's service; it was a force consisting largely of Gurkhas which defeated the Indonesians in the recent struggle for Malaysia.

---

the aggression committed against her in 1956, Britain was outraged; when, soon afterwards, Israel launched a *blitzkrieg* after the manner of Pearl Harbor, Britain applauded. Although it was clear that there were rights and wrongs on both sides of the conflict, the prevailing British view of it was one-eyed. In the crisis of May and early June 1967 we lacked both the sense of justice to make our neutrality impartial and the resolution to make our partisanship effective, lest it should provoke a Russian counter-stroke and precipitate the destruction of the world. The French, by contrast, were able to avoid friction with the Arabs merely by observing a genuine neutrality, even though it was they who had equipped the Israeli air force. The experience of 1967 should confirm the lesson which we failed to learn properly in 1956, that attempts to dictate to the Arab world merely increase its alienation from the West and confirm its hatred of Israel by making Israel appear – however absurd the appearance may seem to us – to be the spearhead of Western imperialism; and that our own interests and those of everyone else are best served by limiting our activity in the Middle East to the pursuit of amicable commercial relations and the offer of technical assistance.

Are we to conclude, then, that British interests did not suffer in any way as a result of India's independence? Unfortunately we can only return a qualified answer to this question. Britain's interests were, as they had been for centuries, those of a trading nation, requiring free access to markets, prospering if her markets expanded, and suffering loss if they shrank as a result of mis-government, lawlessness or war. It did not matter whether India was governed by Englishmen or by Indians; it did not matter whether, after attaining full control of her own affairs, she was willing to call herself part of the British Empire or demanded recognition as an independent republic; but it did matter that she should be honestly and efficiently governed, that her economy should be competently managed, and that she should be kept secure against internal and external violence. It was not India's independence which Britain had cause to deplore, but the fact that the attainment of independence was accompanied by partition.

I have no wish to attempt the controversial and unprofitable task of allocating responsibility for the division of India between the politicians of Congress and those of the Muslim League, or of enquiring to what extent British mistakes contributed to the disaster. It is enough to mention the effects. The most immediate was the slaughter of about half a million people in the communal riots in the Punjab.[1] The lasting consequence was that the internal peace of the sub-continent was rendered precarious, and the Indian army, which ought to have been standing united to guard the Himalayas, was divided into two mutually antagonistic forces, and resources and energies which ought to have been put to constructive uses have been wasted on a futile dispute which has left the Chinese to acquire the undisputed leadership of Asia, and postponed indefinitely the day when there will be any adequate Asian counterpoise to Chinese power. Yet in spite of all this I think we can regard the transfer of power as a qualified success for British policy, rather than as a failure. If we look at the matter in the narrowest terms of national self-interest, we find that our

---

[1] The scale of the massacres has been variously estimated, but few, I think, would agree with Sir Penderel Moon that the dead may have numbered fewer than 200,000. Dr Percival Spear concludes that 'we shall probably be somewhere near the mark with Judge G. D. Khosla's conclusion, after a very judicious analysis, of about 500,000': *A History of India*, II (1965) 238. The killings were accompanied by the burning of homes and the expulsion of millions of refugees.

exports to India and Pakistan combined are larger than our exports to the whole of Latin America, and one and a half times as large as our exports to the Soviet Union and eastern Europe; though I must add, for the sake of due proportion, that we now export more than ten times as much to western Europe as we do to India and Pakistan combined. Taking a larger view, we observe that there has not been a collapse into chaos or tyranny; in India democratic government still survives, and in Pakistan it has been partially restored. Economic growth has precariously kept pace with the growth of population.[1] Under the threat of Chinese aggression, India has enjoyed the joint protection of the United States and the Soviet Union, which she would certainly not have enjoyed if she had still been under British rule. Suppose, indeed, that Indian independence had not already been achieved and consolidated by the time China had been re-united under Communist control: what an opportunity the situation would have presented to Mao Tse-tung and his famous methods of insurgency!

It will perhaps be thought strange that I have said so much about the old Dominions and India, and have scarcely mentioned tropical Africa. The reason is that the African dependencies, when first acquired, were merely on the periphery of the British Empire, and it was only after India had gained its independence that they emerged into prominence as a result of their own increasingly vociferous demands that they should become independent too. When Britain assumed control of vast tracts of tropical Africa in the late nineteenth century, it was not because she was dissatisfied with the pattern of relationships which had developed during the preceding generation. At the Niger delta she had a flourishing trade in palm oil, which had no need of any colonial administrators to stimulate it; but it did seem to need to be protected against the Germans when they suddenly exhibited an interest in colonial acquisitions, and accordingly Britain declared a protectorate over the area to forestall them. In East Africa it was

---

[1] These statements do not imply optimism about India's prospects, either politically or economically. Although Congress politicians cannot fairly be blamed for the failure of the monsoon, they have much to answer for, and it is doubtful if they can continue to fend off disaster for much longer. Yet this in no way invalidates the conclusion that the present situation would have been far worse than it is if Britain had refused to relinquish her Indian Empire.

not a desire for tropical products or protected markets which brought in the British, for East Africa had next to nothing to offer in either respect. The British had worked out an inexpensive and fairly satisfactory arrangement with the Sultan of Zanzibar, by which they utilised his authority to suppress the Arab slave trade along the coast, and they wanted nothing more. Here again it was Germany which transformed the situation, by seizing what became Tanganyika. Likewise in Nyasaland, the British declared a protectorate, not because they wanted it for themselves, but because the Portuguese were in process of invading the area. The British Treasury was most unwilling to be burdened by such unprofitable acquisitions, British ministers were hesitant, and the demand for intervention was humanitarian far more than commercial. It is significant that the new acquisitions were protectorates, not colonies, and that for the first ten years or so they were under the Foreign Office, not the Colonial Office. It was hoped that by not annexing them, and accepting only a vaguely supervisory responsibility for them, the commitment could be minimised. Of course the hope was vain. The rudiments of administration had to be established, internal peace had to be maintained, justice had to be administered, communications improved, revenue collected, and economic development encouraged. The longer British control continued, the more deeply involved we became, so that a protectorate became virtually indistinguishable from a colony. The African dependencies gradually came to have a certain modest economic importance. Their administrations became almost if not entirely able to pay their way without grants-in-aid from the British Treasury. During the inter-war period they seemed more like assets than liabilities, and it was assumed that British rule would continue for many generations, because it had not yet become intellectually fashionable to believe that the difference between civilisation and barbarism is merely a prejudice of the western European bourgeois mentality, and it was assumed that civilisation could not be built up in frantic haste if it was to have any quality and power of endurance.

But I do not think there was ever any desire, on the part of any significant element in this country, to hold down the African populations in perpetuity against their own interests and wishes. British rule would not be withdrawn as long as the probable alternative to it would be annexation by another European power;

and in the 1930s it was those who were most concerned about African welfare who were insistent that Tanganyika must not be restored to Germany as part of the attempt to appease Hitler. But the transfer of power to the Africans themselves was quite a different matter.

The position was, indeed, complicated by the establishment in parts of central and eastern Africa of communities of white settlers, who, although not large in numbers, provided the main thrust to develop the economy and create the material fabric of a civilised life, and therefore assumed too readily that the interests of the whole territory were identical with their own, and that their own voice in the politics of the country ought to be decisive. Much the largest of these communities, outside the Union of South Africa, was in Southern Rhodesia. In 1923, when that country ceased to be administered by the British South Africa Company, it was immediately handed over to white settler control, with certain qualifications; and the consequences of that decision vex and harass us today. Elsewhere, in Kenya and Northern Rhodesia, the settlers gained a great and almost dominating influence; but in both these territories the British government always retained some residual control, and its reason for so doing was that the interests of the African majority were paramount, and that it could not abandon its own responsibility as trustee on their behalf. This doctrine had been officially laid down as early as 1904, when it was stated that 'the primary duty of Great Britain in East Africa is the welfare of the native races'. In 1923 it was expressed in a famous White Paper, and from then on the British government was publicly committed. If it was to be honoured, it meant, in the short term, that self-government must be denied for as long as only an immigrant minority were competent to exercise it; but at a later stage, even if it was in the very long term, it could hardly mean anything other than the grant of self-government, when the progress of civilisation among the mass of the inhabitants would have made this possible and right. Still, throughout the inter-war period it was unusual to look so far ahead. At that time, what the prevailing orthodoxy required was the preservation and the maximum employment of traditional tribal institutions, rather than the increasingly effective representation of Africans at the territorial level. Indeed, it was supposed that the proper way to associate Africans with the central legislature would be through the representation of tribes rather than of individuals. The ultimate objective of self-government was seen only dimly in the distance, at the end of a long and ill-defined process of political evolution, necessarily accompanied by social evolution and nurtured by economic growth. Let me quote a statement made by Mr Malcolm MacDonald when he was secretary of state for the colonies:

The great purpose of the British Empire is the gradual spread of freedom among all His Majesty's subjects in whatever part of the world they live. That spread of freedom is a slow, evolutionary process. In some countries it is more rapid than in others. . . . It may take generations, or even centuries, for the peoples in some parts of the Colonial Empire to achieve self-government. But it is a major part of our policy, even among the most backward peoples of Africa, to teach them and to encourage them always to be able to stand a little more on their own feet. That love of ours of freedom, not only for ourselves but for others, inspires policy right through the Colonial Empire.

Those words were spoken at a time when it was not yet considered necessary to avoid the word 'backward' and to use 'underdeveloped' or (better still) 'developing' as a polite synonym for it. They were spoken in 1938, before the beginning of the Second World War. The war, when it came, hastened political evolution in Africa just as the First World War had hastened it in India. Compare with the statement I have just quoted the words used five years later, in 1943, by Colonel Oliver Stanley, and you will notice how, while the general meaning is the same and there is the same sincerity of purpose, there is a greater clarity of definition and a greater sense of urgency:

We are pledged to guide Colonial people along the road to self-government within the framework of the British Empire. We are pledged to build up their social and economic institutions, and we are pledged to develop their natural resources. . . . It is no part of our policy to confer political advances which are unjustified by circumstances, or to grant self-government to those who are not yet trained in its use, but if we really mean as soon as practicable to develop self-government in these territories, it is up to us to see that circumstances as soon as possible justify political advances and to ensure that as quickly as possible people are trained and equipped for eventual self-government.

Therefore, to my mind, the real test of the sincerity and success of our Colonial policy is two-fold. It is not only the actual political advances that we make, but it is also, and I think more important, the steps that we are taking, economic and social as well as political, to prepare the people for further and future responsibilities.[1]

You will observe that he defined the objective as being 'self-government within the framework of the British Empire', and that this was precisely the objective of British policy for India as Montagu had defined it a quarter of a century previously. And, as in the case of India, the eventual outcome was the status of full independence within the Commonwealth.

Why was it that this eventual outcome was reached, not after generations or even centuries, but after a mere ten or fifteen years from the end of the war? The answer is that the whole intellectual and moral climate of the post-war world served as a hothouse to force the growth of colonial independence. It affected opinion in Britain as well as at the United Nations, though of course much less strongly; it influenced colonial administrators as well as the colonial nationalists whom they sometimes found it necessary to imprison. But – to return to the previous metaphor – the road along which we were hustled and chivvied with indecent haste was the road along which we were already firmly resolved to travel. It is quite untrue that Britain gave up her empire because her post-war impoverishment and weakness made her unable to retain it. The Communist insurrection in Malaya was relentlessly worn down and extinguished, and the Mau Mau gangs were hunted down and overpowered in the forests of Kenya. In Nyasaland the grip of the security forces was only briefly weakened. The fact that in all these instances the restoration of peaceful conditions was followed by an accelerated transition to independence was due to the British dislike of repression, to the belief that merely negative policies were no more useful to Britain herself than to her colonies, and to the assumption that even among an ignorant peasantry the moral right to govern depended upon the consent or at least the acquiescence of the governed. So in the last resort a territory was deemed to be ready for self-government, not when it satisfied certain objective criteria of economic and

[1] These and other relevant quotations will be found in the Hansard Society's publication, *Problems of Parliamentary Government in Colonies* (1953) 130–1.

political viability, of educational attainment and of social maturity, but simply when a sufficiently intense demand arose among its own inhabitants that they should control their own affairs. And the length of the transitional phase between dependence and independence was what the nationalist politicians could be persuaded in their own interests to accept; it became shorter and shorter with the territories which were last in the queue.

It has often been alleged that British policy was foolish and narrow-minded in 'imposing the Westminster model' of parliamentary government and cabinet responsibility as the condition of independence, without regard to local circumstances and traditions. To make this charge is to ignore innumerable experiments with federations, written constitutions, bills of rights, entrenched clauses, safeguards for minorities, weighted representation – all the dust and rubble of laborious legal ingenuity devoted to meeting the special needs of societies which were recognised to be neither homogeneous nor fully mature; all of it swept away into oblivion by the rushing torrent of nationalism. It was the nationalists themselves, whether in Ceylon before the war or in Africa after it, who insisted on straightforward uncomplicated cabinet government, with 'one man one vote'. And it is well worth mentioning that in Ceylon, though not in Africa, parliamentary democracy as we understand it has been retained as the accepted means of sustaining and replacing the government, as indeed it has also been in the West Indies.

What those who scoff at 'the Westminster model' are really saying is that in the African territories Britain ought to have established the one-party state on her own initiative. Since so many Africans say that the one-party state is the truly African form of democratic government, Britain ought, according to this view, to have shown respect for their traditions and their wishes by giving them what was good for them, not what she found good for herself. But I would ask you to observe that it is only those Africans who happen to be in power, with their adherents, who appreciate the peculiarly African excellences of the one-party state. A year or two ago it was still considered intellectually respectable, even enlightened, here and in the United States, to point out how splendidly Dr Nkrumah embodied the national will of the people of Ghana. But today one may fairly ask whether British policy in the Gold Coast would have been more deserving of respect if it had placed even fewer obstacles than it did in the path of his arrogant self-will.

The truth is, of course, that it was wildly optimistic to suppose that democracy as we understand it could flourish in Africa after scarcely more than half a century of initiation into the heritage of civilised mankind.[1] That the Africans have managed no worse than they have done is greatly to their credit. If circumstances had permitted them to remain under British tutelage for a longer period, I do not doubt that they would have managed considerably better. British governments may indeed be criticised for the self-deception by which they convinced themselves that their legal experts could prefabricate a substitute for political and social maturity, in the form of paper safeguards for individual rights and minority interests. They may be criticised for supposing that any majority community would for long be satisfied with a weighted franchise designed to protect minorities from being swamped.[2] They may be blamed for showing a lack of respect for long-term African interests when they created the unhappy federation of Nyasaland and Northern Rhodesia (now Malawi and Zambia) with Southern Rhodesia; and they may be censured for pretending that the dissolution of that federation, although urgently necessary, was anything other than a breach of faith. The criticisms may be multiplied; and most of them are criticisms which were made at the time, without benefit of hindsight. Yet they are all, relatively speaking, matters of detail. In its broadest essentials, British policy was surely right. It was right to relinquish sovereignty while it could still be done with a measure of co-operation from the nationalist leaders. It was right to insist on a transitional phase of internal self-government, before sovereignty was finally transferred. And it was also right that we should try to introduce the Africans in our protectorates to what was best in our own political experience. To suggest that, on the contrary, we ought to have encouraged them to believe that for them, as

[1] The remoter parts of the interior did not come under effective administration until almost the eve of the First World War.

[2] And yet, in spite of all experience with such expedients (none of which, of course, is borrowed from 'the Westminster model'), we are still obstinately trying to persuade or compel the Rhodesians to adopt additions to such paper safeguards as they already have, for the immediate purpose of protecting the black majority, and for the ultimate purpose of protecting the white minority after the local balance of power has tilted against them.

distinct from the rest of the human race, the ideal form of government is a ramshackle form of boss rule – this, most certainly,
would not have been broad-mindedness; it would have been a
racial insult.[1] We have no need to regret that instead of adopting
such a course Britain made an honest, serious attempt to set them
on the path of genuinely free, democratic government, and we
may still hope that after many stumblings they will find their way
back to it.

FURTHER READING

1. *Collections of Documents*

The Development of Dominion Status, 1900–1936, ed. R. M. DAWSON
(Toronto, 1937), includes some illuminating newspaper comments as
well as official documents, and has a masterly introduction.

Selected Speeches and Documents on British Colonial Policy, 1763–1917,
ed. A. B. KEITH (Oxford, 2 vols, 1918; 1 vol. reprint, 1948), with its
sequel, *Speeches and Documents on the British Dominions, 1918–1931*
(Oxford, 1932), conveniently bring together most of the basic
official documentary material; they have been supplemented by
Imperial Constitutional Documents, 1765–1965, ed. F. MADDEN
(Oxford, 1966).

Documents and Speeches on British Commonwealth Affairs, 1931–52, 2 vols,
and its sequel, *1952–62*, both ed. N. MANSERGH (1952 and 1963): a
magnificent collection, including some material on the transition of
the dependencies to independence, although mainly concerned with
the relations between Britain and the older members of the Commonwealth.

The Evolution of India and Pakistan, 1858–1947, ed. C. H. PHILIPS
(Oxford, 1962).

2. *Secondary Works*

HANCOCK, Sir W. K.: *Survey of British Commonwealth Affairs*, 2 vols,
vol. II in 2 parts (1937–42) is a work of great penetration, especially

---

[1] 'To advocate double standards, one for Africa and another for the rest of the
world, is a great insult to Africa.' These words were written by a distinguished
African, Dr E. Njoku, former Vice-Chancellor of the University of Lagos, in a
foreword to *University of Lagos: the Truth about the change in Vice-Chancellorship*
by G. K. Berrie and others (published by the authors, P.O. Box 437, Yaba, Lagos,
1965).

in its examination of the British response to Dominion nationalism. It is supplemented and continued by N. MANSERGH, 2 vols (1953–8).

WHEARE, K. C.: *The Constitutional Structure of the Commonwealth* (Oxford, 1960) brought up to date the same author's standard work on *The Statute of Westminster and Dominion Status* (1st ed., 1938).

MILLER, J. D. B.: *The Commonwealth in the World* (1958) illustrates admirably the viewpoint of a decade ago.

JENNINGS, Sir I.: *The Commonwealth in Asia* (Oxford, 1951). A brief survey by an eminent authority.

TINKER, H.: *South Asia: a Short History* (1966) covers India, Burma and Ceylon; it is a work of reflection as well as scholarship, and is admirably written.

—— *Experiment with Freedom: India and Pakistan, 1947* (1967) discusses the transfer of power with exceptional lucidity, and judiciously places it in the wider context of British imperial policy.

MENON, V. P.: *The Transfer of Power in India* (1957). A substantial study which includes an account of constitutional developments from the beginning of the century, written with detachment and scrupulous fairness by a distinguished Indian who played a prominent part in the events of the time.

MOON, Sir P.: *Divide and Quit* (1961). Brilliant and incisive; important for its account of events in and near the Punjab.

MONROE, E.: *Britain's Moment in the Middle East, 1914–56* (1963) brings out the essentials with great clarity.

PERHAM, Dame MARGERY: *The Colonial Reckoning* (1961). A series of Reith Lectures, by the greatest living authority on British rule in Africa.

OLIVER, R. and ATMORE, A.: *Africa Since 1800* (Cambridge, 1967) contains, in the African rather than the imperial context, a good clear account of the ending of colonial rule, and includes a substantial bibliography. A fuller account, now in preparation, will be given in AUSTIN, D.: *Africa, the Transfer of Power*, to be published in Macmillan's series on 'The Making of the Twentieth Century'.

HUNTER, G.: *The New Societies of Tropical Africa* (1962) is a sympathetic but clear-sighted examination of a number of African states as they emerged from British and French rule.

Index

Kimberley, John Wodehouse, 1st Earl
of, 177–80, 184, 186
Kipling, R., 242
Kishm, 96, 103
Kleffens, E. N. van, 215–16
Kossmann, E. H., 14
Kosygin, A. N., 235 n.
Kowloon, 183
Kuala Lumpur, 177
Kuchin, 181

La Rochelle, 39
La Vauguyon, P. F. Duc de, 133
Labuan, 183
Lahore, 86
Landes, D. S., 176
Langhorn, Sir William, 98
Lansdowne, H. C. K. Petty-Fitz-
maurice, 5th Marquess of, 171
Lauderdale, John Maitland, 1st Duke
of, 52
Laurier, Sir W., 236 n.
Lawas river (Borneo), 184
Leeward Islands, 84
Leiden University, 56–7, 154
Lenin, V. I., 174–5, 177, 186, 188, 246
Liège, 142
Limbang river (Borneo), 184
Limburg, Dutch province of, 149–50,
152
Limburg Stirum, J. P. van, 200, 203
Linggadjati, Agreement of, 222
Linhares, Conde de, 91
Lloyd George, David, 241
Louis XIV, King of France, 13, 31, 33,
39, 40, 50–4, 106, 110, 114, 119–20
Louis XVI, King of France, 134
Louvois, F. M. Le Tellier, Marquis de,
48
Lucas, Sir Gervase, 101
Lucaszoon, Pieter, 77
Lundu river (Borneo), 184
Lurgan valley, 119
Luxemburg, 53; Grand Duchy of, 142,
153, 167

Macao, 63
MacArthur, Douglas, 216
Macassar, 63–5, 68, 87, 90, 93–5
MacDonald, Malcolm, 251
Machiavelli, N., 24
Mackenzie King, W. L., 241
Macmillan, Harold, 234
Madagascar, 91

Madras, 84, 97–8, 102, 104–5
Madrid, Treaty of, 85
Maetsuycker, Johannes, 73–7
Malabar, 65, 87, 93, 100–1
Malacca, 63, 85, 87, 176, 185
Malawi, 236–7 n. See Nyasaland
Malaya (Malaysia), 69, 104, 176–80,
184–5, 246, 252; tin mines, 69, 178
Malino, Conference of, 222
Mallaby, Brigadier, 220
Malta, 160, 236
Manipur, 185
Mao Tse-tung, 248
Maoris, 238
Marathas, 100
Mare liberum, 28, 71
Maria Theresa, Empress, 124
Marlborough, James Ley, 3rd Earl of,
85
Marlborough, John Churchill, 1st
Duke of, 52, 115
Martinique, 127
Masselman, George, 58
Masulipatam, 87, 93, 96–7
Mataram, 75–6, 87, 94
Maurice, Stadholder, 17
Mazarin, Cardinal, 30
Medlicott, W. N., 168
Meerman, Johan, 30
Mehemet Ali, 163–4
Mergui, 105–6
Methwold, William, 91
Metternich, Prince, 146
Meyer Ranneft, J. W., 224
Michelet, Jules, 148
Michiels van Verduynen, E. M. F. J.,
216
Middle East, Britain and the, 244–6
Millman, Richard, 164
Milner, Sir Alfred, 1st Viscount, 169
Minorca, 122, 128
Mocha, 93
Moira, F. Rawdon-Hastings, 2nd Earl
of, 183
Moluccas, the, 65, 71
Montagu, Charles, 51
Montagu, E. S., 243–4, 251; Montagu–
Chelmsford Report (1918), 200
Montesquieu, 25–6
Mook, H. J. van, 209, 216–17, 222–3,
226, 231
Morier, Sir Robert, 167
Morley–Minto reforms, in India, 243
Mosse, W. E., 166